Childhood and the
Philosophy of Education

Philosophy of Education by Richard Pring
Thinking Children by Claire Cassidy
The Right to Childhoods by Dimitra Hartas
Children's Futures by Paul Croll, Carol Fuller and Gaynor Attwood

Childhood and the Philosophy of Education

An Anti-Aristotelian Perspective

Andrew Stables

continuum

Continuum International Publishing Group

The Tower Building
11 York Road
London SE1 7NX

80 Maiden Lane
Suite 704
New York, NY 10038

www.continuumbooks.com

British Library Cataloguing-in-Publication Data
A catalogue record for this book is available from the British Library.

ISBN: 9780826499721 (hardcover)

Library of Congress Cataloging-in-Publication Data
The Publisher has applied for CIP data.

Typeset by Newgen Imaging Systems Pvt Ltd, Chennai, India
Printed by the MPG Books Group in the UK

Contents

Contents

Introduction:
The Conception of Childhood

There are two ways of conceiving children, although one is not generally the business of philosophers. By the same token, how we think about children is not the same as how we deal with them, though how we think about them does affect how we deal with them in various ways. For example, our desire to protect our children, and our care for their welfare are not principally matters of conceptualization, yet the history of childhood is one that reveals considerable differences in spontaneous human relationships between the old and the young; and to some extent such differences appear in comparative studies of contemporary societies, so it appears that such matters are not completely free from conceptualization either (Alanen and Mayall, 2001). On the more formal, organizational plane, how we think about childhood clearly bears on how we formulate policy relating to children, and how we set about educating them.

At the same time, as philosophers including Hume and Wittgenstein have variously reminded us, we cannot move unproblematically from the 'is' to the 'ought', in adult–child relations or any sphere of life. Studies of the history, psychology, sociology and even philosophy of childhood cannot dictate the moral and practical decisions we make with respect to children, but they will inevitably inform such decisions.

It is therefore important to reconceptualize childhood from time to time, or at least to examine how we conceive of it, though such a rethinking will by no means end all debate about how children should be treated in every situation. It is my contention that such a reconceptualization is due.

The problem is not one of shortage of educational research. Of course, one can always have more of a good thing (assuming educational research to be generally a good thing, despite recent critiques, such as those by Tooley and Darby, 1998). However, empirical research has to work on a series of assumptions: for example, research into effective schooling has to assume the desirability of schooling. Philosophy of education, by contrast, is more useful in repeatedly taking us back to such assumptions, reminding us that there are always questions prior to those that inform data collection. Such questions might include the following:

- In what senses, and to what extent, might schooling be validly held to be a universal, social or private good?
- (To what extent . . .) Is compulsory schooling justifiable?
- (To what extent . . .) Should children enjoy adult rights?
- (To what extent . . .) Should children be regarded as legally responsible?
- How should childhood be defined, and at what ages should children be granted adult rights (of consent, marriage, purchasing, driving, inheritance, etc.)?

From time to time we need to remind ourselves that these questions have not necessarily been answered once and for all. (Has any question ever been answered once and for all?) At the time of writing, the UK government has recently announced its intention to raise the school leaving age to 18. Regardless of the many contextual questions this poses, there is a normative question too: Should all children beyond a certain age (currently five in the UK) be forced to be in full-time education? And a question is raised for the philosophy of education: Does increasing compulsory education always and necessarily benefit individuals and societies more than the feasible alternatives? And if not: What are the desirable and undesirable effects of increased compulsory schooling, and under what circumstances do the desirable effects outweigh the undesirable?

These questions form the principal motivation for writing this book, though they cannot be fully divorced from the other bullet-pointed questions above, which also deserve consideration in the following pages.

The work to follow is organized into four parts. The argument of Part 1 is that if the conception of childhood is important, and conceptions of childhood have been insufficiently challenged in recent times, then a new conception of childhood is required. In this section, I trace Western attitudes to childhood back to Plato and (in particular) Aristotle, and show how key Aristotelian assumptions about childhood have coloured modern history, and how they are in many respects still taken for granted in the modern discourse of childhood. I shall argue that there are four key historical 'moments' acting as contributory factors towards contemporary assumptions about the education of young people. The first is the Classical: the writings, in particular, of Plato and then of Aristotle. I think Aristotle is particularly influential here, and will describe the modern history of childhood and education as, in many ways, a 'series of footnotes to Aristotle', to misquote A. N. Whitehead's remark about Plato – and that these influences are apparent in many non-Western cultures. The second is the Puritan strand within the Christian tradition which, in countries such as those of Northern Europe and North America, assumes the child to be naturally sinful but possibly redeemable through hard work, devotion and discipline. The third is the liberal, Enlightenment tradition which, in the West at least, construes the child as a rational agent and education as liberation from ignorance and servility. The fourth is the Romantic tradition – again, largely in the West – which construes childhood as innocent but the adult world as tainted, and so demands of education that it both protect the young and keep childlike powers of imagination and sympathy alive in a hostile world. Although I have employed the term 'moment' here, it is important to note that these are complete and self-sufficient approaches to childhood, each of which has held sway for a discrete period of time. Rather, each is an aspect of our thinking about childhood from place to place and time to time (in the Western tradition at least), though each has had its period of relative ascendancy over the others so that a historical pattern, though rather fuzzy round the edges, is indeed discernible.

I maintain that these traditions have each affected the thinking about childhood and education across much of the world to some extent, but I do not attempt to speak for everywhere, nor to deny that other traditions will also have enduring effects on educational thinking outside Europe and the English-speaking countries. While conceptions of childhood are not merely descriptions of cultural practices, they are not context-blind. The primary focus of the present work is Britain (specifically England); the secondary focus is the United States and the rest of the English-speaking world; and the tertiary focus Continental Europe. I am aware that there are great traditions that get little or no attention. These include the specifically Jewish tradition, Islam, Hinduism, Sikhism and Buddhism, and the twin influences of Confucianism and Daoism in the Chinese world. I have also excluded what I assume to be the myriad of indigenous perspectives around the world, some of them documented, some not. The book is less interesting for these omissions. However, given imperialism, globalization and the spread of Western science, culture and economics, I am confident that the discussion has global resonance, even if its significance varies from place to place. I believe that much of it is largely applicable elsewhere.

The second phase of the argument (Part 2) builds on the work I have undertaken for a series of prior publications in which I have developed a 'fully semiotic' perspective on education and learning: a view of living as comprising responses to environmental signs and signals. Based on the premise that 'living is semiotic engagement' and the associated claim that this assertion can act as 'a foundational statement for a post-foundational age' (Stables, 2005a, 2006a–c; Stables and Gough, 2006), I argue here that if living can validly be conceived as semiotic engagement, and if children are fully alive, then children are as fully 'semiotic engagers' as adults. At the crux of what it means to be human, therefore, children are not incomplete, unprepared or lacking purpose. This begs an anti-Aristotelian reconception. It also builds on the work of commentators such as Gareth Matthews (1994) who have already expressed their scepticism concerning the developmental accounts of childhood that dominated twentieth-century educational thinking – particularly that of Piaget.

In Part 3, I argue that if children are as much semiotic engagers as adults, and social policy is intended as much to protect the interests of children as those of adults, then social policy, including educational practice, must regard children as 'already fully engaged' rather than 'not yet ready'. In relation to this, I examine the history of compulsory schooling in Part 3 and some potential ways forward in Part 4.

In all this, I am generally taking 'childhood' to refer to life from birth to 18. However, this is merely a default position, and sometimes I shall depart from it. Not only can childhood be variously defined with respect to historical periods (Ariès, 1962) but its meaning in contemporary discourse is also multiple. To this end, current conceptions of childhood in ordinary language might lead us to identify *Child 1*, *Child 2* and *Child 3*.

Child 1 is the child of one or more parents. Anyone with living parents is a *Child 1*; it is not a matter of age. People with beliefs in an afterlife may feel they continue as *Child 1* after their parents have passed away. Indeed, the entire history of ancestor-worship rests on positioning all persons as *Child 1*. It is a position that calls forth respect for tradition, gratitude, duty and sacrifice. Christians, for example, pray to 'Our Father, Who art in Heaven'.

Child 2 is the person of an age at which adult rights and responsibilities have not been bestowed: the default position identified above. In Britain, the status of *Child 2* used to run from birth to 21; now it is birth to 18 (though it varies somewhat from context to context: you can get married before you can drive or drink in public). Being positioned as *Child 2* bestows protection at the cost of individual freedom; it implies lack of readiness and a period of constrained preparation but with few responsibilities. Only the youngest sector of the population has *Child 2* status.

Child 3 is the novice, he or she who is relatively incapable or uncivilized: who has 'not yet learnt' or is 'not yet ready'. We speak with sympathy of the young mother, or victim of disease who is 'just a child herself'; we speak of the poor football team pitched against Manchester United as 'boys against men', and the British used to call male servants 'boy' in Colonial times. *Child 3* status calls forth condescension. A *Child 3* has responsibilities but limited means to undertake them. However, whether one is a *Child 3* is a matter of context: the absent-minded professor or unworldly celebrity may be the object of extreme respect or disdain depending on which activities are under scrutiny. We are all *Child 3* from time to time.

It is important to make these distinctions because discussions about the conception of childhood can all-too-easily proceed on partial assumptions. For example, Ariès (1962) argues that pre-modern societies had little or nothing of our conception of *Child 2*, but they certainly acknowledged *Child 3*, and there is plenty of evidence (beyond Ariès' brief) that they have acknowledged *Child 1* since time immemorial and may do so less now than hitherto. If we are to aim for any progression in our conceptions of childhood, we must acknowledge their existing variety. In particular, we should be wary of attributing a one-dimensional, all-or-nothing character to childhood, particularly as purely *Child 2*. I shall argue that such a reductionist view is in the interest of neither 'child' nor adult, and, in the concluding chapter, will consider how contemporary society balances these three conceptions of what it means to be a child against the Aristotelian, Puritan, Liberal and Romantic assumptions that have influenced our thinking about childhood generally. I shall conclude that over-adherence to several of these assumptions runs counter to the *Zeitgeist*, and that existing models of schooling and attitudes to children in general have been insufficiently responsive to other social changes.

Part 1
The Aristotelian Heritage

How Anti-Aristotelian Can One Be?

1.1.1 Introduction to Part 1

In Part 1, I shall attempt to reveal the strong Aristotelian influence on the modern history of childhood. While conceptions of childhood have certainly not remained static over the past millennium – and are not universally uniform now – our assumptions about how we should deal with children all have strongly identifiable roots in the Aristotelian tradition. In this key respect, I shall argue that childhood has not been adequately reconceptualized, particularly given that other Aristotelian assumptions have faced very significant challenges. This provides the background to the 'fully semiotic' reconception of childhood offered in Part 2.

In Chapter 1.1, I attempt a balanced evaluation of Aristotle's key ideas relating to childhood following the linguistic turn of the past century. Chapters 1.2 and 1.3 explain Aristotle's position more fully, first by making clear Aristotle's debt to Plato. The remaining chapters in this section re-evaluate existing understandings of childhood since the Middle Ages in relation to Aristotle, culminating in reflection on the place of the child in Postmodern or Late Modern society.

While this book is subtitled, 'An anti-Aristotelian perspective', it is important to be clear about which aspect of Aristotle's thought is to be critiqued, since his influence over the contemporary worldview generally is so great that a comprehensive anti-Aristotelianism would amount to significant self-denial.

There is a strong Aristotelian influence on virtually every aspect of our thinking: about science, politics and law, the arts, ethics and morality, and (of particular present relevance) the nature, functioning and development of the human subject. There are many elements within this thinking that will be accepted in the course of developing the present argument. However, I shall argue that the various aspects of the 'linguistic turn' of the last century problematize some of Aristotle's key assumptions and distinctions.

First, I shall attempt a brief general summary of Aristotle's legacies in the areas listed above. I shall then summarize his metaphysical system, which forms the basis of his contributions to the thinking about childhood and education. These summative statements will serve as a necessary background to the critiquing of that system from a particular contemporary perspective. This critique will form the basis of Part 2.

1.1.2 Aristotelian Legacies

1.1.2.1 Science

Aristotle is, in some important respects, the father of modern science.

In sharp contrast to his tutor, Plato, Aristotle (whose father was a physician) was a committed empiricist. That is to say, he believed that reasoning should be undertaken on the basis of experience, and that experience therefore offers a valid basis for reasoning. (Chapter 1.2 will explain Plato's views in relation to this.) This is a central tenet of modern science, even though physics since Einstein has often had to proceed on the basis that empirical justification may be impossible in the short term (e.g. we cannot see into a black hole). This tenet has generally been applicable to both cosmology and quantum mechanics: to science at both the largest and smallest scales of operation. Although theories of multidimensionality and 'branes' (Hawking, 2001) challenge even the 'large–small' distinction, the deeply held belief remains that theory is ultimately testable in practice. The enduring power of this belief is evident in the huge spending on facilities for experimental science, such as the particle accelerators at CERN (the Centre Europeenne de la Researche Nucleaire) in Geneva, which are designed to 'capture' and thus firmly identify subatomic particles that the theory insists must exist.

Aristotle's commitment to detailed observation is exhaustively illustrated in works such as *The History of Animals, On the Parts of Animals* and *Meteorology*. However, this is not his only legacy for science.

Aristotle also held both that there is a scientifically rigorous way to conduct enquiry, and that different methods and distinctions are, to a greater or lesser extent, appropriate to different areas of enquiry. He identified different forms of human reasoning and different areas and foci of enquiry. The currently held distinctions between physics and biology, as well as among logic, psychology, metaphysics, ethics and politics can all be traced back to Aristotle.

The *Nicomachean Ethics* provides the clearest exposition of Aristotle's distinctions between ways of knowing, distinctions that will re-appear regularly during the conduct of the present argument. These are *theoria* (knowledge gained through detached contemplation, cf. the modern 'theory'), *praxis* (human knowledge-in-action based on *phronesis* – judgement – as in the modern 'practice', but always with a strong moral and ethical dimension), *techne* (skill, know-how, cf. 'technology' – literally 'knowledge of *techne*') and *poesis* (making, a concept much reduced in the modern 'poetry'). What we now understand as 'science' corresponds largely to *theoria.*

1.1.2.2 Politics and law

Although modern political scientists draw sharp distinctions between the Ancient Greek city-state and the modern nation-state, Aristotle's work in *The Politics, The Laws* and elsewhere has been highly influential in the development of contemporary understandings of state and citizenship. Aristotle saw politics as a practical science and therefore includes specific examples of how cities might be governed, argued from the basic assumption that good political management should resonate with good management of a household. Following Plato, he describes and critiques various forms of government in terms that are still used today: monarchy, tyranny, oligarchy, aristocracy, polity and democracy. Overall, his thinking on these matters, as was Plato's, is strongly meritocratic, though he is less damning of democracy than was his tutor.

One of Aristotle's major contributions to modern thinking about law, and indeed about ethics, is his thinking about justice, which Aristotle conceived as a virtue – a trait of good character – rather than a disembodied state of affairs. Aristotle is responsible for the still highly relevant distinctions among retributive, distributive and procedural justice.

1.1.2.3 The arts

The Poetics contains a number of ideas about the arts that have significantly affected aesthetic and critical judgements to the present day.

Plato had little respect for the creative arts. He believed that the world as presented to our senses consisted of imperfect copies, or representations, of rational and abstract ideas. By extension, anything that purported to mirror the sensory world (as, say, a poem or play) can have the status of no more than a copy of a copy. Thus, his ideal society, represented in *The Republic*, would have little use for such activities.

As stated above, however, Aristotle believed that study of the 'real world' could give access to transcendent truths. Furthermore, such a study could validly take different forms. This leads Aristotle to the starkly anti-Platonic conclusion that a play might give a more valuable impression of reality than a work of history, as the latter has to be true to life at the level of detail, whereas the former gains its verisimilitude at the level of general truths about the human condition: each is truthful, but in a different way. (Of course, this is not totally anti-Platonic, as there remains a belief in fundamental truths, a point to which I shall return in Section 1.1.3.) Thus, for Aristotle, a play was not merely an exercise in illusion, but a study of character issuing in action. Furthermore, Aristotle offered an explanation of why we respond positively to unpleasant representations in the arts: to a good tragic drama, for example. He claimed this was because such a drama offers *catharsis*, emotional purging. This simple insight has provided fodder for debate about the arts that continues to this day, and is also one of Aristotle's important contributions to the development of psychology.

1.1.2.4 Ethics, morality and the human subject

As with justice, so in all other areas, Aristotle's ethics rest on finding balances between unacceptable extremes: thus courage might be seen as a mean between foolhardiness and cowardice. The *Nicomachean Ethics* lists many virtues and attempts to explain them in this way; I alluded to justice as a further example in Section 1.1.2.2.

Despite the stereotype of the Ancient Greek as a believer in fate, Aristotle's philosophy is strongly humanistic, with a strong emphasis on individual character. In these senses he prefigures the liberal conceptions of the human subject that have dominated Western thinking since the Enlightenment of the seventeenth century. However, Aristotle was not a modern liberal who construed people as autonomous rational beings responsible for choosing their own social roles. Rather, for Aristotle, the person is defined by his or her social ends, which are not chosen, in the way most modern people would understand the term. This point will be developed in Section 1.1.3.

Nevertheless, Aristotle put great emphasis on moral agency and personal responsibility. His conception of *praxis* is deeply moral. The aim of philosophy for the Greeks generally was the pursuit of the good life (*eudaimonia*), in all three modern senses of 'good': as intellectually, emotionally and morally satisfying. Aristotle is the founder of modern virtue ethics insofar as he regards right action, feeling and thought as personal characteristics, or inclinations, and education as the means to develop them.

In many ways this is a very modern view of the person and of the developing person. However, to appreciate fully the differences between Aristotle's views on these matters from our own, it is necessary to examine his metaphysics and how this drives his systems of classification. Only then does it become clear just how deeply Aristotle's assumptions about childhood might differ from some of those embraced today.

1.1.3 Aristotle's Metaphysics

Plato was a rationalist, not an empiricist (see Chapter 1.2). If we simply contrast Aristotle's empiricism to Plato's rationalism from our modern perspectives, however, we can easily gain a false impression. Plato dismissed the perceived world as a poor substitute for that of pure forms. Aristotle rejects this, but he nevertheless retains an essentialist belief in form. To quote J. L. Ackrill (in Urmson and Rée, 1989: 25):

> . . . his word *ousia* (literally 'being') does duty both for our substance and for our 'essence'.

and:

> Form is *immanent* [italics in original]: the form of table exists only as this table or that table. . . . There is no separately existing transcendental Platonic Form of Table.

In other words, Aristotle puts more faith than Plato in real-world experience as a guide to understanding forms; he is no post-Enlightenment empiricist for whom all understanding flows from sense-data (or, more recently still, practices of signification – as discussed in Part 2).

To Aristotle, therefore, the form of everything is within it; everything has its own nature, if you will. On this view, actuality and potentiality are very closely related. That is to say: if everything contains form within it, and form is expressed in the multifariousness of the experienced world, then what happens to any particular thing in that world is determined by its inner form. This is a deterministic account, according to which what something *is* cannot be understood separately from what it will *become*. As Ackrill puts it: 'The actuality is the end for the sake of which the potentiality exists' (Urmson and Rée, 1989: 25). It is on this basis that we should consider Aristotle's view of the child: a task to be undertaken in the next but one chapter.

According to Aristotle, the form and function of any particular substance can be understood with reference to four 'causes'. The material cause comprises what something is made out of; the formal cause comprises its essence; its efficient cause comprises what brought it into being; and its final cause comprises its purpose or ultimate function. In Aristotle's own words (as translated by W. D. Ross) at the beginning of Part 3 of Book 1 of *Metaphysics*:

> . . . causes are spoken of in four senses. In one of these we mean the substance, i.e. the essence (for the 'why' is reducible finally to the definition, and the ultimate 'why' is a cause and principle); in another the matter of substratum, in a third the cause of the change, and in the fourth the cause opposed to this, the purpose and the good (for this is the end of all generation and change. (retrieved from www.classicallibrary.org/aristotle/metaphysics 8 May 2007)

Alternatively, in *Physics*, Part 3 of Book 2 (translated R. P. Hardie and R. K. Gaye):

> In one sense, then, (1) that out of which a thing comes to be and which persists, is called 'cause', e.g. the bronze of the statue, the silver of the bowl, and the genera of which the bronze and the silver are species.

> In another sense (2) the form or the archetype, i.e. the statement of the essence, and its genera, are called 'causes' (e.g. of the octave the relation of 2:1, and generally number), and the parts in the definition.

> Again (3) the primary source of the change or coming to rest; e.g. the man who gave advice is a cause, the father is cause of the child, and generally what makes of what is made and what causes change of what is changed.

> Again (4) in the sense of end or 'that for the sake of which' a thing is done, e.g. health is the cause of walking about. ('Why is he walking about?' we say. 'To be healthy', and, having said that, we think we have assigned the cause.) The same is true also of all the intermediate steps which are brought about through the action of something else as means towards the end, e.g. reduction of flesh, purging, drugs, or surgical instruments are means towards health. All these things are 'for the sake of' the end, though they differ from one another in that some are activities, others instruments. (retrieved from <classics.mit.edu/Aristotle/physics> 8 May 2007)

To Aristotle, therefore, what things are tells us a good deal about what they are meant to be, and this applies as much to people as to inanimate objects.

Thus to Aristotle, the purpose of the farmed or hunted animal is to be eaten by people; the purpose of the slave is to serve, and so on. By modern standards, it is a teleological and deeply conservative philosophy: there is a natural order and each organism or object within that order has a specific purpose in life.

1.1.4 Limits of Aristotle's Metaphysics

From a late modern, or postmodern perspective, Aristotle's view (like Plato's before him) is rigidly absolutist and insensitive to differing perspectives. Aristotle was a man of his time, not of ours, though he speaks to us in many important ways, and there are many distinctions and complexities in our social situation that were not present for him. We see this clearly on a reading of the *Politics*, where he argues for good governance of the state as an extension of the household; meanwhile, Phillippe Ariès has argued that the Aristotelian concept of household is not synonymous with the modern understanding of family (Ariès, 1962). Thus the private-public distinction is not in evidence in Aristotle, nor distinctions between community, region, nation and state – let alone a Postmodern awareness of cultures as characterized by the often conflicting practices of subcultures (Lyotard, 1984). This leaves three interrelated aspects of his metaphysics open to question: his essentialism, his inattention to cultural difference, and his limited view of language and other semiotic systems.

1.1.4.1 Essences

Aristotle's belief in the clear identification of 'causes' (a concept he embraces in a more comprehensive sense that we are wont to do) is made possible by the prior belief that potentiality lies within an object or organism and is not an interpretation of it. To this, Aristotle might validly respond, 'But when we see a child, we do know that it is on the way to becoming an adult; this is an invariable truth, confirmed by experience!'

Indeed so: as with much of Aristotle's thinking, this seems undeniable – as far as it goes. If we take some liberties with numbers, we might argue as follows:

• Children (of a certain age) will get bigger until their late teens (true in 99.9 per cent of cases).

- Children will live to become legally adults (true in 99 per cent of cases now – though not so many in Ancient Greece).
- The child will live to enjoy full adult rights and responsibilities (true in 90+ per cent of cases; not true for some of those with various forms of disability – disregarding for a moment the fact that not all adults in Classical Athens were granted equal rights and responsibilities).
- The child will become a full representative of an ideal of adulthood: autonomous yet socially responsible, self-motivated yet sympathetic to the needs of others, physically strong and so on (true in a very small percentage of cases, possibly none); furthermore:
- Children will become teenagers before they become adults (true for all now, none in Aristotle's time, since there was no conception of the teenager).
- Children will be youths until they are over forty (not true for Aristotle or for us – but according to Ariès [1962], early modern literature uses the term 'youth' in this way).

On examination, it appears that it is not so much inevitable as probable that the child is destined to become the adult. Experience leads us to have certain expectations, but this falls short of justification for the view that the adult is latent within the potentiality of the child.

Also, Aristotle takes it for granted that a human being has a soul (*anima*) and a mind (*psyche*). While these terms remain current, philosophers have long been unwilling to grant them *a priori* status. The onus in the more recent past has been on justifying and refining such conceptions, not assuming them. Thus philosophy of mind is concerned with problems around any conception of mind. In neither case can it merely be assumed that such a thing simply exists within a human being. By contrast:

> In *De Anima*, Aristotle makes extensive use of technical terminology intro-duced and explained elsewhere in his writings. He claims, for example, using vocabulary derived from his physical and metaphysical theories, that the soul is a 'first actuality of a natural organic body' (*De Anima* ii 1, 412b5–6), that it is a 'substance as form of a natural body which has life in potentiality' (*De Anima* ii 1, 412a20–21) and, similarly, that it 'is a first actuality of a natural body which has life in potentiality' (*De Anima* ii 1, 412a27–8), all claims which apply to plants, animals and humans alike. (retrieved from http://plato.stanford.edu/entries/Aristotle-psychology 9 May, 2007)

Aristotle's conception of the unproblematized soul is the ground of his virtue ethics. In other words, what chiefly defines a person is his or her moral attributes and strength of character. Much of the *Nicomachean Ethics* is devoted to defining such desirable characteristics, with no hint that different conceptions of the human good might develop according to context. For example, might liberality have developed as a virtue in an egalitarian, but desperately poor society in which no one enjoyed an excess of basic goods?

1.1.4.2 Cultural differences

What terms mean ('adult' and 'child', for example) varies over time (diachronically) and between contexts at the same time (synchronically). Diachronic variation in conceptions of childhood has been addressed by Ariès and other historians of childhood and will be further addressed during the course of the present argument. Synchronic variation is charted by numerous anthropological and sociological studies. To be a child, or an adult, is not quite the same in Place A as in Place B (even insofar as it is the same for persons A 1 and 2 or B 1 and 2), just as it was not quite the same in Time X as in Time Y. If we were privileged enough to be able to experience both, say, Place-Time AX and Place-Time BY, we might be surprised to find that, albeit there are similarities, the 'human condition' encompasses significant variation, even after generalizing across populations.

That there are points of contact between contemporary and Aristotelian worldviews is, therefore, beyond doubt, but they should not blind us to important differences.

For example, take Aristotle's views on money and trade. Consider the following passage from Book 5 of the *Nicomachean Ethics* (translated by Ross):

Let A be a builder, B a shoemaker, C a house, D a shoe. The builder . . . must get from the shoemaker the latter's work, and must himself give him in return his own. If. .. first there is proportionate equality of goods, and then reciprocal action takes place, the result we mention will be effected. If not, the bargain is not equal, and does not hold; for there is nothing to prevent the work of the one being better than that of the other; they must therefore be equated....For it is not two doctors that associate for exchange, but a doctor and a farmer, or in general people who are different and unequal; but these must be equated. This is why all things that are exchanged must be somehow comparable. It is for this end that money has been introduced, and it becomes in a sense an intermediate; for it measures all things, and therefore the excess and the defect – how many shoes are equal to a house or to a given amount of food. The number of shoes exchanged for a house (or for a given amount of food) must therefore correspond to the ratio of builder to shoemaker. For if this be not so, there will be no exchange and no intercourse. And this proportion will not be effected unless the goods are somehow equal. All goods must therefore be measured by some one thing, as we said before. Now this unit is in truth demand, which holds all things together (for if men did not need one another's goods at all, or did not need them equally, there would be either no exchange or not the same exchange); but money has become by convention a sort of representative of demand; and this is why it has the name 'money' (*nomisma*)-because it exists not by nature but by law (*nomos*) and it is in our power to change it and make it useless. There will, then, be reciprocity when the terms have been equated so that as farmer is to shoemaker, the amount of the shoemaker's work is to that of the farmer's work for which it exchanges . . . And for the future exchange – that if we do not need a thing now we shall have it if ever we do need it – money is as it were our surety; for it must be possible for us to get what we want by bringing the money. Now the same thing happens to money itself as to goods – it is not always worth the same; yet it tends to be steadier. This is why all goods must have a price set on them. (Retrieved from http://classics.mit.edu/Aristotle/nicomachean 9 May 2007)

The key phrase is 'all goods must have a price set on them'. Aristotle is a price-fixer. He believes that absolute judgements can be made about relative worth. No successful modern government indulges in widespread price-fixing; all, to a greater or lesser extent, allow market forces to determine prices, because they accept that no commodity or service can validly be held to have a fixed value *vis-à-vis* other commodities and services, simply because people vary in their preferences, within and between cultural and social groups and across time. There is a general acceptance that a more-or-less free market produces economic growth (though whether it results in fair shares is more open to contention) and that highly restrictive trade practices are counterproductive overall. Aristotle, however, believes that the governors of the society can and should determine the right price for everything as a means of exercising virtue in the public sphere. This may be interpreted as a measure for stability but not as one for economic growth, and it takes no account of differing priorities among consumers, or the relative capacities or value-systems of, and within, different societies. It is simply one example of Aristotle's failure to recognize the importance of cultural differences.

1.1.4.3 Language and other sign systems

As the soul, and its ends, defines the person, so language and other means of communication must take a dependent and instrumental role in Aristotle's overall scheme. Indeed, Aristotle pays little attention to such matters, though he does consider the 'language arts', particularly in the *Poetics* (of which only fragments remain) and most memorably with respect to drama.

Drama, in the *Poetics*, operates principally through story. It offers universal truths about the human condition and engages its audience through the arousal of emotion: in the case of tragedy, pity and fear. Aristotle therefore sees the language of the play as a vehicle for conveying messages about the human condition which call forth certain responses in an audience. Plot expresses character in action; in tragedy, the protagonist's tragic flaw, or *hubris* results in appropriate retribution. Although the play is artifice, therefore, it works by summoning forth qualities internal to the human subject. The language gains its power not from its selection and organization, but from what it seeks to convey.

In a less essentialist, less metaphysical age, attention inevitably switches to an interest in language itself: both in how it conveys what is assumed to be within (and which therefore remains hidden from direct view), and in how it may itself contribute to the experience of reality. In all its major forms, philosophy since the turn of the twentieth century has taken a 'linguistic turn'. As one of the major figures associated with this, Ludwig Wittgenstein ended his first published work, the *Tractatus Logico-Philosophicus*, first published in 1921, with the assertion (variously translated from the German), 'What we cannot speak about, we must pass over in silence' (Wittgenstein, trans. Pears and McGuinness, 1974: 74: often remembered as 'Whereof I cannot speak, thereof I must remain silent'.). In his most significant later work, the *Philosophical Investigations* (Wittgenstein, 1967; first published 1953), he went further than before in arguing that concepts only make sense within the contexts of the 'language games' in which they are played, and that these 'language games' or the 'forms of life' to which they are related (we might now talk of 'cultural practices' to embrace both) provide the 'bottom line' as far as our rational understanding is concerned. Nothing we know in experience is proved or presupposed by pure logic, according to Wittgenstein, and often our attempts to solve philosophical debates, particularly of the metaphysical sort, result in nonsensical answers, as we attempt to answer questions arising in one language game in the terms of another: almost as though, to coin an example, we were to accuse someone of cheating by playing hide-and-seek.

Wittgenstein's *milieu* – though to some extent he undermined it – was Anglo-Saxon and Northern European analytic philosophy; he studied principally at Cambridge, initially under Bertrand Russell. In the French-dominated world of Continental philosophy, structuralism, poststructuralism and semiotics all used an interest in language, or in *semiosis* (communication *via* any and all sign-systems) as the means to understand human identity, society and culture, sometimes in ways completely at odds with the humanistic tradition that owes so much to Aristotle. These influences will bear heavily on the conception of childhood to be developed in Part 2. Meanwhile, the next chapter will explain in greater depth how Aristotle's view of childhood builds on that of his predecessor, Plato.

1.2

Aristotle's Debt to Plato

As would Aristotle after him, Plato devoted considerable space in key works to the consideration and treatment of the young. In this chapter, I shall explain briefly how Aristotle's metaphysics draw on Plato's before examining the latter's approach to childhood.

1.2.1 Plato's Metaphysics

Plato's works are written as dialogues, and thus tend to be exploratory rather than conclusive. Having acknowledged this, the conversation is generally rather 'one-way', involving the character Socrates and one other, with one developing a thesis while the other responds appropriately, but passively, to each stage in the argument, often simply agreeing to that which has just been proposed. Sometimes, therefore, we get a strong sense of Plato's philosophical position, but at others, only of his concerns, since his characters (notably Socrates) cannot counter all the opposing arguments and find it difficult to settle on a position. In discussing Plato's theory of the Forms, therefore, we are discussing something that seems fairly settled in some texts, but is portrayed as contested and often unsatisfactory in others.

Where one text is taken as definitive of Plato's philosophy as a whole, it is the *Republic* (Plato's Utopia), while the *Parmenides* is one of his most difficult and apparently self-critical dialogues.

Consider the following from Book 5 of the *Republic* (translated by Lee, 1987: 208-9). Here the first speaker is Glaucon, the second Socrates.

'Then who are the true philosophers?' he asked.
'Those who love to see the truth.'
'This is clearly right, but what does it mean?'
'It would be difficult,' I said, 'to explain it to anyone else; but you, I think, will agree with me on the following point.'
'What point?'

'That, since beauty and ugliness are opposites, they are *two*.' [italics in
original]
'Of course.'
'And as they are *two*, each of them is single.'
'That is so.'

. . . .

[Socrates] 'I use this principle to distinguish your sight-lovers and art-
lovers and practical men from the philosophers in the true sense, who are
the subject of our discussion. . . . Those who love looking and listening
are delighted by beautiful sounds and colours and shapes, and the works
of art which make use of them, but their minds are incapable of seeing
and delighting in the essential nature of beauty itself.'
'That is certainly so,' he agreed.
'And those who can reach beauty itself and see it as in itself are likely to
be very few.'

In other words, the philosopher seeks the truth concerning abstractions
such as beauty, while the ordinary person merely enjoys beautiful things,
and is thus distracted by them from the pursuit of truth. In the same text,
Plato gives us his 'myth of the cave' wherein he depicts most people as cave-
dwellers mistaking the shadows caused by the flickering of the fire on the
cave wall for reality, which can only be encountered by those brave enough
to leave the cave, where they will initially be blinded by the light. This
absolutist view of truth as indivisible and beyond mere sensory experience
drives Plato's political and educational prescriptions for his Republic, a
state to be ruled by philosopher-kings. These prescriptions include detailed,
and sometimes draconian, instructions for curriculum and the general
training of the young, which will be addressed below.

On a reading of the *Republic* alone, it would be relatively straightforward
to define Plato's metaphysical stance. In brief, there are many beautiful
things or just things but there is only one beauty or justice. Philosophers
should not be misled by the multifarious examples but should seek to know
the one truth: the ideal form of beauty, truth or whatever. However, in earlier and later works, the theory of Forms is presented (or assumed) as much
less clear and unproblematic.

Perhaps the most notable extended problematization of the theory of
Forms (or Universals) is the *Parmenides*, which dates from a similar period
to the *Republic* (around 370 BC, when Plato was in his fifties). This dialogue
is unusual insofar as much of it involved Socrates in a passive role, while the
argument is largely developed by the older man, Parmenides. Here, if you
like, we see Socrates given some doses of his own medicine.

Parmenides develops four objections to the theory of Forms. These are briefly:

1. A beautiful thing partakes of the Form of beauty. Through this process of multiplication, or division, the Form is no longer one.
2. The so-called Third Man argument stipulates that the series of large things includes the Form of largeness itself, which calls forth a second form of largeness to embrace everything in the series, and so on *ad finitum*.
3. If a Form is a thought, or concept, it must be a concept of a Form, resulting in another example of infinite regress.
4. The things of our world are related to each other, and not to the Forms: thus the master owns the slave, but does not own either mastery or servitude. What is more, the gods who dwell in the divine world of Forms can have no knowledge of us. The world of Forms and human experience cannot meet.

Unlike *The Republic*, where Plato/Socrates speaks with confidence and certainty (albeit in making a series of propositions for government that could be countered), in the *Parmenides* we find Socrates very much 'on the back foot', as the following examples illustrate:
[In relation to (1) and (3) above]

> But may not the ideas, asked Socrates, be thoughts only, and have no proper existence except in our minds, Parmenides? For in that case each idea may still be one, and not experience this infinite multiplication.
> And can there be individual thoughts which are thoughts of nothing?
> Impossible, he said.
> The thought must be of something?
> Yes.
> Of something which is or which is not?
> Of something which is. (Translation by Benjamin Jowett, retrieved from http://ww.sacred-texts.com/cla/plato/parmeni.htm 21 May 2007, p. 5)

[In relation to (4)]

> I may illustrate my meaning in this way, said Parmenides:- A master has a slave; now there is nothing absolute in the relation between them, which is simply a relation of one man to another. But there is also an idea of mastership in the abstract, which is relative to the idea of slavery in the abstract. These natures have nothing to do with us, nor we with them; they are concerned with themselves only, and we with ourselves. Do you see my meaning?

Yes, said Socrates, I quite see your meaning.
. . . Then the nature of the beautiful in itself, and of the good in itself, and all other ideas which we suppose to exist absolutely, are unknown to us? It would seem so. (ibid. 7–8)

All in all, the *Parmenides* is a difficult text, but it seems that the strongest defence that can manage these objections is that dialectic must proceed in relation to the tensions between being and not-being and the particular and the universal, and even this is more strongly proposed by Parmenides than by Socrates.

Regarding a typical Platonic view, it is therefore necessary not merely to attend to the clearest and most polemical expressions. Whether or not Plato 'is' Socrates, what characterizes the dialogues is a series of concerns rather than a firm commitment to conclusions: concerns with the value and limits of dialectic and, of more immediate pertinence, with the relationship between the universal and the particular.

How might a twenty-first-century philosopher respond to the problems Plato grapples with in the *Parmenides*?

One response is that the 'linguistic turn' in philosophy of the last century locates Plato's problems in the nature of language rather than of reality. The argument might proceed as follows.

In philosophical terms, Plato's approach is strongly realist. That is to say, there is a strong conviction that every 'thing' that is postulated in language relates to some 'thing' in the real world: that every signifier has a referent. To Plato, this must be true for abstractions such as 'beauty' as well as for concrete objects such as a 'tree'. Thus when I see a beautiful tree, I see both a tree (which is clearly evident to my senses) and a manifestation of 'beauty', which must exist in reality too, but which I cannot see, as it lies within a world of ideal Forms that I can only perceive (if at all) through the exercise of my reason. This view of language as either a mirror (reflecting reality) or a vehicle (carrying information about reality) has a long heritage, as does the belief that human reason, expressible in language, acts as a bridge between limited human experience and the divine. It is a view that permeates the Judaeo-Christian tradition, *inter alia*: a tradition that draws strongly on both Platonic and Aristotelian ideas.

Plato therefore assumes that, as 'beauty' is a word that applies to all beautiful things, and that there must be a referent for 'beauty', as there is for everything else, it follows that there is a real world – that of the Forms – that is separate from that which we encounter day by day. We might counter this by proposing that we use the word 'beauty' to pass a sort of value judgement on certain trees, based on characteristics we find useful, affecting or whatever, and which we see repeated across all the trees we respond to as beautiful. In other words, there need not be any referent for 'beauty' at all. Furthermore, there is no requirement for us to use the same criteria of beauty in relation to, say, trees, members of the opposite sex and buildings. This is not to deny that there might be certain underlying aesthetic principles that do apply to all these sets of judgement, relating perhaps to symmetry, proportion or colour, but while this would be an argument with Platonic connotations, it would not be a theory of Forms.

The language of the beautiful itself might thus create the illusion of a Form of beauty, rather than the other way round. More recent work in philosophy, linguistics and social and cultural theory is broadly sympathetic to this position, stressing the role of language in creating, and not merely conveying, human reality. While this 'linguistic turn' has many sources and many manifestations, including the pragmatism of C. S. Peirce in the late 1800s, and the analytic philosophy of Bertrand Russell in the early 1900s, one of its most important roots lies in the linguistic theory of Ferdinand de Saussure. Saussure argued that languages are socially constructed systems of signs. Therefore: (i) words derive their meanings not from referents in 'the real world' but from the other words they relate to; meaning is, as the later poststructuralists would stress, defined by difference not identity; and (ii) the relations of signs to referents are therefore arbitrary, or uncallable, as are the relationships of elements of the sign (the signifier and the signified, i.e. broadly, the word and its meaning). To put it crudely, we call a dog a dog for no better reason than that it is our cultural practice so to do; this does not imply any absolute, rational conception of dogginess, though we use scientific analysis to define the species. (For a general introduction to the ideas within Saussure's *Course in General Linguistics*, see Culler, 1976.)

Furthermore, if languages are socially constructed systems of signs, then they are in one sense analogous to other, non-verbal sign systems. Thus Continental European thought, in particular, drew on Saussure in developing modern theories of Structuralism, Poststructuralism and Semiotics, using studies of language and other cultural practices in fields such as anthropology and sociology, as well as philosophy and cultural theory, to explain the human condition. Such approaches are anti-humanist, anti-essentialist and therefore anti-Platonic.

Within the predominantly Anglo-Saxon analytic philosophical community, Ludwig Wittgenstein also came to recognize the primacy of language. Apparently ignorant of, or indifferent to Saussure, Wittgenstein's later great work, *Philosophical Investigations* (1967: hereafter *PI*) is influenced by the 'ordinary language' philosophy of J.L. Austin, who stressed the 'performative' power of language (e.g. in Austin, 1962). For example, if an employer tells an employee 'clear your desk', this results in a series of actions that might include serious personal breakdown. Language in itself makes things happen.

Wittgenstein's great blow against the Platonic tradition in *PI* is to argue that conceptions and truths can only be held to be valid within the contexts of the 'language games' or 'forms of life' in which they are employed. A trivial example, not used by Wittgenstein, might be that the term 'multiply' means 'make greater in number' in most contexts (such as the Biblical order to 'go forth and multiply') but does not mean this within mathematics, where one might multiply by a fraction. There is no absolute, decontextualized multiplication. It follows from this that philosophy's function should not be to try to answer unanswerable questions, such as 'What is the true nature of multiplication?', because questions can only be answered from within the language games that pose them. Rather, philosophy serves to guard against 'the bewitchment of our intelligence by means of language' (Wittgenstein, 1967: Aphorism 109). On this account, Plato was bewitched by language into assuming that beauty must exist as surely as the beautiful tree exists. Wittgenstein would argue that beauty exists as a concept within a language game of aesthetics, and can only be understood thus.

As with beauty, so with childhood, one might infer – except that Plato did not discuss childhood as a Form directly.

1.2.2 Plato on Childhood

It is easy to see how Plato's concern with the relationship of the particular and the universal could influence Aristotle's beliefs about potentiality and actuality. The main difference lies in the value ascribed to human experience, and here Aristotle might be held to have resolved many of the problems Plato found in reconciling human and 'divine' knowledge, of the human world and the world of Forms respectively. However, despite Aristotle's generally greater bias towards the empirical, when it comes to child-rearing and education, Plato (albeit in his Utopias, the *Republic* and the *Laws*) is much the more prescriptive of the two.

Of the three common senses in which one is a child, Plato was principally interested in *Child 3*, the not-yet-competent rather than the person of limited age. He does often specify age in relation to education, but the education of the guardians, in both the above texts, extends far into what we now consider adulthood, while he pays little attention to the emotional needs of younger children. In Book VII of the *Republic*, for example, he specifies that the training in philosophy to be undertaken by future leaders – the final stage of their education for guardianship – should extend from 35 to 50: shortly after the period in which men should be compelled to marry in Book IV of the *Laws*! Indeed, whenever Plato discusses the curriculum, there is little awareness of the protected or special state we associate with childhood, other than the acknowledgement (in Book VII of the *Laws* and elsewhere) that early training should be in gymnastics, as it exploits children's natural inclinations to play and move.

What Plato does find in children, as would Aristotle, is natural potentiality. In *Republic* Book III, he tells the tale of how the gods put gold, silver, iron or bronze into the souls of children, thus determining their natural course in life. True justice and education consist in training each child according to what is in his or her soul (for Plato foresaw some female guardians), bearing in mind that sometimes golden children can be born to silver parents, and so on. This vision of education according to innate ability bears a striking resemblance to Britain's 1944 Education Act. A possible difference is that Plato always discusses young people in terms of their future usefulness to the state, never in terms of their leading any other kind of worthwhile existence; whether this was significantly different in the 1940s is a matter of debate, but the tone is certainly different in, for example, the 1967 Plowden Report on primary education (CACE, 1967). Overall, Plato had little or no philosophical interest in *Child 2*, the sate of being young *per se*. In this sense, Plato was more interested in education than in childhood.

On one level, this interest is very broad, if we regard his whole philosophical output, with its development (and subsequently partial abandonment) of the Socratic dialogue as educational in itself. However, when he explicitly discusses education in terms of curriculum, he does so solely in the limited context of his concern with rational government and good social order. While Plato offers the earliest systematic formulation of curriculum in these works, the purpose of the discussion is not to understand child development *per se*, but to determine how best people should be prepared for their future roles in the state. It is an entirely top-down, narrowly meritocratic prescription, tempered only by the acknowledgment that young people vary in potential. In both the *Republic* and the *Laws*, education exists in its fullest form to prepare a small minority of people for positions of leadership within a totalitarian state governed according to an inflexible and absolutist form of reason. While it is intended as benevolent, the form of government envisaged contravenes many liberal democratic principles, even more strongly in the *Laws* than the *Republic*. Examples include controlling prices and wages; punishing activities other than those for which a person is known professionally; specifying the time of marriage and punishing the childless; invoking the death penalty for many offences, and infanticide under certain circumstances; controlling population levels; specifying that men and women should exercise naked together regardless of the humiliation; forbidding travel unless permitted; offering no rights to slaves, and teaching children about war by taking them to war. The conception of reason in these two texts is narrow insofar as it is not subjected to the critique offered in, for example, the *Parmenides*. Rather, certain assumptions are taken as given: assumptions that, in many cases, continue to have considerable resonance in contemporary debates about education and the curriculum. These particularly relate to assumptions about the relative worth of branches of study.

Readers may recall school reports from the days before computers, in which subjects were listed with comments relating to progress against them. Sometimes these comments were cursory: 'satisfactory', for example. (Satisfactory according to whom and to what?) Such comments betray one Platonic legacy: It is up to the elders to decide what is appropriate knowledge, progress and understanding for each child according to the latter's potential. Schools still make such value judgements, albeit in more sophisticated ways: for example, by comparing students' progress against their scores on standardized tests designed to measure various forms of 'intelligence'. Also interesting was the way in which subjects were listed. In my own experience, 'difficult', abstract subjects – Mathematics and Science – along with English, the home language, came at the top of the list, while 'arts and crafts' were at the bottom. This, too, is Platonic. Plato's 'philosopher-kings' moved through a curriculum that took them from the concrete and kinetic through to the abstract, a progression also remembered in the current practice of calling our highest degrees doctorates in philosophy, regardless of whether they are technically philosophical in any recognizable modern sense.

Plato responded to an Athenian tradition of largely private education, specializing in the literary arts, by insisting that children should be removed from their parents and educated in schools by the state (for the origins of compulsory state education are to be found here, and not in the liberal Enlightenment tradition, wherein compulsory schooling did not form part of the social contract in the writings of, for example, Hobbes, Hume, Locke or Rousseau – as will be discussed in later chapters). Once under the safe control of the guardians, their training would be strictly controlled and their exposure to works of art strictly censored. They would begin with training in gymnastics, as preparation for military activity and a highly constrained conception of music, as training of the 'soul', or mind (*Republic* Book II). (Towards the beginning of Book VII of the *Laws*, the possibility is even entertained of gymnastic training for those yet unborn by making pregnant women deport themselves in specified ways, though the subject is dropped on the grounds that such rules would be ridiculed: a rare reminder in these texts that Athenian society in reality differed greatly from Plato's prescriptions for his ideal republic.) Their exposure to literature must be strongly constrained, as the following interchange makes clear:

> 'Shall we therefore readily allow our children to listen to any stories made up by anyone, and to form opinions that are for the most part the opposite of those we think they should have when they grow up?'
> 'We certainly shall not.'
> 'Then it seems that our first business is to supervise the production of stories . . . ' (*Republic* translated by Lee, 1987: 72)

Those selected as suitable for higher offices of state would eventually move through a more specialized curriculum with much emphasis on mathematical training in areas such as geometry, before the future leaders are ready for their long training as adults in philosophy, or 'dialectic'.

It is in relation to this hierarchy of concerns that Plato suggests certain young people should be trained for leadership, though they will by no means be young on attaining high office. (They will serve as guardians from 50 to 70, according to the *Laws*.) Although he sees his curriculum as potentially fit for girls as well as boys, he supposes that, on the whole, the boys will outperform the girls, and it is not intended for slaves. Very few young people will experience its higher reaches. By modern standards, his vision is of a one-dimensional society with a restrictively narrow conception of the social good. However, in many respects, it is a vision enacted in many places in the contemporary world, and when we consider curriculum, we often continue to do so on the basis of key Platonic assumptions. Indeed, it might be argued that contemporary conceptions of *Child 2* draw heavily on Plato's treatment of *Child 3*: the not-yet-ready, to be trained and selected on the basis of natural predisposed potential in relation to a monological conception of reason and the good that we nowadays tend to call 'intelligence'. It is still largely on this basis that we prescribe and enforce the upbringing of the young.

1.3

Aristotle: Children as People in Formation

To a great extent, Aristotle's work serves as a series of responses to Plato, and it is often held that in so responding, Aristotle offers the final major expression of Ancient Greek thought; Bertrand Russell, for example, refers to him as the last great creative force within that tradition in his *History of Western Philosophy* (1945/1972). It is therefore not surprising that his influence on subsequent cultures – including our own – has been so significant.

As well as being Plato's respectful but often critical student, Aristotle can also be regarded as putting in place one of the key foundations of modern science, including social science: his grounding and testing of theory in observation. This is one of his seminal contributions to the history of childhood. In studying children as animals as well as future citizens, Aristotle set the agenda for the scientific study of child development.

Aristotle's second great contribution is to refine Plato's Theory of Forms such that it becomes a Theory of Form and Matter: of potentiality and actuality. This gives a much stronger view than Plato of children as emerging adults reliant on appropriate environmental conditions to thrive.

His third contribution, arising in part from the first two, rests in setting the seeds for the development of the modern conception of the nuclear family. Like Plato, Aristotle was more interested in households than families, and regarded households as political units; unlike Plato, and crucially, however, he did not believe in children being removed from their parents for communal education. He saw spiritual development as arising from individuated care, not merely from training in curricular disciplines; in short, he argues that children should be nurtured. Finally, in pursuing this intention, Aristotle offers development of Plato's initial prescriptions for the educational curriculum.

1.3.1 Children as Biology: Growth and What to Make of it

As stated in the Introduction, there is a modern tendency to regard the child as predominantly *Child 2*: as a person in the first few years of life, irrespective of their experiences or attributes. This is doubtless in part because we tend to hold the post-Darwinian view that humans are fundamentally animals, and therefore that biological development is central to the development of the person. Aristotle was not Darwinian, of course, but he does ground his study of children, as of so much else, in detailed observation of the physical. His theories regarding children are drawn from such observations and ascribe their validity to their 'fit' to them. This is the basis for all modern empirical science, albeit Aristotle did not test his hypotheses through experimentation and attempts at falsification. It is also the basis on which the modern mind tends to locate childhood firmly in the early years of life. It is important to appreciate the significance of this, because without such a belief childhood (as *Child 1* or *Child 3*) is rather a state of being than a period of time. Indeed, other ancient texts often offer a view of childhood as a state of non-worldly, or uncorrupted being, a view that draws indirectly on Plato and has also influenced the strong counter-strain in modern views of childhood: the Romantic view. This view will be explored more fully in subsequent chapters, but it is worthy of note at this stage that, for example, the pre-Socratic Heraclitus wrote: 'Time is a child moving counters in a game. The royal power is a child's' (Wheelwright, 1960: 71). Such a view sees the immature body rather as a sign of childhood than vice versa. Aristotle shifts the focus very strongly to the child as an emergent, growing body and soul.

It is an important feature of Aristotle's argument that body and soul are truly inseparable. The material and spiritual are each aspects of the emergent organism. Thus we find Aristotle's remarks about young people in *The History of Animals* (*sic*) combine the scientist's dispassionate observation with the moralizer's unproblematized attribution of causes. Quotations are from the *Internet Classics Archive* text translated by D'Arcy Wentworth Thompson (http://classics.mit.edu/Aristotle/history,retrieved18/07/2007: Book VII):

> When twice seven years old, in the most of cases, the male begins to engender seed . . . About the same time, the voice begins to alter, getting harsher and more uneven, neither shrill as formerly nor deep as afterward, nor yet of any even tone . . . Now this breaking of the voice is more apparent in those who are making trial of their sexual powers; for in those who are prone to lustfulness the voice turns into the voice of a man, but not so in the continent. For if a lad strive diligently to hinder his voice from breaking, as some do of those who devote themselves to music, the voice lasts a long while unbroken and may even persist with little change.

The chain of events is quite different in the case of girls, however:

> Girls of this age have much need of surveillance. For then in particular
> they feel a natural impulse to make usage of the sexual faculties that are
> developing in them; so that unless they guard against any further impulse
> beyond that inevitable one which their bodily development of itself
> supplies . . . they contract habits which are apt to continue into later life.

There is a compelling mixture here, as throughout Aristotle's work, of
rigorous description and false certainties. What comes over very clearly,
however, is that the child as agent cannot be divorced from the child
as body. The will and the material on which it acts appear to be in a sort of
dialectical tension. This is not a perspective from which it is easy to argue,
for example, that the enlightened one will be like a child.

1.3.2 Children as Potential Adults

Aristotle's metaphysics has already received some attention. He departed
from his master, Plato's, Theory of Forms, in valorizing the real, observable
world rather than the world of abstractions such as beauty and justice. However, he did not depart from a faith in absolute reason and, therefore, in a
clear hierarchy among forms of life, and among people.

In *The Cambridge Encyclopaedia of Child Development*, Celia Moore explains
how Aristotle combined ancient assumptions with new forms of scientific
thinking, leaving an enduring, though not entirely attractive legacy:

> Aristotle . . . presented the first detailed conception of development,
> along with a vivid natural history of embryology in diverse life forms, in
> *On the Generation of Animals.* He replaced the atomistic preformationism
> of earlier thinkers with an epigenetic conception in which the embryo
> differentiates progressively from a homogeneous origin, with parts such
> as heart, lungs, and limbs and their spatial arrangement only gradually
> taking shape. . . . The central features of Aristotelian epigenesis derived
> from his material, efficient and final causes. These included a distinction
> between the material cause from which the embryo is produced and
> nutrients to support the growth and maintenance of the embryo; an
> explanation of differentiation as the action of a non-material generative
> principle in the semen of males (the efficient cause) on the formative
> material from females (menstrual blood of humans, the white of a bird
> egg etc.); and an explanation of the particular form taken by an organism

and its parts in terms of final causes (purpose or plan). The central epi-genetic idea was that there was a male principle that acts on generative material secreted by females, setting developmental processes in motion that progressively actualize potentials inherent in the material. . . . Aristo-tle . . . defined the major developmental questions and led the way for empirically minded successors to continue the inquiry some two millen-nia later.' (Retrieved from www.cambridge.org/us/catalogue/catalogue. asp?isbn=9780521651172&ss=exc 20 June 2007)</Ext>

Where were these 'developmental processes . . . progressively' leading? Towards a happy and fulfilled life of speculative reason, the highest state of human being. In Part 3 of *Physics* (for example), Aristotle makes absolutely clear that the essence of humanity is fixed, and that growth is the realiza-tion of potential, not 'alteration'. He writes: 'it would seem absurd . . . to speak . . . of a man or house or anything else that has come into existence as having been altered . . . acquired states, whether of the body or of the soul, are not alterations.' (Translation by R. P. Hardie and R. K. Gaye: retrieved from http://classics.mit.edu/Aristotle/physics 20 June 2007.) What differentiates between realized human natures, therefore, is degree: different people, or groups of people, are not to be judged against different criteria. Human nature is not altered by growth. However, where Aristotle moves us on from Plato is in the emphasis he puts on the importance of correct environmental stimulation to turn potentiality into actuality. Book 3 of *Physics* stresses that 'that which is potentially possessed of knowledge becomes actually possessed of it not by being set in motion at all itself but by reason of the presence of something else: i.e. it is when it meets with the particular object that it knows in a manner the particular through its knowl-edge of the universal'. Thus 'the use and activity of the intellect aris[e] from a man's becoming sober or being awakened' (ibid.).

The particular challenges of progressing children towards their highest feasible adult states are addressed most fully in the *Politics* and the *Nicoma-chean Ethics*. Despite its title, the *Politics* is concerned primarily with the management of households, for Aristotle sees the household as the model for the state (arguably the reverse of the assumptions in Plato's *Laws*). The household is the basic unit of social organization, in which the master-slave, husband-wife and parent-child relationships model those of both soul-and-body and king-and-subject. Within this highly rational organizational system, children must learn subservience in order to prepare for leader-ship, or to fulfil lesser functions in as fully adult a way as possible. The soul itself comprises reason (the basis for rule) with non-reasoning feelings that are subject to rule. Newborns have the most basic of these feelings, but reason can only develop much later.

A perhaps unfortunate consequence of this strongly hierarchical view is that happiness, or fulfilment (*eudaimonia*), is not possible for children. Without proper education and training they can and will never be happy. This view, like the rest of the Aristotelian offering, has its enduring counterpoint in Western culture in the Romantic view that the adult is corrupted, that children are 'trailing clouds of glory' (Wordsworth's *Ode: Intimations of Immortality*) and that our schooldays are the best of our lives. This Romantic reaction will be considered later, but it might be noted that it carries its own Aristotelian legacy, expressed in Wordsworth's paradoxical assertion that 'the child is father of the man' (*My Heart Leaps Up When I Behold*). This, of course, is an ironic reversal, as we expect, as did Aristotle, the father to be wiser than the child.

While Aristotle's belief in the superiority of the mature, philosophical condition is also Platonic, his emphasis on the household calls particular attention to parental, particularly fatherly responsibility. To Aristotle, the household is not merely a microcosm of the state, therefore, but its engine-room, and this has implications for the treatment of children.

1.3.3 The Care of the Child: From State to Household to Family

Although Aristotle is scarcely a modern liberal democrat, some seeds of liberal democracy are sown in his critique of Plato and Socrates. This is nowhere clearer than in Book 2 of the *Politics*, where he asserts, 'liberality consists in the use which is made of property' (Translated by Benjamin Jowett; retrieved from http://classics.mit.edu/Aristotle/politics 21 June 2007). In this striking phrase, Aristotle strikes at the heart of the Platonic utopian vision by claiming that virtue rests on individual responsibility, which in turn rests on a degree of individualism. He arrives at this conclusion through consideration of the relationship of family, household and state:

> . . . since the nature of a state is to be a plurality,
> and in tending to greater unity, from being a state, it becomes a
> family, and from being a family, an individual; for the family may
> be said to be more than the state, and the individual than the family.
> So that we ought not to attain this greatest unity even if we could,

reasonable life is the path to happiness, and that there is, at least potentially, a best expression of that life. This is the simplest and safest basis for
curriculum planning, insofar as no doubt is entertained as to whether reasonable adults know what is best for their merely wilful charges. What is best
for them is what reasonable adults say is best for them, and certainly not
what they may want for themselves: Aristotle's social settlement has no more
place for a free market in ideas than in goods and services.

Aristotle has no modern concept of readiness for education, so his
curriculum begins at birth. Infants, though unreasonable, should still be
habituated, for such habituation forms the basis for the development of
deliberative reason. Thus, according to the *Politics* (Book 7), the natural
inclinations of babies should be steered into virtuous patterns of behaviour:
they should be exposed only to positive influences (e.g. not slaves; Aristotle's
curriculum is for citizens), and their natural energy and receptivity should
be exploited by encouraging them to play movement games and listen to
suitable stories. They should be raised initially on milk, and be hardened to
the cold. Virtually the same recommendations, against both swaddling and
spoiling children, would be made again in the eighteenth century by both
John Locke (in *Some Thoughts Concerning Education*) and Jean-Jacques Rousseau in *Émile*, each of which will be discussed in forthcoming chapters.

According to Aristotle (as, it might be argued, according to us), the principal years of general devotion to study should be from 7 to 21, with a
demarcation between approaches at puberty. (Aristotle is relatively less concerned with the education through adulthood of future rulers; his is more
recognizably a concern with *Child 2*.) The general principles underlying
this education are best expressed in the *Nicomachean Ethics*; the substantive
details in Book 8 of the *Politics*. In the former, Aristotle gives his fullest
account of the importance of habit in the development of virtues, and of
the nature of specific virtues. Aristotle's contribution here is in his insistence on virtue as a mean between extremes: thus the brave man is neither
foolhardy nor temperate. In most respects, contemporary societies tend
to follow Aristotle on this, though there are exceptions. One particular
challenge relates to pride, which the Christian tradition condemns as the
greatest sin of all. To Aristotle, there was a proper level of pride and self-
love, between blind arrogance and submissiveness; after all, how can a
man be generous if he has no sense of self-worth? Here is another example
of Aristotle simultaneously setting the tone for modern Liberal societies
while being at the same time quite at odds with them. Western societies (at
least) currently value self-worth because they value individual freedom of
thought and agency; this is true notably of the United States, which is also

strongly Christian. It might be said that self-worth is a necessary precondition of market economies: individuals must have preferences as consumers and marketable skills as producers. However, Aristotle is not interested in markets or any other conception of the voluntary interchange of free individuals, except insofar as they exercise their virtues in the interests of the state. Within this context, it would be an irresponsible citizen who were to give all his possessions to the poor, for example.

As to the content of the curriculum, its main elements should be reading and writing, physical training, drawing and music. In all cases, skills in these are developed so that the individual can contribute at the highest possible level to the state, but not in the modern sense of offering services to others. For example, musical skill should be developed as training of the character, not with a view to playing for the enjoyment of others, and certainly not as a paid entertainer, for such a person would forego his (*sic*) sense of civic duty by effectively prostituting himself thus. In these, as in all activities, attention must be paid to due balance. For example, too much emphasis on physical training will promote savagery rather than reason; too little, weakness and timidity. Therefore Aristotle suggests relatively easy physical training before puberty, a break from it for three years, and then a tougher régime.

Yet again, Aristotle's approach now seems paradoxical. This is a recognizably 'liberal' education – an education in the arts, to a large extent – yet it exists to prepare young people, inter alia, to fight in war (though Aristotle, unlike Plato, puts emphasis on the warrior virtues also being moderated). Furthermore, it is an education geared very strongly towards the enjoyment of leisure. However, by 'leisure', Aristotle did not mean the passive pursuit of pleasure. The man of leisure was the man of reason, not the wastrel or the slob, for leisure was the time of deliberation; threats to the social order were more likely to come from the overactive and unreflective. Thus drawing, music and gymnastics are all about training the mind, inducing calm senses of order and reason and the capacity to reproduce them in one's own company. These are the necessary foundations for responsible adult life, whether as farmer, soldier or statesman, and for the advanced training in mathematics and dialectic that Plato had already stipulated as necessary preparation for the latter. Aristotle stresses that every citizen, as head of a household, needs to be a responsible statesman, if not of the status and power of a Platonic philosopher-king.

(Interestingly, Platonic and Aristotelian conceptions of music as rational and spiritual harmony remained strong throughout the early modern period. In Shakespeare, for example, characters are judged by their responses to music. Thus Caliban, the half-human, part 'noble savage' – part mere savage – in *The Tempest* hears music on the enchanted isle that 'delights, and hurts not', whereas Shylock, the vengeful – but cruelly treated – Jew of *The Merchant of Venice* complains of 'the vile squeaking of the wry-neck'd fife'. Clearly these are each problematic characters, for whom Shakespeare is arguably inviting conflicting responses, but the use of music in these cases draws on a long, strongly Aristotelian tradition.)

Overall, Aristotle's influence on modern education is very great and yet deeply paradoxical. Young people are potential adults; they are crucially important for society; they have natural inclinations which must be supported and channelled rather than suppressed; they must learn to value themselves, to be responsible, and to be balanced and moderate in all things except for general strength of character, in which they should excel (an unacknowledged irony in Aristotle's position). At the same time, they (i.e. those who are male free citizens), should defend the social order, scorn the slaves and entertainers whose services they require, and, while exercising their democratic rights as free citizens, regard all the subservient members of their households (i.e. everyone else: women, children, servants, slaves) as property. In general, they should value private property but restrict trade and ban profit. Aristotle offers us a society in which everyone is fully human but very few can enjoy full human rights, as currently understood; furthermore, it is not a social order that Aristotle sees fit to attempt to change.

Histories of Childhood:
Footnotes to Aristotle?

1.4.1 The Ariès Debate

In one of the most quoted remarks by a modern philosopher, A. N. Whitehead wrote of the history of philosophy as 'a series of footnotes to Plato' (1978 [first published 1929]: 39). Since Aristotle built on Plato's foundations in his thinking about childhood and education, histories of childhood might be considered 'a series of footnotes to Aristotle'. Although history is not philosophy, and there are many important influences on the development of modern conceptions of childhood that are not recognizably either Aristotelian or anti-Aristotelian, I shall argue that much of the debate has moved on Aristotelian assumptions, and that contemporary thinking and policy about education remain strongly rooted in such assumptions.

The literature in history of childhood is extensive (only a limited selection will be referred to here), offering numerous insights into the lives of young people in the past, in the contexts of home, work and school. It is also riven by debates about the concept of childhood.

In general, most of this literature can be understood as Modernist, in two senses. First, it tends to take as its scope the modern era: that is, from Medieval, or 'Early Modern' times to the late twentieth century. Secondly, it tends to interpret changes over this period in terms of progression: that is, the writer's aim is to show how the modern, relatively enlightened treatment of children has developed gradually from the privations and cruelties of former times. Set against this is a much smaller body of work that is deeply critical of contemporary practice, and that might, therefore, be construed as Postmodernist.

The Modernist tendency is exemplified strongly in two of the most cited works: Phillippe Ariès' *Centuries of Childhood* (1962) and Lloyd deMause's *The History of Childhood* (1974). Of these, Ariès is probably the more influential; indeed, following Whitehead, a case could be made that late twentieth-century histories of childhood were often 'responses to Ariès'.

While many of these responses have been critical of Ariès in various respects, few, however, have questioned his progressivist orientation.

Ariès' thesis is that childhood is essentially a modern construct. That is to say, until about the seventeenth century, childhood was not conceived as a separate category: there was no particular interest in *Child 2*, the child as person of limited years. Rather, children's status was as mini-adults, whose *Child 3* characteristics (i.e. their relative incompetence) must be taken account of, though it might also be fair game for adult humiliation. Thus children did similar work to adults, where they could, and joined in the same games. Rather than schooling being a preparation for life, many went away to school after a period of employment: There was no assumption that education would prepare one for work in the broadest sense, but only for particular forms of work. Children could have fun with adults and be made fun of in their turn. To illustrate this, Ariès draws on the relatively extensive record of Louis XIII's childhood compiled by his doctor, Herouard, in the early seventeenth century, in which great amusement is had at the expense of the child's sexual precocity, aided and abetted by the adults around him. (For example: 'He was one year old: "In high spirits." Notes Herouard, "he made everybody kiss his cock". This amused them all.': [Ariès, 1962: 98]. There are several further instances cited.) It is, however, interesting that these sexual references are dealt with separately by Ariès from a longer account of Louis' upbringing, earlier in the book, that contains little that is remarkable beyond its attention to detail and resonances with modern childhoods, albeit games were then shared with adults (1962: 50–55). With documentary evidence increasingly weak the further one goes back in time, Ariès took much of his evidence from representations of children in art. On these grounds, Ariès argues that late modernity gradually developed an interest in, and respect for childhood, as *Child 2*, in its own right, to the point where children are granted their own rights and are simultaneously offered extensive protection and education. There is, however, a 'down side' to Ariès' account, for while it is progressive in the terms just stated, it renders the mid-twentieth-century context for growing up as rather narrow and restrictive. Thus Ariès concludes *Centuries of Childhood* with a rather downbeat assessment:

> The concept of the family, the concept of class, and perhaps elsewhere the context of race, appear as manifestations of the same intolerance towards variety, the same insistence on uniformity. (Ariès, 1962: 399)

All in all, Ariès' thesis is one of the increasing separateness of childhood, for good and ill. Lloyd deMause's account is significantly more progressive in this sense, though it has also been influential. DeMause's analysis of the historical importance of parent-child relationships charts a progression from a long period in which children were seen as dispensible, or worse, towards the increasing dominance of an empathetic response, or 'helping mode' in the late twentieth century. He claims, 'the history of childhood is a nightmare from which we have only recently begun to awaken' (1974: 21) and that 'Ariès' central thesis is the opposite of mine' (1974: 5). DeMause's 'psychogenic' account is deeply influenced by psychoanalytic theory, so that he details three possible ways in which an adult can interact with a child: a projective reaction, using the child as expression of his or her unconscious desires; a reversal reaction, in which the child becomes a substitute for a lost or missing parent; or an empathic reaction, sensitive to the child's own needs and perceptions. DeMause's account is a chilling one, not only for the numerous examples of barbarity and projected guilt that often characterized, and can continue to characterize, the child's experience, but also (and in contradiction to Ariès) for his insistence that, 'All of this is not to say that parents didn't love their children in the past, for they did' (1974: 17): it was not the sentiment that was at fault but its expression. The parent, particularly in the past, lacked the 'emotional maturity' to 'see the child as a person separate from himself' (ibid.).

Like Ariès, deMause refers to Herouard's records of Louis XIII, arguing that 'his picture of the baby shifts between projective and reversal images' (DeMause, 1974: 21). Indeed, deMause interprets the numerous references to Louis' apparent sexual precocity as adult wishes for, and assumptions about, what is appropriate for a future king. In many other cases, he understands infanticide and other forms of child cruelty as projective, noting that 'Urges to mutilate, burn, freeze, drown, shake, and throw the infant violently about were continuously (*sic*) acted out in the past' (1974: 31). All this is chilling and compelling. More controversial is deMause's conviction that the evidence is strong enough to support measurement of the frequencies of these practices, and furthermore, that such measurements can validly form the basis of a strong historical thesis. Thus, in graphical form on page 53, the thesis is presented that the dominant child-rearing mode before about 300 BC was 'Infanticidal', then 'Abandoning' till the late Middle Ages, 'Ambivalent' till about 1700, then, in turn, 'Intrusive', 'Socializing' and finally 'Helping' as we approach 1974. Given the steepness of the graph, it would be interesting to know deMause's evaluation of the situation at the time of writing. One wonders whether progress can really be so clear, dramatic, consistent and sustained. From such perspectives, the present condition of childhood marks a significant advance on all previous ages, implying that the major characteristics of this condition, including our extensive provisions for education, are all worthy of strong endorsement.

These two accounts, however, and particularly Ariès', have been subject to extensive critique, including from those who share modernist, progressive assumptions. Ariès' interpretations of the evidence are often open to question. For example, the fact that Montaigne remarked of his children 'All mine die in infancy' does not necessarily imply, as Ariès assumes, 'indifference' (Ariès, 1962: 37).

Hugh Cunningham offers an unusually full account of the debate after Ariès', first noting that Ariès' position was not entirely original but was broadly pre-dated by the Swiss historian, Norbert Elias (Cunningham, 1995; Elias, 1978 [first published in 1939]). Childhood historians of the 1970s, however, (including deMause) were principally conscious of Ariès and, indeed, had few other extensive texts to draw on, thus their works are very much responses to him. In this vein, Edward Shorter agreed with Ariès that the modern family was a recent invention, but went further than the latter in claiming that mothers have only become preoccupied with infant welfare over the last two hundred years, and that this change occurred even more slowly among the poor, whose material circumstances did not allow them to make this shift (Shorter, 1976). In contrast to Shorter, Lawrence Stone concentrated on the middle and upper classes, finding the key features of the modern family to be in place in England by the middle of the eighteenth century though he stresses the variety of practices evident both then and in earlier times (Stone, 1977).

All the above commentators see the past as more brutal than the present, but in the 1980s some historians came to challenge this view. Michael Anderson expressed some doubts about the rigour of the methods of earlier writers (Anderson, 1980). Linda Pollock (Pollock, 1983), however, offered a more radical critique. As a medievalist she simply rejected many of the earlier assumptions, refuting the conclusion that children were generally badly treated in the Middle Ages. Focusing on demographic and economic evidence rather than attempting to construct a history of sentiment from an often very limited range of sources, Pollock and other writers since the 1980s have returned to a much more sceptical and open position regarding adult-child relations in earlier times without assuming that the present must mark the end of a progressive history.

1.4.2 The Postmodern Turn

Since the 1980s the progressivist tendency has been replaced by a more critical view of the present and a more appreciative and nuanced one of the past. Medievalists, in particular, have been keen to insist that the Middle Ages were not chiefly characterized by cruelty or indifference towards children.

Shulamith Shahar, for example, specifically refutes Ariès' thesis that there was no valid conception of childhood in the Middle Ages, and is described by Cunningham as 'the acknowledged authority on the period' (though Cunningham retains some sympathy for Ariès, as he feels the translation of the latter's '*sentiment*' as 'concept' is somewhat misleading: Shahar, 1990; Cunningham, 1995: 30).

Perhaps the most extreme, yet widely recognized, expression of this postmodern, or late modern scepticism is Neil Postman's thesis of the 'disappearance' of childhood. (Postman, 1994, first published 1982). Postman's position is Postmodernist (though he does not employ the term) insofar as he does not regard current conceptions of childhood as progressive; rather, he shares with Postmodern theorists such as Jean Baudrillard the thesis of an increasingly infantilized society in which child–adult distinctions are blurred. Instead of being a preparation for adulthood, childhood has, according to Postman, become sexualized and commodified while simultaneously valorized: in short, childhood has become a state to be desired rather than sanctified and protected. Adults have increasingly lost any sense of the need to nurture children, as they have lost the distinction between commercial and spiritual values and have therefore become uncritical pawns of a mass media culture themselves. Postman's thesis will be critiqued in a later chapter, but it is appropriate to summarize his argument here.

Like other major commentators, Postman is, in important respects, responding to Ariès. That is, Postman accepts that childhood, though it 'has a biological basis', 'cannot be realised unless a social environment. . . . has need of it' (Postman, 1994: 144). Therefore, following Ariès, it is valid to conceive of the 'invention' or 'discovery' of childhood – as opposed to biological infancy – and to locate it as the social construction of a particular period of history. Postman regards 1850–1950 as the period with the most powerful conception of childhood. In other words, childhood thrived during the late industrial period, and has lost much of its power during the post-industrial period or Age of Information (again, terms not employed directly by Postman). In arguing this, Postman joins a tradition of critical twentieth-century thought embracing both disillusioned Liberal Humanists such as F. R. Leavis and politically radical commentators such as Theodore Adorno and Walter Benjamin, all of whom were deeply sceptical of mass culture, and particularly of mass visual culture (Leavis, 1930; Adorno, 1970; Benjamin, 1968). What unites these commentators, and also drives Postman's thesis, is that literate culture promoted an enhanced adulthood, a cultural achievement that has been increasingly eroded by the infiltration of the largely visual mass media (film, television and so on) that are themselves prey to commercial forces of late capitalism.

In other words, from Postman's perspective, television has turned thinking, literate, responsible people into unthinking, passive and irresponsible consumers. Postman sees the effects of this in many areas of life. Regarding dress, for example, children used to wear small versions of adult clothes; then clothes specifically for young people emerged with the youth culture of the 1950s and 1960s; subsequently, adults began to adopt these fashions. Regarding sport and leisure: children used to join in with adult games (Ariès wrote much on this); then children had their own games, songs and the like (as catalogued by Peter and Iona Opie in *The Lore and Language of Schoolchildren*: Opie and Opie, 2001); subsequently, adults would travel thousands of miles to support their children in sporting tournaments while the children themselves knew nothing of the practices detailed by the Opies (Postman, 1994: 129-31). Regarding behaviour and the law: children would become increasingly criminalized, with adults increasingly apparently unable to stop them (134-6).

In comparison to Ariès, therefore, Postman puts a great deal of emphasis on the development of print as the key driver of the invention of childhood, for reading is both a private activity and is esteemed, and it requires formal instruction, preferably from a young age. Reading creates private space and individuality, thus enhancing the state of adulthood, to which children must aspire: 'In a literate world, children must become adults' (Postman, 1994: 13). It is not merely a matter of skills and knowledge, however. Again following Ariès, Postman notes the lack of privacy in the medieval household, so that even sexual practices could not be kept secret. Increasing privacy correlates with an increasing sense of shame, and of what is appropriate for children to know, see and do. Postman notes that a conception of childhood rests on 'a well developed sense of shame' (1994: 9). He finds the first evidence of this in the writings of Romans such as Quintilian, who wrote of his sense of discomfort concerning what children saw adults getting up to; he does not find evidence of any such sense of shame in Plato, Aristotle or other Greek writers. The late medieval and Renaissance periods rediscovered this sense of shame as they rediscovered Classical civilization and, in tandem with this, promoted mass literacy. Mass literacy in turn demanded mass formal education, thus allying a new conception of childhood with a new belief (this time resurrected from Plato and Aristotle) in the necessity of compulsory schooling, organized according to a sequential curriculum – an issue to which we return below.

However, a visual medium does not promote either self-control or critical, individual, thought to the same extent as literature. Central to Postman's thesis is the view that 'Language is an abstraction from experience, whereas pictures are concrete representations of experience' (Postman, 1994: 73). In Part 2, this assumption will be subjected to critique from a later theoretical perspective, but it cannot completely be overturned, as it is clearly the case that the information environment has changed and that, from film and television onwards, the visual has played a relatively greater role with respect to the verbal; anyone doubting this might compare the layouts of newspapers from different periods, for in recent times there has been much greater domination of space by the visual even in 'highbrow' publications such as *The Times*. (See also, for example, the work of Günther Kress: e.g. 2003.)

Nevertheless, Postman's thesis was developed around 1980 so it is appropriate to consider whether it should still be considered the key thesis on childhood in the Information Age. For example, does Postman's analysis of television apply to the internet?

To some extent, Postman addressed this himself in *Technopoly* (1993), in which he paints a bleak view of computers, very much extending his earlier critique of television. Again, he identifies only a tiny privileged minority as in a position to use computers to enhance their lives, while most lives are effectively impoverished by them, and in the later book he urges educators to preach resistance against the technological media (much as Leavis and others had done in the rather different context of the 1920s and 1930s). This, of course, was before the mass use of the internet. However, many of the trends Postman identified have clearly continued into the early years of the twenty-first century. Under capitalism, and now not merely in the West, many adults attempt to hide the effects of ageing and aspire to the aspirations of youth, as evidenced by their clothing, leisure activities and viewing and reading interests. Regarding reading, J. K. Rowling's 'Harry Potter' series (recently completed at the time of writing, and aimed at children) has hugely outsold any competing adult literature, and the impact of the film series has intensified this effect. The cult of celebrity invests individuals who are not highly literate or critical with greater social status than those who are. In the 1950s, an Arsenal first-team footballer apparently earned about the same as an Oxford professor; in the 2000s some of the former earn in a week what the latter earns in a year. While people have had greater access to information, their interest in politics has waned. Furthermore, large areas of the world, such as the Far East, have become increasingly Westernized and consumer-orientated, and exhibit many of the same cultural characteristics as the USA and the UK. None of this, however, provides full support for Postman's central thesis concerning literacy and the effect of visual culture. To evaluate this, we must consider whether the trends he associated with television have been continued or reversed since the introduction of the internet, with its own forms of interactivity.

When Postman was writing around 1980, computers were new and their social effects could only be a matter of conjecture. However, what Postman wrote on this has turned out to be remarkably prescient (Postman, 1993: 149–50). In the early 1980s, computers required a degree of understanding of programming in their users. Thus, in answer to the question, 'Are there any communication technologies that have the potential to sustain the need for childhood?', Postman cites the computer on the grounds that its use requires 'complex analytical skills' (1993:149). However, Postman is wise enough to note that this may not continue to be the case. His conclusion to this short section is chilling, though it could be argued that he does not take into consideration the computer's potential for genuine interactivity and creativity:

> There are . . . economic and political interests that would be better served by allowing the bulk of a semi-literate population to entertain itself with the magic of visual computer games, to use and be used by computers without understanding. In this way the computer would remain mysterious and under the control of a bureaucratic elite. There would be no need to educate the young, and childhood could, without obstruction, continue on its journey to oblivion. (Postman, 1993: 149–50)

Not all recent commentators share Postman's pessimism, however.

1.4.3 The Millennial Debate

Since Postman, commentators have been starkly divided on the issue of the new information technologies and the interactivity associated with them. David Buckingham (2000) provides a balanced overview of positions on this, up to that date. Buckingham's concern is to 'challenge' the 'totalizing rhetoric' of 'essentialist views of childhood and of communications media' (Buckingham, 2000: 6), concluding that the new technologies offer considerable potential for young people to use to the good, but there is a social need to prepare them to do so; thus education in media literacy is of paramount importance.

Buckingham points out that positions on these issues in the 1990s were starkly divided, with children often seen as either in danger or as dangerous

(2000: e.g. 3). However, what unites these perspectives is an acceptance of the child as outside the mainstream of society. He writes:

> . . . in the recent history of industrialized countries, childhood has essentially been identified as a matter of *exclusion*. (Buckingham, 2000: 13. Italics in original.)

Indeed, Buckingham's further explanation of this is remarkably Aristotelian in tone. He regards the discipline of developmental psychology as central to contemporary understandings of childhood, and the psychologists' understanding of childhood as 'a teleological process of development towards a preordained goal' (2000: 14). Buckingham also notes the continuing presence of the Romantic reaction to this position in contemporary society's continuing belief that the adult retains an 'inner child', playful and uncorrupted. Under this (largely Aristotelian) settlement, children are evaluated in terms of age-appropriate expectations of their behaviour and formal education is organized around same-age groupings and a fixed sequential curriculum. Buckingham is very aware of the irony of this: that Postmodern commentators work unquestioningly with assumptions drawn largely from the Pre-Modern world, though his recommendations for education differ somewhat from those developed in the present volume.

Buckingham's critique of Postman is particularly incisive. Like other writers of his time (see Chapter 1.8), Postman is accused of an essentialist view of both the child and the technology, resulting in a 'one-dimensional' and morally conservative understanding of the consequences of their coming together (Buckingham, 2000: 24–7). This narrowness is particularly evident in Postman's treatment of literacy and the literate mind. Drawing on his own research, as well as that of others, Buckingham shows how children use media texts as stimuli for reflection, discussion and the development of self-identity, and that they are sceptical, and often sophisticated, in their responses to media outputs, drawing sharp distinctions between levels of realism in different forms of programming, for example, and thus distinguishing between different forms of screen violence (a key issue, given widespread concerns about children as passive consumers of such violence: Buckingham, 2000: 108ff).

In other words, it is not merely print literacy that develops reasoning; media literacy has the capacity to do this as well, but formal education – still too influenced by the likes of Postman – pays insufficient attention to developing children's critical reasoning in these areas and thus impoverishes childhood while attempting to protect it. Furthermore, we no longer live in Postman's world, characterized by either television or books: media have been increasingly integrated, both proliferating and converging. Furthermore, media texts have become increasingly intertextual, ironic and interactive, and representations more ambiguous and problematic (Buckingham cites Michael Jackson as example of man–woman, black–white and adult–child; 2000: 91). Thus the difference between literacy and response to the visual is considerably less obvious and clear-cut than Postman and others held it to be. Furthermore, Buckingham accuses Postman of ignoring important religious influences on the early social effects of print literacy, citing the differing examples of France and Germany in the Early Modern period (2000: 37).

Following Buckingham, one might ask: if literacy is necessary to produce abstract thought, how do we explain Socrates? If print literacy preceded such thought, there would be no Classical philosophy, and the printing press could not have been invented. This insight by no means undermines all of Postman's thesis, but it certainly problematizes it. Plato, for example, was deeply sceptical of writing, seeing it as a threat to memory. Indeed, the Greek root of the word 'school' (*skhole*) meant 'leisure': it was assumed by Aristotle and others that, given time away from necessary duties, people – the best people, anyway – would naturally turn to contemplation and debate, though there was no widespread availability of books. Clearly, however, the current debate around childhood is strongly concerned with conceptions of literacy and the associated role of education.

1.4.4 Implications for Education: So Far From Aristotle?

Postman's message for education is fairly clear: The civilized human being is the literate human being, and education's role is to produce literate adults, thereby countering the pernicious effects of the visual media. Buckingham's is quite different: education needs a broader conception of literacy.

However, is formal education the answer at all? One of the most powerful critiques of recent government initiatives to boost literacy levels in the US and the UK comes from James Paul Gee (Gee, 2003). Gee's study of young children's uses of video games suggests that they develop reading skills beyond their expected age levels (as well as visual literacy) through their playing of such games. For example, to understand the complex strategies required to undertake 'cheats' in such games, children successfully interpret text at a level way beyond that with which they seem able to cope effectively at school. Furthermore, the ethnic, gender and social class differences that always appear in levels of academic achievement in schools are missing in relation to use of computer games. To Gee, these startling findings are not so startling after all: as a pragmatic linguist, he is committed to the idea that meaning is always meaning-in-use. Thus the children in his study understood complex texts because they were involved in complex sets of actions, and they were involved in such actions because they were motivated so to be. In other words, they learnt more from computer games than from school because, in effect, they wanted to learn more from them and concentrated more on them.

Critiques such as Gee's remind us how far current assumptions about education remain Aristotelian. The system of compulsory schooling rests on the assumptions that children are potential adults, that adults are reasonable and that children are not, that reason is timeless and not dependent on culture or technology, and that children's own interests and preferences are not worthy of serious consideration. A future chapter will consider the future of schooling when these assumptions are rejected. However, in attempting an overview of histories of childhood, it is tempting to conclude that perhaps the problem concerns not so much what we mean by 'children' as what we mean by 'literacy' and 'education', for there is no timeless essence of the child. Childhood is, to a large extent, a social construction – but there are cultural practices that shape children at any historical moment, and these, too, must be questioned by anyone seeking a better settlement for the young.

Pessimism and Sin: The Puritan Child

1.5.1 The 'footnotes' to Aristotle

In this chapter and the next, three cultural-historical movements are identified and discussed as the principal 'footnotes to Aristotle' from within the Judaeo-Christian tradition. Two of these movements – characterized as the Puritan and Romantic tendencies – offer responses to the question of Original Sin, understood in the broadly Aristotelian context of the incompleteness of the child. The third – characterized as the Liberal Enlightenment tendency – offers a scientific view of the child as an initial 'blank slate' with the innate capacity for reason, and of this capacity working on sense data to create the autonomous rational individual. Each of these traditions impacts on our understanding of the contemporary 'Late Modern' or 'Postmodern' child. The first two of these tendencies are discussed in the present chapter, the third in Chapter 1.6.

1.5.2 The Weight of Sin, Death and Duty

In his 2006 publication, *The Invention of Childhood* (produced in conjunction with a radio series for the BBC), Hugh Cunningham offers numerous insights into the world of extreme Protestant childrearing, beginning with the 'child-prophets' of the sixteenth and seventeenth Centuries (Cunningham, 2006: 64): strange cases of children possessed by religious fervour, such as that of William Withers, an 11-year-old who, in 1580 'fell into a deep trance'. After ten days in a coma, he 'regained consciousness and began to denounce the sin and immorality of the age. Unless, thundered William, his bed trembling with the vehemence of his speech, there was "spedie repentance", the Lord would shake the villagers' houses and cause the earth to open up and swallow them alive' (ibid: 62). Such events – and there are records of a good number – illustrate, at the very least, the demons that haunted the dreams of children during a period of deep religious instability in England.

It should be noted at this point that, although these religious differences were apparent throughout much of European civilization, they were not universally played out with such vehemence, and with such consequent *angst* in parent–child relations as in England. In the Netherlands, in particular, newfound wealth resulted in relative indulgence of children (Schama, 1997), though, even here, enjoyment of an embarrassment of riches was tempered by a sense of guilt and religious uncertainty. Overall, however, the Puritan influence was very great, and spread way beyond the British Isles. As Steven Mintz illustrates in his book *Huck's Raft: A History of American Childhood* (2004), Puritanism was particularly strong in the USA as a legacy of the original settlers. Mintz takes his title from the insight that the characters in Mark Twain's *Huckleberry Finn* represent Puritan and Romantic conceptions of the child and of child-rearing in dramatic contrast. Thus Huck, despite his drunken abusive father and outcast state, has a heart of gold uncorrupted by the ways of the world. In contrast to the repressed children of Puritanical parents who surround him, and to many modern children, 'Huck . . . enjoyed . . . opportunities to undertake odysseys of self-discovery outside the goal-driven, overstructured realities of contemporary childhood' (Mintz, 2004: 384).

Mintz points out an irony at the heart of the Puritan educational tradition, especially in the USA: that is, the Puritans actually went to America for their children, to escape instability on this side of the Atlantic. Their children were their future, in whom they had invested everything. They were strict with them to protect and to save them, and must have been mortified by the obvious preference to stay with Indians that many expressed after they had been kidnapped! According to Mintz, seventeenth-century American parenting must have been characterized by 'intense anxiety' (ibid: 31). Anyone familiar with the witchcraft trials in Salem, Massachusetts, described with only limited exaggeration by Arthur Miller in his play *The Crucible*, will be aware of just how deep that anxiety could run.

On both sides of the Atlantic, therefore, the Puritan tradition was influential. It influenced the new rash of publications, discussed by some historians of childhood, which dealt with child-rearing. While, in general, the father was still held up as the primary educator of the child, in the Aristotelian tradition, the seventeenth century saw some publications intended for children to read for themselves. Perhaps the most famous, or infamous, of these was James Janeaway's *A Token for Children, Being an Exact Account of the Conversion, Holy and Exemplary Lives, and Joyful Deaths, of Several Young Children.* This book has been variously described as 'probably the most influential children's book ever written' and (albeit nearer the time) as 'the most entertaining book that can be' (quoted in Cunningham, 2006: 68–9), its thirteen case studies of children who died young intended as an inspiration to its readers.

Janeaway's book serves also to illustrate how Puritan ideas influenced Protestant culture as a whole: it was not written for a highly limited audience. Although, strictly speaking, the Puritans were a small sect within an often fractured rebellion against Catholicism, some of the Puritans' key ideas embody the Protestant spirit to the extent that it is justifiable to characterize a mass movement in attitudes towards children as 'Puritan'. In relation to conceptions of childhood, Puritanism can be taken as an important cultural trend, characterized by a belief in the essential sinfulness of the human being and the desire to purify the soul as much as possible through prayer, devotion and good work before an often untimely death. Puritan childrearing was the response of a fearful people to difficult social conditions and a belief in Original Sin.

Nevertheless, it is important not to assume that a Puritan childhood was necessarily an unhappy one. Indeed (and perhaps counter-intuitively), the historical evidence suggests that, in Britain at least, there may have been more positive cruelty towards children in the early nineteenth century than in the sixteenth or seventeenth. With respect to this, it is important to clarify a working definition. The Puritan tendency, for the present purpose, is that tendency that sees children as essentially corrupt – at the very least, as easily corruptible – until corrected and guided by adults qualified to lead them to salvation. This is a specifically Christian gloss on the Aristotelian tradition, insofar as it is a response to the doctrine of Original Sin, though one in contrast to the earlier (and later) Humanist construals of children as pure like the infant Jesus. It might be argued that it is more strictly a Protestant than a Puritan response; however, for present purposes, 'Protestant' seems too broad, as most nineteenth and twentieth-century conceptions of childhood in the UK and related countries are dominated by Protestantism (a general belief in freedom of will and conscience and the desirability of work to achieve the common good, if not religious salvation), but are not dominated by the Puritans' obsession with the need to reject worldliness and devote oneself to avoiding damnation in the face of ever-present danger. While the Protestant tradition can, in some of its manifestations, seem positively easy-going, this is not a charge easily levelled at the Puritans and those who shared their orientations towards the upbringing of children.

The key point here is that while the Puritans (and those who were not self-styled Puritans but shared their views on children) were deeply religious and deeply concerned, they were not necessarily cruel. Sternness is not cruelty. Linda Pollock (Pollock, 1983) offers an extensive analysis of diaries and autobiographical evidence of childhood experience from 1500 to 1900; Stephen Mintz (2004) focuses on the Puritans in North America. Both Pollock and Mintz paint a relatively sympathetic picture of Puritan childhood. Each had been led by earlier histories of childhood, such as that by Stone (1977), to focus on the Puritan belief in breaking the will of the child, but even Stone had noted that the Puritans substituted 'prayers, moralising and threats of damnation' for beatings (Pollock, 1983: 19). Rather than the insensitivity implied by the 'breaking the will' thesis, and intensified in accounts such as deMause's (1974) – which Pollock describes as 'a history of child abuse and not of childhood'(Pollock, 1983: 57) – Pollock's evidence leads her to focus on the Puritans' earnest and sincere intentions: 'Puritan parents were intensely concerned with the salvation of their children – even though it was impossible to know who had been elected and who had not' (ibid.: 53).

Although Pollock found many seventeenth-century diaries referred to children as sinful, they regarded adults as sinful too. She found no references at all in these diaries to breaking the will of the child (ibid.: 103). However, she notes that the famous liberal, John Locke, advised this! (ibid.: 116) Rather, Pollock finds cases such as that of Byrd, who chastised his wife for making their daughter eat against her will (ibid.: 116), and of Mather, who regarded whipping as a failure of discipline (ibid.: 155), and she refers to frequent conflicts between parental emotions and the duty to submit to God's will (ibid.: 131). Pollock does, however, find some evidence of a Puritan tendency insofar as 'Children were seen by a few parents as being depraved in the 17th Century, innocent in the 18th and as both depraved and innocent in the 19th' (ibid.: 140) in addition to the piety and awareness of imminent death.

Overall, however, Pollock's message is that childrearing and childhood experience have been varied in all periods, just as individuals and families vary in their responses to cultural conditions today. This is not to deny that there are Aristotelian influences or Puritanical tendencies, but rather to avoid falling into the trap of allowing one such influence to explain all the practices and experiences of childhood in any one time and place. Indeed, as I shall argue with respect to Romanticism and, to some extent, Liberalism, certain cultural movements may not have their most significant effects at the time of their inception; it is perhaps most pertinent to think of them as identifiable influences on the way we tend to think about children today.

Nevertheless, Puritanism had its period of greatest influence, and this was during a period of considerable religious and social uncertainty. For the

North American settlers, conditions must have seemed particularly harsh, as Stephen Mintz relates. Even here, however, Puritan childrearing was strict rather than cruel. On the one hand, the Puritans did indeed differ from Anglican traditionalists and humanists in their emphasis on the sinfulness of the child, according to Mintz (2004: 11); on the other, the very reason they went across the Atlantic was to offer their descendents a better future on Earth, escaping the instability in England (ibid.: 10). Their care for children, Mintz argues, is further shown by their opposition to wet-nursing (ibid.: 12–13). It seems that even Puritan parents wanted the best possible lives for their children on Earth.

1.5.3 The Softening of the Puritan Tradition

All commentators seem to agree, however, that a Puritan upbringing implied a degree of discipline, simplicity and austerity. This might be seen as an almost inevitable response to economic conditions and religious heritage. There is, however, also a consensus concerning a considerable softening in attitudes to children during the eighteenth century, with increasing documentary evidence of increased sentiment towards them and enjoyment of their childish ways. This change is evident to both Pollock and Mintz. Pollock notes the number of references in her sources to children bringing pleasure in the eighteenth century (Pollock, 1983: 103ff.) and that children's own diaries of this, and later, periods generally point to happy childhoods (ibid.: 253–60). Mintz states that in the eighteenth century, 'relations with families grew more affectionate' (Mintz, 2004: 40), and even that 'Between 1749 and 1780 from one-fourth to one-third of all brides in one Virginia parish were pregnant on their wedding day' (ibid.) Indeed, Mintz reckons the Quakers (a Puritanical movement) to have been in many respects emotional and indulgent parents in eighteenth-century America (ibid.: 48). Philosophically, this softening coincides with the development of Liberal, Enlightenment ideas from the previous century and the germs of the Romantic reaction that would flower in the next.

The changes in attitude during the eighteenth century are partly attributable to Liberal Enlightenment thinking, and the history of the Liberal, Enlightened child is the subject of the next chapter. The polar opposite of this tendency is the one best characterized as Romantic, the subject of Chapter 1.7.

Optimism and Enlightenment:
The Liberal Child

1.6.1 Enlightenment and the Origins of Liberalism

Insofar as Puritanism was characterized by anxiety, the Enlightenment brought hope: not principally for salvation in the Afterlife, but rather for personal liberty and social progress on Earth. While the philosophical revolution of the seventeenth century coincided to a considerable degree with Puritan practice, it would eventually come largely to displace it; hence the considerable relaxation in attitudes to children noted by several of the historians cited in preceding chapters.

Before considering Classical Liberalism, and then its most influential philosopher of education – John Locke (though he might have been surprised to be so remembered) – it seems appropriate to clarify 'Enlightenment' in this context.

Generally understood, the term 'Enlightenment' refers to the philosophical and scientific revolution of the seventeenth century and its impact on the social and political upheavals of the eighteenth, and subsequently nineteenth. It is a very broad term encompassing a change of attitude. Perhaps above all, 'Enlightenment' signals a positive belief in freedom of rational enquiry, and its effects on individual and social life. Although Enlightenment thinkers tended to be religious, Enlightenment thinking heralded a more secular age with its emphasis on improvement in the here and now rather than possible salvation in the world to come. Key Enlightenment thinkers include Francis Bacon, whose work arguably propelled the scientific and technological revolution more than any other.

Ironically, Francis Bacon owes a debt to a much earlier Bacon – Roger – a medieval philosopher whose experiments with alchemy can be argued to mark the beginning of modern experimental science, building on the empirical commitment that was one of Aristotle's greatest legacies. Particularly in his *New Organon*, first published in 1620 and now available electronically at www.constitution.org/bacon/nor_org.hym, Francis Bacon argued, much more fully than his Medieval namesake, for a new commitment to methodical empirical enquiry and analysis, bringing the rational human mind to bear on the material world in order to create understanding and apply it for practical ends. That this seems such an obvious commitment today bears testimony to its subsequent influence. In deeply religious times, Bacon's motivation was itself religious. In contrast to the deliberately unworldly Puritans, Bacon sought understanding as a potential escape from Satanic manipulation; to distort a phrase from later times, he did not want the Devil to have the best ideas. Rather than focusing on the Biblical warning about tasting the fruit of the tree of knowledge of good and evil in the Garden of Eden, Bacon was more inclined to regard dwelling in ignorance as playing into the Devils' hands. Rather than fear and superstition, people should devote themselves to rational contemplation of God's Creation. This was a broadly Aristotelian development of the Protestant belief in individual conscience and hard work that would have very different social consequences from the fearful partial fatalism of the Puritans. Bacon led the way for Newton and others to develop a mathematically based, scientific worldview that has dominated global culture for three hundred years.

The seventeenth and eighteenth centuries are often remembered in terms of a debate between rationalism and empiricism. To cast the times in this way, however, masks the deeper truth that the Enlightenment relied on a commitment to both: to the rational use of empirical evidence in the development of science, and its rational application for practical ends *via* technology and, eventually, social intervention. Where the debate seems conflictual is in terms of which is prior, and here a sharp distinction is evident between, most notably, René Descartes and the British philosophers, John Locke and David Hume.

Descartes (1596–1650) famously argued '*cogito ergo sum*', usually translated as 'I think therefore I am' (Descartes, ed. Cottingham, 1996). By this, he meant that subjective existence precedes all knowledge: that is, I can even doubt I exist, but there remains an 'I' who is doubting. Locke (1632–1704), and subsequently Hume (1711–1776), were more sceptical, and their stronger empirical biases would set the tone for new approaches to understanding childhood and practising education.

1.6.2 Locke

While there are grounds for regarding Hume as the more convincing philosopher, it was Locke's earlier work that would be applied to a revolution in childrearing. The philosophical basis was laid out in *An Essay Concerning*

Human Understanding (first published 1690), while the enormously influential text *Some Thoughts Concerning Education* appeared in 1693. These are both sprawling and somewhat piecemeal works, the former worked at for over two decades, the latter a series of pieces of personal advice about the upbringing of an acquaintance's son. In terms of coherent and watertight argument, each is flawed. Despite this, Locke's advice about childrearing held sway with many for over a hundred years, while the *Essay* remains a landmark in the development of empiricist thought. Given their flaws, it may seem odd that this is so, but this would be to overlook Locke's immense influence as a political philosopher, arguably the father of modern Liberalism.

Locke's most enduring contributions to the philosophy of childhood and of education can therefore be summarized under the following headings: epistemology, politics, and education.

1.6.2.1 Locke's Epistemology

Locke's epistemology, or theory of knowledge, was much influenced by his reading of Descartes, against whom he proposed an empiricist explanation of mind: that is, he argued that no understanding can precede experience. His empiricism notwithstanding, he adopted Cartesian substance dualism in holding that there are two kinds of substance, broadly material and immaterial. We thus understand the world through our 'ideas', which are invisible, but which can only arise in the mind.

Contra Descartes, however, he held that there can be no understanding prior to experience of the world. People are thus both rational and shaped by their experiences: they are distinct and autonomous rational beings. In a sense, while Descartes is principally a child of Plato, Locke's forebear is Aristotle.

1.6.2.2 Locke's Liberalism

Locke's epistemology explains, or reflects, his Liberalism, depending on the relative strengths of his formative influences. Again like Descartes, Locke insists that what makes people special are their own thoughts and feelings about the world: people can, and do, think for themselves. This is generally an optimistic view, one that continues to underpin the relatively 'high trust' orientations of liberals, as opposed to those with more authoritarian political sympathies. Although their explanations differ, therefore, both Descartes and Locke stand as radically anti-authoritarian figures in the contexts of their times, each opposed to the Divine Right of Kings.

Although Locke's epistemology is essentially individualist, his interests were essentially political, and he was concerned with how autonomous rational individuals could and should ensure social harmony. In relation to this, he drew on the 'Social Contract' theory of Thomas Hobbes (1588–1679). Hobbes himself did not offer an optimistic account of human nature. Particularly in *Leviathan* (MacPherson, 1980; first published 1651), Hobbes also construed people as naturally free, but as purely self-interested. Thus in a 'state of nature', according to Hobbes, people would be continuously at war with one another; for their own protection, therefore, they must agree to forego their individual liberties for authoritarian monarchical rule.

Locke did not agree that it was always in the free individual's interest to be ruled by others. However, he did propose a milder form of the Social Contract, under which free individuals agree to work together under a restricted monarchy to protect as much of their freedoms as is feasible. Although the Social Contract would be reinterpreted by, among others, Rousseau (see Chapter 1.7), Locke's approach is broadly that which has held sway in liberal-democratic countries ever since.

1.6.2.3 Locke on Education

Locke believed three things about a new-born child: its mind was a 'blank slate' until it had worldly experience to work on; the child was therefore trainable; and the child was an emergent free individual. These three themes feature strongly in the rather long-winded, but educationally seminal treatise, *Some Thoughts Concerning Education.* (The following references to this text are from the online *Modern History Sourcebook*, retrieved from www.fordham.edu/halsall/mod/1692locke-education.html 27 September 2007, with 'S' referring to Section.)

Locke begins S2 with the words: 'I imagine the minds of children as easily turn'd this or that way, as water itself'. Comparing the mind to water stresses its immateriality, but until the child has experienced the world, the mind has nothing to work on and cannot therefore set its own course. It is therefore hugely, if not infinitely, malleable and responsive. Early training is therefore of paramount importance, and it is inevitably parents who must take responsibility for this, for 'A compliance and suppleness of their wills, being by a steady hand introduc'd by parents, before children have memories to retain the beginning of it, will seem natural to them, and work afterwards in them as if it were so, preventing all occasions of struggling or repining' (S44).

Aristotle also viewed the child as a trainable and potential rational being, but Locke's system achieves more than Aristotle's. Aristotle would have education produce good, rational citizens, albeit different in their capacities. Locke has education producing good rational citizens who are genuinely diverse, autonomous agents, thinking for themselves but not necessarily drawing the same conclusions. Locke's citizens would be agents in a largely free market of goods and services with an emphasis on private property, yet as children they are extremely trainable. The training of free, autonomous citizens (Locke's glorious paradox) requires a deep commitment and sense of moral authority on the part of those practising it.

Initially, it requires attentive and responsible parenting. It then requires teachers of considerable personal calibre. Locke believes that it is 'education . . . which makes the great difference in mankind', accounting for 'nine parts of ten of what [people] are' (S1). However, education serves autonomy, as 'Men's happiness or misery is most part of their own making' (S1). This exalted role for education in producing free citizens has remained part of the liberal tradition to the present day, echoed by theorists such as John Rawls (1993, 1999).

For Locke, as for Plato and Aristotle, correct training begins at birth, and involves making babies as physically tough as possible, for 'a strong constitution, able to endure hardships and fatigue' (S3) is a necessary prerequisite for future success. Locke thus promotes a general lack of 'cockering and tenderness' (S4) including not dressing children too warmly (S5), giving children leaking shoes so their feet get used to cold water (S7), exposure to sun and wind, for boys and girls (S9), loose clothing (S11–12) and a 'plain and simple' diet (S13). There should even be a contrived introduction to 'pain' (S115). To many modern minds, there will seem to be as much cruelty as common sense here, but Locke would doubtless find the Millennial parent dangerously indulgent. It must be remembered, too, that Locke's overall drift in this advice is away from stilted and damaging formality, from swaddling and dressing children in fashionable clothes. On this interpretation, it is Locke's view that sometimes seems the more progressive. (It would also, without doubt, leave a smaller 'carbon footprint'!) Indeed, as the text progresses, we find increasing examples of a recognizably modern form of 'liberalizing' in his prescriptions. Thus children should eat when they feel like it rather than be kept to regular mealtimes, so they learn to regulate their hunger naturally (S15), though they should be kept away from alcohol (S19); they should be fully indulged when it comes to sleep, 'nothing contributing more to the growth and health of children' (S21), yet they should sleep on firm beds (S22); they should not be subject to much corporal punishment, which is 'lazy' and 'unfit . . . to be us'd in education' (S47) and is ineffective compared to 'esteem and disgrace' (S56), with very young children being 'very sensible of praise and commendation' (S57); they should not be subject to too many rules 'which they often do not understand' (S64) – indeed, there should be 'rather fewer than more than seem absolutely necessary' (S65). Overall, 'children love liberty; and therefore they should be brought up to do the things that are fit for them, without feeling any restraint laid upon them', other than curbing their own tendency to 'dominion' (S103).

As long, therefore, as they do not indulge their children with unnecessary toys, clothing or comforts (for children should learn to be self-sufficient as far as possible), parents alone can play a highly significant role in raising the Liberal, Enlightenment child. However, while Locke does not believe that 'anything goes', he believes even less that 'anyone goes'. He argues that there comes a point in the education of a gentleman (*sic*) when he must be protected from the influences of servants and tutored formally by a scholar of moral distinction.

It is at this point that Locke's thinking departs most strongly from that of Rawls's generation. There are two clear points of departure here: the first is Locke's strong preference for private tutoring over mass schooling; the second is his conviction that mixing with those of lower social class is largely anti-educational.

However, it is again tempting to exaggerate the differences. Locke did not write the *Thoughts* for the poor, yet his advice on parenting could equally apply to all strata of society (and he makes a point of mentioning fathers and mothers together, so parental responsibilities are shared); the impression given is that he would recommend that those of the lower orders improve their practices, while urging those of greater discrimination to avoid contact with them. There is no necessary inconsistency here, on Locke's terms, since his prescriptions for the early stages of education require neither great material resource nor much social interaction: if parents have the right attitudes, they can do much for their children. In terms of formal education, meanwhile, Locke simply does not consider its feasibility for those without the means to purchase private tutoring.

There is a robust naturalism in much of Locke's advice to parents. However, his wishes regarding tutors may be seen as wishful thinking, notwithstanding his failure to address the issue of how such an intensive system of education and personal tutoring could ever be offered to any bar the most privileged. Set against this is Locke's repeated insistence that good education is a priority, justifying 'doing without' in other areas: 'Spare [money] in toys and play-games, in silks and ribbons, laces, and other useless expenses, as much as you please; but be not sparing in so necessary a part as this' (S90). Nevertheless, the good-enough tutor will be a rare commodity indeed. '. . . he will never be able to set another right in the knowledge of the world, and above all in breeding, who is a novice in them himself' (S94).

Much of the later sections of the *Thoughts* concern Locke's detailed views on the curriculum, and much of this reads as unwarranted opinion rather than close argument. The discussion ranges over the importance of Latin and grammar, and the usefulness of mathematics and physics: common concerns of the time. There is, too, an emphasis on motivation and readiness to learn, again features that have characterized Liberal educational thinking ever since. Locke argues, "Tis better it be a year later before he can read, than that he should this way get an aversion to learning' (S155). Furthermore, the motivation to learn is a much more important consideration than the content of the curriculum: 'his tutor should remember, that his business is not so much to teach him all that is knowable, as to raise in him a love and esteem of knowledge; and to put him in the right way of knowing and improving himself when he has a mind to it' (S195). Again, Locke proves himself to be more progressive than may at first appear.

Locke's influence has been great, but is certainly not unproblematic. While his form of Liberal thinking sets much of the agenda for the contemporary debate, it has two major shortcomings. The first has been recognized for some time, and Locke is a prime example of it as a seminal figure in Classical Liberalism: that is, there is little attention to the mass of humankind and the feasibility of offering them any kind of systematic education at a high level. The second is a broader, and increasingly compelling critique of Enlightenment more broadly: it is exploitative of Nature (while in praise of it) in regarding the natural world, including the animal kingdom, as a giant machine, which the human mind (that remains immaterial, and so not part of the machine) can and should exploit without compunction. The first of these critiques has so far received much more attention in the philosophy of education than the second.

1.6.3 Dewey and Social Liberalism

Classical Liberalism, indebted to Locke, now forms only part of the Liberal agenda. During the nineteenth century, a form of Liberalism emerged that was sceptical of *laissez-faire* economics and demanded an increased role for the State in attempting to ensure that the less well off could enjoy significant 'liberty'. Social Liberalism now dominates mainstream Liberal thought (i.e. the thinking of politicians who designate themselves as Liberals) in both the UK and the US, while Libertarians and the so-called 'Neo-Liberals' are generally associated with the politics of the Right rather than the reforming Centre-Left. In Britain, there is considerable shared ideological commitment between the Liberal Democrat party and the mainstream of the Labour party, while the Conservative government of the 1980s, under Margaret Thatcher, was heavily influenced by the broadly Classical Liberal, pro-free market Friedrich von Hayek (particularly Hayek's *The Constitution of Liberty*: 1960).

This change of dominant orientation is dramatically marked in the career of John Stuart Mill, whose *On Liberty*, first published in 1859, stands as a seminal text in the development of Classical Liberalism, but who charts in his *Autobiography* an increasing belief in legislation to protect the poor. The following refers to the 'third period' of his 'mental progress' and is from Chapter VII (retrieved from www.utilitarianism.com/millauto 1st October, 2007:

> . . . our opinions were far more heretical than mine had been in the days of my most extreme Benthamism. In those days I had seen little further than the old school of political economists into the possibilities of fundamental improvement in social relations . . . in short, I was a Democrat, but not the least of a Socialist (. . .) now . . . our ideal of ultimate improvement went far beyond Democracy, and would class us decidedly under the general designation of Socialists.

Mill had a longstanding interest in education, and bemoaned the ineffectiveness of the mass schooling then available. However, his heirs in the Social Liberal tradition, such as John Rawls, have placed considerable faith in the potential for schools to deliver what we now tend to refer to as 'equality of opportunity'. By far the most influential Social Liberal model of education was developed at the turn of the twentieth century by John Dewey.

Dewey published prolifically from about 1890 to 1950, and his work encompassed philosophy, psychology and education. He was a university professor of both education and philosophy, and ran a Laboratory School in which to conduct educational experiments. He has been a huge influence on educational thinking, particularly in North America, and is arguably the most influential modern philosopher of education.

Dewey moved assumptions about the individual within Liberalism about as far as possible from the model of autonomous rational agency associated with Hobbes and Locke. To Dewey, the individual cannot be separated from her social environment; Dewey's is in many respects a communitarian form of Liberalism. Given this, it is not surprising that Dewey had, at least towards the beginning of his career, a huge faith in the power of schools to transform society, particularly in *My Pedagogic Creed* (1897), *The School and Society* (1915) and *Democracy and Education* (1916).

I shall argue in Chapter 2.1 that this faith was, up to a point, misplaced; indeed, that Dewey may have come to realize this himself. A more detailed account of his educational philosophy than that below will appear later, therefore. At this point in the argument, three elements in Dewey's thoughts will be introduced to indicate his enormous influence on the debate.

Dewey drew on two new and controversial areas of study to discuss childhood and the nature of learning: the theory of evolution and the science of psychology.

First, he saw the child as someone who grew in, and with, her environment – with particular reference to the social environment. This seems unremarkable to us but was a radical position in the days when Darwinian thinking was struggling to establish itself.

Secondly, in so doing, he came to a view of the child as a creature of action, neither a passive machine nor a disembodied brain, but an organic whole that both responds to and interprets environmental stimuli. Early psychologists had focused on stimulus-response mechanisms; Dewey argued that the two could not be neatly separated. Learning is 'conative' rather than 'cognitive' or 'behavioural' according to Dewey. That is, the human being, as organism, interacts with his environment; it is response that determines what constitutes stimulus, for example (Dewey, 1896). The person as actor and meaning maker can never be dissociated from the context in which she operates.

Thirdly, therefore, he believed that learning was both social and active, and that if a community could express its worthiest activities through its schools, then its schools would produce worthy citizens. In short, Dewey's child was a social-psychological entity in a recognizably modern way. A hundred years later, Dewey continues to be regarded as the pre-eminent Liberal thinker about childhood and education.

One of the reasons for Dewey's stature is his bold (in its time) rejection of Cartesian mind–body substance dualism: the belief, reinforced by Descartes, that mind and body are each substances but of different orders. This belief, shared by Locke, Newton and other seminal influences on modern science and politics, continues to have a considerable influence on social attitudes – another theme to which I shall return in Part 3, where

Dewey's thinking about education will be explored further and subjected to some critique.

1.6.4 Humanism vs. the World as Machine: The Dark Side of Enlightenment

There will be some extended discussion in future chapters of the Humanist and Enlightenment legacies in terms of their limitations on the development of conceptions of the child. Here, again, it is appropriate to lay down some 'markers' to contextualize that debate.

Whenever we speak of 'mind' (or 'soul') and 'body' we are adopting a dualist perspective of some sort. We are dualists simply by virtue of our acceptance of these contrasting terms. If we accept the need for a 'healthy body' as well as a 'healthy mind' then a qualitative, if not a substantive, difference between the two concepts is applied. Furthermore, mind/soul–body dualism is not unique to Western Enlightenment culture: it is evident in Plato, early Christianity, Buddhist and Hindu cultures, for example.

However, the way the mind (soul)–body duality is conceptualized, and thus operationalized, within traditions and cultural practices does vary. In Hindu and Buddhist teaching, for example, there is a tendency to regard the mind as immanent, existing (albeit at different levels) in all living things. Thus the body may be mechanical – 'the temple of the spirit' - but also sacred: the eternal lodged within the temporal, one might say. In Descartes' scheme, by contrast, mind (soul) and body are entities of quite different sorts, with mind (soul) supervening upon matter. Thus: (a) there is not one nature, with the temporal and eternal co-present within it, but rather (in the Judaeo-Christian tradition) two natures: (bodily) Nature and (divine) Supernature; and (b) only human beings partake of the divine on Earth, so 'human nature' is part natural, part supernatural, while (for example) animal natures lack mind (or soul). On this metaphysical account, Creation is not so much ordered as starkly divided, with humans in the position of overseers, in God's own image, temporarily implanted on Earth with a duty to govern and manage, but with an ever-present realization that human life is sacred while non-human life either is not, or is so only in an attenuated sense.

This starkly dualist tradition is manifest in a number of related but distinct fields of life: in the development of the broadly Humanist, or at least heavily anthropocentric, ethics of the past four centuries (depending on how you define humanism); in the belief that human reason is best employed in the development of science and its application in technologies that exploit natural 'resources' to further the human interest; and in the belief that human duty is almost exclusively to self, other people and (in religious cases) God. All these affect current conceptions of children and educational practices. At a more specific level, the Cartesian legacy is strongly evident in both curricular, disciplinary practices (such as the practice and teaching of science) and in theories of learning and pedagogy (the cognitive–behaviourist divide).

The implications of this for education and childrearing more generally will be examined more fully in subsequent chapters. Suffice it now to assert that Cartesian dualist Enlightenment thought has had two unfortunate, and highly significant sets of consequences: The first relates to naïve conceptions of what counts as 'intelligence' and thus educational potential, while the second concerns the attitude that human intelligence can exploit the natural environment without fully realizing the implications of such use of natural resource, resulting in the current environmental crisis.

The cultural movement that first challenged some of these assumptions was Romanticism.

Trailing Clouds of Glory: The Romantic Child

1.7.1 Rousseau: Enlightenment at Odds with Society

Jean-Jacques Rousseau (1712–1778) is a pivotal figure with respect to our three 'footnotes to Aristotle'. Writing in the middle and latter half of the eighteenth century, he is influenced by both the Puritan and Liberal-Enlightenment traditions. In his responses to these traditions, he prefigures Romanticism. He is preoccupied with the sin and corruption of the world and believes strongly in the power of reason and the appeal of liberty, yet his pessimism concerning society leads him to wish to keep it very much 'at arm's length' as regards childrearing and education. He can be seen, therefore, as either a very positive and a very negative figure, whose prescriptions for personal fulfilment can equally be read as a doctrine of escapism.

Romanticism is a cultural movement concerned with a return to Nature as a means of both escaping and reinvigorating society. In this, it both takes up and subverts a theme common to earlier Enlightenment thinkers: that of the 'state of nature'. Both Hobbes and Locke (Chapter 1.6) had made use of this concept in their social philosophy: for Hobbes it represents the unhappy state people would be in without a ruler, while in Locke it is the source of the natural rights of liberty and property which must be transacted and moderated through civil society by means of the social contract. In neither case does the 'state of nature' actually exist, and both Rousseau and subsequent Romantic thinkers can be accused of mystifying 'nature' to suit their own ends, appealing to this mystical Nature as a source for the cure for the ills of society. (For a fuller exposition of this perspective, see Stables, 2008a.)

Against this, it might be argued that Nature has been mystified and idealized in the Western tradition for centuries: in Montaigne's sixteenth-century concept of the 'noble savage', for example. It is certainly the case that the strongly empirical Locke often refers to Nature in an unquestioned way in his *Thoughts Concerning Education.* Perhaps it is inevitable that Nature will be invoked as an explanation of that which transcends or eludes the rational insofar as 'Nature' is the reverse of 'Society'. Thus understood, Rousseau and the Romantics represent disillusionment with industrialization, urbanization and other undesirable consequences of the Enlightenment, rather than a real philosophical alternative to it.

Indeed, both Rousseau and Romanticism adopt key Enlightenment insights: namely, a basic belief in human goodness and the power of liberty set against despair at social corruption. Like their predecessors, these thinkers reject subservience to superstition, fear and totalitarianism (though Romantic excess, with its renewed valorization of mysticism, has often been associated with the later rise of Fascism) and Romantics tend to believe in individuals coming to their own conclusions and making their own pacts with society. Furthermore, even Rousseau does not simply advocate living in an amoral state of nature to the complete exclusion of society; rather, he despairs at the prospect of the society he knows being able to bring the best out of people. In Book 1, Paragraph 14 of *Emile*, Rousseau writes, 'We are born weak, we need strength; we are born lacking everything, we need aid; we are born stupid, we need judgment. All that we lack at birth and that we need when we are grown is given by education', and (para. 15), 'This education comes to us from nature, from men, or from things.' Whatever the philosophical impact of Romanticism, however, there is no doubting its very significant influence on practices of childrearing and education.

Rousseau's key educational treatise is *Émile, or On Education,* published in 1762. This, and *The Social Contract,* published in the same year, are probably Rousseau's best-known and most influential works, and each begins in a very similar manner:

> 'Man is born free; and everywhere he is in chains' (*The Social Contract,* retrieved from www.constitution.org/jjr/socon_ol.htmb 10 January 2008).

> 'Everything is good as it leaves the hands of the author of things, everything degenerates in the hands of man' (*Emile,* retrieved from www. columbia.edu/pedagogies/em_eng_bk 1.html 3 October, 2007).

The Social Contract is principally a work of political philosophy, whereas *Émile* is a treatise on education, and thus the text to which the remainder of this discussion will refer.

At the most basic level, Rousseau's argument in *Émile* is disarmingly similar to Locke's in *Thoughts Concerning Education.* That is, Nature provides propensities towards good in the human condition (as well as some propensities towards evil, though these do not override the good), and these propensities can be developed to the good of society through correct education. The emphasis of each writer is very different, however. Rousseau conceives of a form of self-love (*amour de soi*) which is natural and not dependent on others – reminiscent, perhaps, of the moderate self-confidence that Aristotle considered desirable in the *Nicomachean Ethics* and elsewhere, as opposed to the emphasis on self-denial in the Christian tradition, at least since St. Augustine in the fifth century. Rousseau contrasts this inherent self-belief with *amour-propre*, which depends on comparing oneself with others. Thus for Rousseau, a whole area of education opens up which was not evident for Locke (nor, ironically, for Aristotle). Locke's emphasis is on the gradual socialization of the child, bearing in mind its level of readiness; Rousseau, by contrast, argues for a considerable delaying of entry into society to allow for healthy self-development to occur before the child is introduced to the ways of the world and to significant social interaction. We hear echoes of Rousseau in every recent claim that 'you have to learn to love yourself before you can learn to love others'.

While this belief in unworldly child-centred education has strong resonances in the present day, it should be noted that Rousseau's belief in natural endowment has its less palatable side. Émile's education must involve learning about sexual relationships, so Rousseau introduces the character of Sophie. However, her 'nature' dictates that she must be subservient to Émile, on the grounds that women are weaker and less independent-minded than men, though cleverer in certain respects. Rousseau's view of gender relations illustrates how the Romantic unquestioning faith in 'Nature' can be as deeply conservative as it is radical. There is a tendency in Romanticism to assume that instinct comes from Nature and is not in any way the product of previous cultural practice.

Émile is likely to leave the contemporary reader with strongly conflicting messages, as does Locke. On the one hand, Rousseau's is a message of compassion (though, as with Locke, his prescriptions are tinged with toughness, even ruthlessness, on occasions). On the other hand, one has a strong sense – a sense that will only be reinforced by a reading of *The Social Contract* – that actually Rousseau has no confidence in society at all, so his ideal education must remain no more than an ideal, a futile attempt to shelter children from an uncaring world. Regarding the former, *Émile* is clearly a progressive text, though not usually a revolutionary one, as many of his ideas were articulated by (at least) Locke. Rousseau thus argues for breastfeeding and against swaddling (e.g. para. 44). What Rousseau offers that Locke cannot is a dramatic and forceful expression of these ideas: for example, para. 48: 'The first gifts they receive from you are chains, the first treatment they experience is torture'. While the point made here is not new, it is certainly driven hard.

Sometimes, Rousseau goes further than Locke in more than rhetoric, however. For example, while Locke addressed both parents, equally, Rousseau spends considerable time stressing the importance of the mother, albeit on the deeply conservative assumptions about gender roles noted above. Rousseau shares with Locke, however, the belief in toughening children up: para. 66 of Book 1 states, 'Experience shows that children delicately raised are more likely to die' while para 68 reminds us, in typically dramatic Rousseauian fashion, 'The fate of man is to suffer at all times'. Other similarities with Locke include disdain for the influence of servants and the arguably impossibly high expectations of a suitable tutor.

It is not merely in the matter of tutors that Rousseau might be considered an impossibilist, however. As early as para. 18 of Book 1 of *Émile*, Rousseau makes clear that his educational prescriptions are unlikely to succeed: 'As much therefore as education is an art, it is almost impossible that it succeed, since the coordination necessary to its success depends on no one person. All one can do by one's own efforts is to more or less approach the goal. One needs luck to attain it.' However, how can one 'attain it' when existing society is so corrupt? Rousseau proceeds to inform us in para. 22 that 'you must choose between making a man and making a citizen, for you cannot do both at the same time', and in para. 32 that 'Public institutions do not and cannot exist, for where there is no longer a homeland there can no longer be citizens.' One can take such assertions literally, or as examples of Rousseau's hyperbolic rhetoric. On the latter interpretation, Rousseau is merely stating dramatically the modern Liberal critique of the Aristotelian rational citizen; on the former, if taken literally, Rousseau is effectively admitting that the whole exercise is ultimately pointless, since there is no functioning society for Émile to enter. One may assume that Rousseau intends a message somewhere between the two, to the effect that, if children are brought up as Émile and Sophie have been brought up, a better society might emerge. Rousseau's immense educational legacy must surely rest on such a generous interpretation.

1.7.2 Wordsworth: From Rousseau to Romanticism

Rousseau did not consider himself a Romantic; he predates the term. Indeed, it is possible to describe him as a revolutionary, an Enlightenment

Liberal, an anti-Enlightenment Liberal, or a Conservative. His influence, however, is apparent on succeeding figures in both philosophy and litera- ture more broadly: on Kant, for example, in terms of his arguably absolutist morality, whereby something is right because it is reasonable and not because of its immediate and contextual social consequences (see, e.g., Guyer, 1992); and on William Wordsworth, in terms of his belief in learning from Nature in solitude.

The following sonnet, published in 1807, touches on the central aspects of Wordsworth's position:

> The world is too much with us; late and soon,
> Getting and spending, we lay waste our powers:
> Little we see in Nature that is ours;
> We have given our hearts away, a sordid boon!
> This Sea that bares her bosom to the moon;
>
> The winds that will be howling at all hours,
> And are up-gathered now like sleeping flowers;
> For this, for everything, we are out of tune;
> It moves us not. – Great God! I'd rather be
> A Pagan suckled in a creed outworn;
>
> So might I, standing on this pleasant lea,
> Have glimpses that would make me less forlorn;
> Have sight of Proteus rising from the sea;
> Or hear old Triton blow his wreathed horn.
>
> (Wordsworth, ed. Hutchinson, 1973: 206)

This short poem sums up what the poet felt about his life and society in his mid-thirties (for the Romantic poets believed in poetry as a vehicle of self- expression, by no means the assumption of previous ages). He sees it as a superficial world dominated by commerce in which more important values have been lost (lines 1–4). It is an over-urbanized, and thus over-restricted, world (5–8). Furthermore, the whole Judaeo-Christian tradition has failed us in leading us into this situation by depriving us of a deep and mystical sense of unity with Nature from which a true sense of the Divine can emerge (9–14). It might be argued here that all Wordsworth is doing is expressing forcefully a sense of yearning for an idyllic past that has characterized pastoral poetry as far back as the documentary evidence can lead, that is, to Classical Greece and Rome (specifically, to Theocritus in the third century BC).

Given this, the question must be put as to why Wordsworth's impact has been so great on conceptions of childhood and education. His poetic skills apart, his historical context, at the height of the Industrial Revolution, might supply part of the answer. Also, and uniquely among the major figures connected with Romanticism, Wordsworth was preoccupied during his most creative period with the nature of childhood generally, and specifically with his own development as a poet. He dealt with this most thoroughly in *The Prelude: Or, Growth of a Poet's Mind*, a vast poem of fourteen 'Books' that occupies nearly one hundred pages in Hutchinson's 1973 edition. Its enduring effect on educational thinking can be seen in the debt Marjorie Hourd owed to it in her writing of one of the seminal works in the training of English teachers, *The Education of the Poetic Spirit* (Hourd, 1949), while his effect on British national life generally can be seen in the way his beloved English Lake District has been transformed in the public imagination from barren wasteland (up to the eighteenth century) to the country's most visited National Park.

Following Rousseau, Wordsworth's view of children is that they are not merely innocent. More than that, children are endowed with gifts that intercourse with the world at large systematically deprives them of. It is from Rousseau and Wordsworth, above all, that we have inherited the idea of childhood as a special time of imagination and creativity. Wordsworth wrote of children in the *Ode: Intimations of Immortality*:

Our birth is but a sleep and a forgetting;
The soul that rises with us, our life's Star,
Hath had elsewhere its setting,
And cometh from afar;
Not in entire forgetfulness,
And not in utter nakedness,
But trailing clouds of glory do we come
From God, who is our home:
Heaven lies about us in our infancy!
Shades of the prison-house begin to close
Upon the growing boy . . .

(ed. Hutchinson, 1973: 460)

This perspective may have philosophical roots in neo-Platonism, a movement of the early centuries AD, whose followers believed in attempting to restore life to the mystical condition whence it came. How aware Wordsworth was of this, or other influences, is not entirely clear. However, in poems such as this, he certainly makes claims for the status of children that go beyond the conventions of the pastoral.

The *Ode* offers an extreme thesis, even by Wordsworth's standards. The more common themes concerning childhood, found throughout *The Prelude* and elsewhere can be summed up as follows.

First, Nature has a moral force of its ('Her') own to which children are particularly sensitive. At one point in *The Prelude*, Wordsworth speaks of being 'led by Her' down to a lakeside, only to be confronted with an experience of Nature's sublime and threatening power as a huge mountain appears to loom over him (Book 1). In *Nutting* (1798), he tells of the guilt he felt in damaging a hazel bush whilst harvesting the nuts, for 'there is a spirit in the woods'. In *The Tables Turned* (also 1798), he claims:

One impulse from a vernal wood
May teach you more of man,
Of moral evil and of good,
Than all the sages can.

(Hutchinson, 1973: 377)

Secondly, this divine power can only be fully felt in solitude. Thus his famous daffodils 'flash upon that inward eye/ Which is the bliss of solitude' (*I Wandered Lonely as a Cloud*, written 1804, ibid.: 149). As with Rousseau, the most important education is that which happens in isolation from society, but in harmony with nature, during the early years (though in '*I Wandered Lonely* . . .' Wordsworth is actually describing an experience as an adult for which such a childhood has prepared him).

Thirdly, as the above example illustrates – and again after Rousseau – the adult with such a richness of natural experience can respond to society with far greater insight, imagination and compassion than the child brought up in it from the beginning. Thus, in *Tintern Abbey* (1798: ibid.: 163) he describes the experience of revisiting a place that had seemed special to him with the experience of increased maturity (Wordsworth was twenty-eight), hearing there 'The still, sad music of humanity' against the backdrop of 'something far more deeply interfused,/ Whose dwelling is the light of setting suns, /And the round ocean and the living air, /And in the blue sky, and in the mind of man' and which retains 'ample power/ To chasten and subdue'.

The influence of Romanticism has been very great, particularly in the English-speaking world. Mintz (2004) makes clear its enormous influence in the USA, where the Transcendentalists of the later nineteenth century, such as Emerson, Whitman and Thoreau, were heavily influenced by it, and where Mark Twain's Huckleberry Finn represents the prototypical American Romantic child, who 'enjoyed...opportunities to undertake odysseys of self-discovery outside the goal-driven, overstructured realities of contemporary childhood' (Mintz, 2004: 384). Romanticism has left enduring legacies, including the belief, or perhaps merely the suspicion, that children can be introduced to worldly things too early, that they are naturally creative, and that they must simultaneously be offered protection and maximal opportunities for self-expression. In other words, Romanticism (coupled with the later development of child psychology) is largely responsible for child-centred teaching.

1.7.3 Nineteenth-Century Childhood: The Dream and the Reality

Cultural movements, however attractive, are not simply relayed through the histories of their times. Indeed, some, such as Romanticism, are very much reactions to their times. As Linda Pollock (1983) has been able to show at some length, English children, at least, had a tougher time of it in the early nineteenth century than at any other time before or since for which evidence exists: they were more often subjected to physical cruelty, for example. While this seems initially counterintuitive, it is easily explained by the fact that the prevailing tenor of the times was not that of Romanticism but of the Industrial Revolution and the urban poverty it engendered, to which Romanticism was the response of the artistic and largely privileged. The strongest marks of the time were those engendered by an extreme Protestant zeal, an obsession with work and profit, fuelled by hordes of refugees from impoverished lives in the countryside. If any time were ripe for a renewal of the pastoral tradition in the arts, it was late eighteenth-century and early nineteenth-century England. Thus Charles Dickens, in *Hard Times*, provides a more accurate social document than Wordsworth ever could in his characterization of education as a cruel and unremitting obsession with 'facts' at the expense of feelings, while many children were denied even this by the demands for child labour, and William Blake's bleak visions of late eighteenth-century childhood in London (in poems such as *The Garden of Love*, *London* and *The Chimney-Sweeper*) offer further insights into the horrors of the world that Rousseau and Wordsworth each sought to avoid and hoped, largely against hope, to renew.

It was largely as a response to industrial exploitation, rather than as a direct expression of Romanticism, that mass schooling emerged in countries such as England. It was principally during the twentieth century that Romanticism began to exert a heavy effect on formal education, and during the 1960s and 1970s that it arguably exerted its greatest influence.

Insofar as Romanticism was, indeed remains, a movement of opposition, it signals the end of the Modernist project of childhood and education itself. According to the Romantics and Postmodernists alike, the future does not necessarily imply progress from the past. The next chapter considers how the broad cultural movements outlined in the last few chapters have been both adopted and subverted in recent years.

The Postmodern Child:
Less Than Not Much?

1.8.1 The Wood and the Trees

If the Modernist project of the child has been based on increased concern for the not yet fully human adult-in-waiting (conceived either as the purely Aristotelian citizen-to-be, the Puritan fallen soul, the Liberal blank slate, or the Romantic innocent facing corruption by the world), what happens to childhood when faith in progress falters? The past century has witnessed a series of jolts to the Enlightenment project, from the First World War, the end of Empire and the Russian Revolution, to climate change and Fundamentalist terrorism; and belief in progress and scientific rationality has suffered in the process.

One answer is that it is not childhood that is diminished so much as adulthood, for the human condition as a whole is problematized by recent events, and it is too early to be clear what this is doing to childhood as a whole. A second is that childhood has, paradoxically, become the end-in-itself that adulthood used to be, so that adults aspire to childhood rather than *vice versa*. A third is that childhood is disappearing as contemporary conditions render it impossible to protect children from all aspects of adult life, while a fourth argues that the emphasis in childrearing has become quite the opposite of this, as children are separated more and more from a world that adults see as increasingly threatening. Across all these possibilities run debates about risk and infantilization: are children experiencing more of a 'risk society' (Beck, 1992), or being increasingly sheltered from risk, and are people as a whole being empowered or disempowered by recent social changes? Have adults become more like children, so that we can no longer make sense of childhood?

It seems clear that, as far as recent history is concerned, we 'cannot see the wood for the trees'. Just as Romanticism took some time to be embedded into formal practices such as pedagogy, so the insights and developments since the mid-nineteenth-century, from Marxism to Freud to television to the internet, have yet to be fully realized or understood in terms of how they affect the everyday practices of childhood and of dealings between adults and children.

The remainder of this chapter deals with the four perspectives above in turn.

1.8.2 The Postmodern Condition?

First, it is important to arrive at a working definition of the Postmodern, since not all commentators agree that Modernity has run its course. Candidate terms adopted include Late Modernity (widely used), High Modernity (Giddens, 1991), New Modernity (Beck, 1992), Liquid Modernity (Bauman, 2000) and Hypermodernity (Charles and Lipovetsky, 2005). Even among those who adopt 'Postmodern', there is some variation.

'Modernity' is, in any case, a loose term, implying simply 'the modern period'. Modernity can be taken to cover the time from the Enlightenment, the Renaissance or the late Middle Ages up to the end of the twentieth century or beyond. Its general characteristic is a belief in progress: that the new is an improvement on the old. Such a belief rests on a prior belief in the rationality, and thus perfectibility, of the human, and thus a simultaneous conviction to both individual liberty and social cohesion. Crudely, the tendency of Modernity has been towards a belief that science can improve society. This is roughly reflected in 'Modernism' in the arts, including architecture, though Modernist art often took experimentation and conceptualism to such disruptive lengths that the avant-garde often seems as much Postmodern as Modern. (See, for example, Jean-Francois Lyotard's *An Answer to the Question, What is the Postmodern,* in Lyotard, 1984.)

Many thinkers construe the general tenor of our times as still recognizably Modern. Anthony Giddens, for example (a strong influence on the British New Labour government of the late 1990s, and arguably coiner of the term 'The Third Way'), regards globalization as evidence of Western Modernity spreading its influence across the globe, and has tended to be very positive about this (Giddens, 1991, 1998). Giddens' concern is rather with the ways in which Modern societies differ from Pre-Modern ones. This difference, according to Giddens, is most strongly characterized by the abstraction of space-time caused by a shift from agricultural living, in which time and duty were understood in response to diurnal and annual rhythms (time to get up, to sow, to reap, to sleep determined by nature), to urban living dependent on standardized clock-time, in which the assumption is that there is no 'Natural Order'. Thus Modern people believe in using their own rational powers to order their own lives and the structure of society, and the development of this tendency results in the lifestyle politics of the Millennium, in which matters as diverse as dress, vocation and religious belief are increasingly matters of individual choice. Giddens is thus also strongly associated with the idea of Identity Politics.

Giddens adopts an unusually optimistic view of recent changes. A similar, but somewhat less sanguine, approach is that of Zygmunt Bauman, whose conception of *Liquid Modernity* (2000) posits people as engaged in a quest for perfectibility but no longer with a belief that perfection is attainable. Bauman adopts the metaphor of liquidity in relation to existing concepts such as that of a 'fluid' labour market. Our times, according to Bauman, remain relatively free (within bounds) and forward looking (without a final destination), yet more anxious than those that preceded them.

The theme of individualization (or 'individuation', to adopt a bleaker term preferred by some sociologists who see even the individual as socially determined) involving increased risk as well as freedom has been most famously developed by Ulrich Beck, whose vision of a New Modernity as Risk Society has both inspired and haunted many other social theorists. Whereas Giddens focused on the abstraction of space and time, Beck's concern was with the abstraction of risk. In Pre-Modern times, risk, and therefore, risk management, was more predictable and contextual than now. Even wars were held between opposing armies through battles on particular sites over claims to identifiable territory. Now – and this has intensified since Beck – global terrorism presents an ever-present risk that is very difficult to measure, evaluate or guard against. One's safety on the London Underground, in the streets of New York or in the nightclubs of Bali no longer depends on the decisions one has made about whether to go to war. Put crudely, we have far more to decide about, but the decisions are much harder to make. Again, this tends to render society increasingly anxious.

'Hypermodernity' is an intensification of Modernity, characterized by superabundance in both goods and information, so that individuals are increasingly able to make choices in the context of multiple 'truths' rather than the one assumed 'truth' acting as a regulatory ideal in previous phases of Modernity. This endless choice is a highly anxious condition, however (Charles and Lipovetsky, 2005).

Set against these reappraisals of the Modern are the Postmodernists. Often satirized as aimless relativists or unhelpful Conservatives, Postmodernists (themselves comprising a range of perspectives) tend to stand against Modernists in their commitment to a metaphysics of difference and absence rather than of presence and identity. That is, Postmodern accounts often differ very little from Modernist ones in their analyses of key aspects of present conditions, but they tend to be grounded in a differing set of philosophical assumptions. Specifically, Postmodern accounts are often also Poststructuralist accounts.

Poststructuralism is a philosophical position grounded as much in the study of language as that of traditional logic, ethics, mind or being. It follows on from Structuralism, which became a major force in twentieth-century literary and social theory, particularly in France.

The fundamental Structuralist insights draw on Ferdinand de Saussure's *Course in General Linguistics* (first published 1917; see Culler, 1976). Saussure argued that languages are not best understood as somehow reflections of an underlying reality but rather as socially constructed systems of signs in which meaning of individual words and phrases are dependent on meanings of other words and phrases: in other words, in which meaning is relational. Structuralists, in fields as diverse as literary criticism and anthropology, drew on Saussure in attempting to understand the underlying codes or sign-systems that make texts, people, institutions and even whole cultures 'tick'.

In this they were also drawing on Saussure's distinction between 'Langue' and 'Parole'. 'Langue' signifies the 'universal grammar' (to borrow a later term from Chomsky) which is invariant and drives a language system, and 'Parole' the infinitely varied world of utterances generated by that system which we hear, speak, read and write. In other words, Saussure-inspired Structuralism proceeded on the belief that cultural systems have invisible but identifiable 'drivers' that it is the job of the researcher to discover. Poststructuralism rejects this assumption of an underlying code.

A seminal text in the development of Poststructuralism was a conference paper delivered in 1966 by Jacques Derrida entitled *Structure, Sign and Play in the Human Sciences* (in Derrida, 1978). In this, Derrida argued that the centre of a structure is just as dependent on the structure as the structure is dependent on the centre. Thus, building on a number of influences including the Existentialist philosophies of Heidegger and Sartre, and the psychoanalysis of Freud and Lacan, Derrida began his development of a philosophy grounded in the idea that the centre is always decentred, and that meaning and truth can never be fully captured, finalized or pinned down. He thus later coined the term 'Différance' to indicate that the meaning of a term, or an event, is characterized both by 'difference' and by 'deferment'. Thus, after the Structuralists, meaning is relational but, *pace* Structuralism, there is no identifiable set of operational rules that determine it. Thus, in philosophical terms, Poststructuralism, and consequently Postmodernism, tends to be more Relativist and Social Constructionist than Realist and Fundamentalist. However, Poststructuralists are not necessarily thoroughgoing Relativists or Antirealists: that is to say, you can be a Poststructuralist without denying that no external reality exists, even if you are not optimistic about ever being sure of its true nature.

Poststructuralists, then, tend to assume that 'at the heart of the matter' are not identity and presence, but rather difference and absence. Those inclined to dismiss this as absurd may be urged to address the development of Quantum Physics. For nearly a century, physicists have grappled with the problem that, at the smallest scale, the subatomic particles which were assumed to constitute matter (the bits of the smallest things – atoms – that the universe was assumed to comprise since Leucippus and Democritus developed atomic theory in the 5th century BC) do not seem predictable or even clearly locatable. Easy assumptions about the universe comprising material that can be divided into smaller and smaller particles until a clear unit of identity can be identified have had to be abandoned or, at least, problematized. It cannot be inferred from this that all, or even many, physicists are Poststructuralists, but it does serve to illustrate that the metaphysics of presence, assumed by all the most significant thinkers of Modernity is, at least, open to question.

Jean-Francois Lyotard has referred to this putative unit of difference, or ubiquitous presence of absence as the '*differend*' (Lyotard, 1988). Where Modernists aspire to consensus and identity, Lyotard aspires to both consensus and 'dissensus', and to identity as non-identity. His work *The Postmodern Condition: A Report on Knowledge* (English edition, 1984) is often taken as a focus point in discussions about the Postmodern. In it, Lyotard defines Postmodernism as 'incredulity towards metanarratives (Lyotard, 1984: xiv), arguing that the faith in the 'big ideas' of Modernity, such as liberty, science and progress, has dissipated into a plurality of 'little stories'; in other words, Postmodern culture is characterized not by grand ideology but by sub-cultures. Followers of Lyotard might point to the more recent adoption of religious fundamentalism as a protest movement in support of this thesis. Lyotard takes up Ludwig Wittgenstein's notion of the 'language game' (Wittgenstein, 1967) to assert that there is no reason to suppose that these 'little stories' ('*petit recits*') are mutually compatible or cohesive.

To Lyotard, therefore, (Post)Modern society is not merely characterized by diverse quests for the truth but by a dismissal of the possibility of one truth; on one level, therefore, it is not very far from the positions of, for example, Baumann, and Charles and Lipovetsky. However, an important element of Postmodern thinking is a rejection of the progressive and linear assumption of Modernist time. That is to say, Postmodernism is not an epoch following the Modern epoch so much as a critical attitude, perhaps allied to scepticism. We did not, Lyotard would assert, suddenly stop being Modernists and become Postmodernists. Postmodern art, music and fashion, for example, draw on the past in playful and idiosyncratic ways, questioning previous assumptions about originality and creativity.

It is not surprising, therefore, to find a range of voices within Postmodernism. Politically, as well as in matters of taste and aesthetics, Postmodernists can range from neo-Conservatives to anarchists. Some, such as Jean Baudrillard (Poster, 1988) ground their analyses in Modernist sociology: Baudrillard argues that society has moved so far from production to consumption that human identity (or non-identity) is caught up in an endless round of recycled images – in 'hyperreality'. Baudrillard's is indeed an anxious society.

For present purposes, current conditions will be described as Postmodern. The full justification for this will be made evident in Part 2, where the theoretical perspective to be developed in this book is explained, and its debt to Poststructuralism is made clear. However, it must be stressed that much of the social analysis of each of the above thinkers tallies with much of that of their contemporaries, notwithstanding the differences in their self-designations and political commitments. There is some general agreement about what characterizes our times.

1.8.3 The Postmodern Adult-Child

Preface: As I drafted this section, BBC news reported that S.V.Hamburg had become the first football club to build a cemetery next to their ground for fans. I leave it to readers to consider whether this has any relevance to what is to follow.

First, what does it mean to be an 'adult' now? While commentators such as Ulrich Beck have stressed the individualization of risk under recent conditions, others have developed what amounts to an infantilization thesis. For instance, Jean Baudrillard's 'hyperreality' is a condition in which reality and fantasy are undifferentiated, such that, in effect, Disneyland becomes the 'real' America' (Poster, 1988: 166). According to Neil Postman (1994: 97), life now commonly passes through three stages: infancy, adult-child and senility: 'The adult-child may be defined as a grown-up whose intellectual and emotional capacities are unrealised.' Such a person transgresses the still dominant Aristotelian assumption of an adult as fully realized, with a clear and productive purpose in life. However, Postman's argument also entails a literacy thesis not employed by Aristotle, for Postman argues that the development of mass literacy in early Modernity redefined the state of adulthood as the literate citizen. In turn, the development of such citizens required a formalized and structured education to become literate for the young. Postman argues that the ascendance of the visual media has effectively disempowered or infantilized adults. Writing in the early 1980s, Postman's thesis is concerned principally with television. However, in his later *Technopoly* (1993), he extends his critique to computers, which he also sees as dehumanizing.

Postman contends that literacy is necessary for abstract thought, accusing the visual media of encouraging the move to irrationalism, as 'language is an abstraction from experience, whereas pictures are concrete representations of experience' (1994: 73). Television, argues Postman, is ephemeral and destroys privacy by decontextualizing, such that 'all events, having no precedent causes or subsequent consequences, are without value and therefore meaningless', as a result of which, 'there is no sense of proportion to be discerned in the world' (Postman, 1994: 106). Consequently, although people may be presented with increased choices, they can neither act on them from a position of rational self-interest, nor even distinguish the commercial from the political or the sacred. Thus brainwashed, American 'childified adult[s] . . . want to be parents of children less than they want to be children themselves' (ibid.: 126, 138). To Postman, the only sector of society capable of deferred gratification, self-constraint and other traditionally adult virtues is that comprising the intellectual élite who have achieved critical detachment from the media.

David Buckingham (2000) attempts to take a balanced overview of perspectives on the new media, mapping a series of responses from Sanders (1994), who strongly supports Postman to the extent of presaging the end of civilization, to Lanham (1993), who stresses the democratic potential of information technology (see Buckingham, 2000: 29, 41).

It is clear that opinions remain divided about the effects of the Late Modern, or Postmodern age, with its dependence on the new technologies, on the human condition generally, and the state of human adulthood or maturity specifically. However, a common thread runs through many of the analyses. On the one hand, people are expected to make huge numbers of choices where such choices did not exist in the past. On the other hand, the abstraction and diffusion of risk, whether or not exacerbated by a weakening of rational capacity, makes such choices increasingly difficult to make, or of increasingly little consequence when they are made.

Both these sets of dynamics, however interpreted, have implications for the states of both childhood and adulthood. Indeed, it can be difficult to tell the two apart. Buckingham refers several times to Michael Jackson as an iconic figure of the end of the twentieth century: neither black nor white, male nor female, adult nor child. Jackson's confusing entanglements with the law in the 2000s have only served to accentuate these confusions.

1.8.4 The Postmodern Child: Opportunities and Constraints

Given the range of responses to current conditions in terms of the human condition generally, it is not surprising that commentators differ in their construals of twentieth, let alone twenty-first-century childhood. Whether or not there ever was, there is certainly no longer one agreed version of childhood, as Allison James and Alan Prout point out (James and Prout, 1997: ix–xvii).

Given Neil Postman's view of the contemporary adult, he is inevitably pessimistic about the Postmodern child. His view could scarcely be further at odds from the optimistic scenarios painted by Modernist historians of childhood such as Ariès (1962) and deMause (1974), for whom current conditions for children are almost paradisal compared to those of the past. Indeed, Postman believes the concept of childhood itself has been devalued, arguing that it depended on 'a well developed sense of shame' (Postman, 1994: 9): in other words, the protection and guidance afforded the child relied in the past on a sense of unworthiness and vulnerability in the adult. Postman finds late twentieth-century children undertaking cultural practices that are scarcely differentiated from those of adults, for instance regarding clothing, crime or games. The days of the '*Lore and Language of Schoolchildren*' (Opie and Opie, 2001) are past, on Postman's account, as the distinctive playground games are increasingly abandoned in favour of football and celebrity gossip. This is a cultural environment in which infancy is succeeded by the child-adult, or adult-child state referred to above, a state in which neither child nor adult can seek fulfilment in an Aristotelian sense, with the exception of a privileged minority, yet in which both child and adult vainly seek fulfilment, or at least comfort, in the practices of the other.

Postman concludes with an ironic echo of Ariès: 'Childhood . . . has a biological basis but cannot be realised unless a social environment has need of it' (Postman, 1994: 144). This thesis is similar to Ariès', but without the optimism.

A sense of unease about the current state of childhood is found in other accounts. David Buckingham notes the ubiquitous sense of danger surrounding children: that they are both dangerous and in danger (2000: 3), even though statistics do not justify this fear. Of course, one can only wish to protect children if one has some special feeling for them. Indeed, Buckingham's analysis reminds us that conceptions of childhood are always dependent in some way on previous conceptions; there can be no complete break. Nevertheless, Buckingham is inclined to the view, as was Postman, that the adult world has tended to become less responsible in its treatment of children. Indeed, Buckingham goes further than this, claiming, '. . . in the recent history of industrialized countries, childhood has essentially been defined as a matter of exclusion' (Buckingham, 2000: 13). However, Buckingham also acknowledges the difficulty in coming to a settled view of the current situation. He cites a wide range of authors who have struggled to come to terms with the relationships of children to the new technologies, for example, and notes a range of conclusions from that of Sanders (1994) who foresees the end of civilization following the death of literacy, to that of Steinberg and Kincheloe (1997) who fear that children may have a super-abundance of knowledge, to that of Lanham (1993) and others, who stress the democratic potential of the new technologies. As Buckingham notes, we all currently seem to be engaged in constructing and reconstructing childhood – or in ignoring it. Buckingham's educational conclusion from all this is that we should concentrate on preparing children for the media age rather than protecting them against it.

In the North American context, Steven Mintz (2004) notes a drift towards *laissez-faire* attitudes to children in the middle of the last century followed by a deepening sense of anxiety at its close. In the USA, young people were noted for their assertiveness much earlier than in Britain. (Mintz offers some possible explanations for this, including a desire to get away from the British influence.) The invention of the teenager (a term coined in 1941), the work of Benjamin Spock (who enjoined parents to trust their, and their children's instincts) and the development of rock culture all exacerbated this tendency. However, Mintz notes that in the libertarian 1960s, there was no effective legal support for children in the USA, and he characterizes the last quarter of the century as a period of moral crisis and panic about childhood, unsupported by statistical data, which fail to show children in ever-increasing danger.

Overall, Mintz notes 'contradictions that lie at the very heart of the contemporary conception of childhood' (2004: 380). On the one hand, Spock has been supplanted by parenting classes (343); on the other hand, there has been some return to a '"pre-industrial" concept of children as "little adults" . . . [who] . . . spend more time alone than their predecessors' (347). However, Mintz sees American culture as continuing to be 'oriented toward mastery and control', and so inclined to view 'childhood as a project' and tolerate 'no tolerance of diversity in paths to adulthood' (383). Thus, for all its Liberal tradition, contemporary American childhood is not painted by Mintz as particularly empowering; he believes Mark Twain's Huckleberry Finn enjoyed a freedom still denied to many, notwithstanding the material hardship and parental abuse the fictional Huck endured.

In general, it can be argued that responses to childhood now are still coloured more strongly by the major influences of the more distant past than by influences of the past hundred years. Indeed, there are grounds for arguing that Postman (for example) has a strong sympathy towards the Puritan view, and Mintz towards the Romantic. These influences, characterized above as Aristotelian, Puritan, Liberal and Romantic, are still strongly evident in the treatment of children in the Information Age: they continue to seem more deeply rooted than later influences, such as that of the sexual child developed by Freud and successors. That is to say, there is still a greater emphasis on the protection of sexual exploitation of children than on their own sexuality, and anxiety concerning the former has certainly not diminished during the 2000s, while the latter is hardly seen fit for public debate, and any such debate might well be viewed as strongly morally suspicious (at least in the UK; the Netherlands have long taken a more liberal view on this). Later developments still, such as the internet, remain too close to be viewed with any degree of critical distance, though revisions of attitudes towards television may now be underway, with anecdotes abounding in journalism and everyday discourse about how television was a less malign influence than previously thought – and, indeed, may have been a benign one – in the days when the whole family sat and watched the same programmes together, and could discuss these at school or work with others the following day.

Nevertheless, publications since the 1980s have tended towards a more negative view of contemporary childhood than their immediate predecessors, and there are few who would now claim that children are enjoying some sort of Golden Age, though an argument could certainly be made for this in the more affluent countries. The belief in progress has been lost by many, and in that sense we are in a Postmodern rather than Late or Hyper-Modern mindset regarding children, unconfident that they will do as well as their baby-boomer parents and unsure about what responsibilities parenting them should entail, while simultaneously afraid to allow them to take risks. We indeed live in anxious times.

If the Aristotelian child was 'not much' in relation to the adult, the Postmodern child may be 'less than not much' in relation to a society of uncertain and immature adults. That, at least, is the impression gained from many who have considered the subject. Few, however, would state the case as strongly as Lee Comer, who as early as the 1970s, expressed a view of childhood in contemporary society the uncomfortable truth of which may now be increasingly recognized:

> . . . children are animals – transitional sub-humans (we tolerate dogs more readily . . .) . . . must literally be locked up . . . Even zoos are open plan these days. While the age of "maturity" falls progressively, we deliberately prolong childhood and dependence . . . we do these things in the name of love. All our theories and practices . . . are nothing short of compensations, sugared pills for the exclusion of children.' (Comer, in Hoyles, 1979: 151–6)

However, it is my intention to show, in Part 2, that a sensitivity to Postmodern perspectives need not lead to such a dismissal of the child. Indeed, Postmodern thinking may rather offer a path away from the restrictions of Aristotelian thinking and its footnotes, developing the very Liberal tradition it problematizes. To make this case will require some prior theoretical discussion in the next chapter.

Part 2
A Fully Semiotic View
of Childhood*

* Some material in this and the two following chapters also appears, or is adapted from, the journal article Semiosis, Dewey and Difference: implications for pragmatic philosophy of education' (Stables, 2008b) published in *Contemporary Pragmatism* 5/1, 2008, and is reproduced with permission from, and acknowledgment to Rodopi publishing.

Living as Semiotic Engagement

2.1.1 Introduction to Part 2

In Part 1, I argued that contemporary conceptions of childhood are heavily indebted to Aristotle, and then to three more recent influences, none of which fully subverts the Aristotelian heritage: Puritanism, Liberalism and Romanticism. Aristotle's view of the child is as not yet fully human because not yet able to carry out a fully adult role as a citizen; the Puritan, or extreme Protestant, view is of the child as corrupt and in urgent need of guidance in devotion and hard work if she is to have any chance of saving her soul; the Liberal view is of the child as innocent at birth with an innate rational faculty that can only work on sense data in the 'real world', and so as highly receptive to education and correct training on the way to becoming a free adult; the Romantic view is of the child as innately superior to the adult, so that the purpose of education becomes to allow her to develop her natural abilities as far as possible before contact with a corrupt and demeaning world. All these, I argue, are elements in the sometimes confused ways in which we think about children, and about their education, today. The three more recent influences are 'footnotes to Aristotle'. That is to say, the overriding view remains of the child as qualitatively very different from the adult: either as insufficiently developed for immersion in society, or (on the Romantic account, still popular among child-centred educators), as too good for it.

The 'semiotic', or *semiosic* view of the child developed in Part 2 challenges the assumption of this qualitative difference and the implications that flow from it, arguing from a perspective according to which children are more like adults (and *vice versa*) than it has been common to recognize.

2.1.2 *Semiosis* as Foundational

In *Living and Learning as Semiotic Engagement* (2005a), I argued that the assertion 'living is semiotic engagement' has the potential to become 'a foundational statement for a postfoundational age' (2005a: 11). By 'a post-foundational age', is meant a Postmodern age in Lyotard's sense of a cultural moment (whether or not clearly definable as a period in history) character-ized by 'incredulity toward metanarratives' (Lyotard, 1984: xiv): in other words, a society that has lost its consensus regarding the validity of religion, mathematical science or the power of human reason more broadly as bases on which to build a brighter future. Such an analysis of a Postfoundational, or Postmodern, condition is often dismissed by academics and others on the grounds that it does not offer sufficient hope for social progress. How-ever, if the analysis has some compelling explanatory power (as I believe it does), it cannot simply be wished away on the grounds that it is not immedi-ately obvious how it is helpful or useful. Such reactions serve to show that the Postmodern analysis creates problems that we have yet to solve.

There is plenty of evidence to support Lyotard's analysis, bearing in mind that it only has to be supportable up to a point for its validity to be granted. Once a consensus is broken, then it is broken. Part 1 showed how histories of childhood no longer universally accept the thesis of continual, or even intermittent, progress over the Modern period. In other areas, too, there has been a marked, sometimes alarming, tendency for people to reject Modernist assumptions. Faith in science has been shaken by the horrors of Modern warfare and the perception of a global environmental crisis; faith in democracy and liberty have been abandoned by religious fundamentalists; faith in social progress has been abandoned by many brought up with great hopes for Keynesian economics and the welfare state. There is less obvi-ously one dominant way of looking at the World than there seemed to be.

As noted in the previous chapter, Lyotard's Postmodern account is also a Poststructuralist account. A view of living as semiotic engagement is a Post-structuralist view. Following the brief definition of Poststructuralism in Chapter 1.8, the argument for regarding living as *semiosis* rests on the following. (A fuller account is in Stables, 2005a, Chapter 1.)

First, 'semiotics' is a broader term than 'language' – it refers to any system of 'signs' – but a language is one sort of semiotic system. Thus there is justi-fication for using theories about language to understand things beyond our normal understanding of 'language'. This is what semioticians do.

Secondly, although semiotics, like linguistics, is generally considered a purely human activity, and, indeed, one limited to certain aspects of human behaviour only (symbolism, advertising, non-verbal communication and so on), it is possible to adopt 'biosemiotic' or 'pansemiotic' perspectives, accord-ing to which humans are not the only 'sign-users'. These perspectives do not make the conventional anthropocentric and humanist distinction between 'nature' and 'culture' and thus the assumption that there is a clear dividing line between 'sign-using' humans and 'signal-responding' non-human entities – from animals to, on the most extreme accounts, inorganic elements.

In the Western tradition, a sign is conceived of as different from a signal. Humans communicate *via* signs; animals (etc.) just respond to signals. However, there has been recent interest in developing broader perspectives. For example, Emmeche (1999) considers the biosemiotic perspectives, whereby every living thing carries messages of survival value. According to this perspective, DNA is a series of codes carrying 'what works' from history. Other authors (including Maran, 2006) have pointed to the possibility of a pansemiotic perspective embracing the non-living as well as the living. However, there has been little exploration of the implications of this, whereas conceptions of biosemiotics have influenced thinking about ecosemiotics, whereby the human/non-human nature relationship is understood in semiotic terms.

According to Cartesian mind–body substance dualism, mind and body are qualitatively distinct kinds of substance. (Descartes argued something much stronger than 'mind is different from body'.) On this account, central to Descartes and developed through modern science, non-human entities effectively respond mechanically to signals, or prompts, without intention or awareness. Of course, science has begun to question this without further resource to philosophy. There is now widespread recognition of kinds of intelligence not formerly noted in certain aspects of animal behaviour: for example, use of tools among chimpanzees and evidence of limited memory, even awareness of death, among, say, elephants. Although such behaviour is not generally accepted as evidence of sign use, some of the research evidence is challenging. For example, the work of the Language Research Centre at Georgia State University has found increasing evidence of the similarities in cognitive processing between, in particular, children and other primates (http://www2.gsu.edu/~wwwlrc/research-main.htm). Also well known in this area is the work of Jane Goodall on chimpanzee language and tool use and other aspects of animal intelligence. Conversely, such discoveries about animals are bound, in time, to affect our conceptions of what it means to be human – as Darwin's discoveries did in the nineteenth century. It is not a case of arguing that a human is a chimpanzee; just that there are considerable overlaps between the two.

Cartesian substance dualism, however, continues to leave its mark on our thinking. One area in which its legacy can be found is that of learning theory, particularly in the 'cognitivism *vs.* behaviourism' debate in education that, although partly superseded, still wields some influence. Cognitive approaches emphasize the minded aspect of human living ('understanding'), and behaviourism the mechanical, and therefore more closely predictable ('behaviour'). The most notable attempt in philosophy of education, that of John Dewey, to overcome Cartesian dualism will be the focus of consideration in the following chapter, where it will be argued that the fully semiotic perspective both reinforces and develops that of Dewey, with significant consequences for his views on educational practice. (See also Stables, 2008b.)

I have coined the term 'sign(al)' as a combination of 'sign' and 'signal' (Stables, 2005a). Both humans and non-humans respond to sign(al)s. As in the body–mind case, this is not to claim that there is 'no difference' between, say, a man and a dog – but it is to claim that the dividing line between human and non-human is nothing like so clear and absolute as has been assumed since Descartes. In making this move, a trend begun by Darwin and others has been accentuated. It is not even that there is nothing special about human beings: simply that we can no longer make grandiose claims such as that only humans can have consciousness, intelligence, or even language. (Of course, a dog cannot have human language, but the reverse is also true!)

It is difficult to define a sign(al) precisely. It is simultaneously a unit of meaning and a prompt to action. Also, as a unit of meaning, it is 'deferred' (after Derrida), and so is not precisely locatable in space-time. (Although meanings happen in relation to time and space and change over time and space, a meaning can never belong or happen at an identifiable point in time and space.) To Derrida and others, meanings are never fixed or fully completed, for we return again and again to a text or an experience and constantly reinterpret it. We can precisely locate a word, therefore, but not its meaning. However, it is possible to explain how a sign(al) might work. This requires an acceptance that processes are more important than substances: that life and the universe are best understood, as physicists understand them, in terms of forces and energy. In Stables, 2008b, I offer a tentative, pansemiotic account of the sign(al) drawing on both process philosophy (particularly A. N. Whitehead's, in *Process and Reality* [1978]) and European poststructuralism (particularly Derrida).

Let us suppose that process creates (the effect of) substance (*via* duration), rather than processes being 'things that happen to substances'. To give an example, a brick, or something equally 'concrete', is understood as a physical phenomenon in terms of the interplay of energy and forces. In addition, process is characterized at the most fundamental level by charged energy, and at the most sophisticated level by consciously-recognized events and experiences – so that experiences are actual events in which we are implicated. In taking the sign(al) to be that which moves us on (or moves something else on), it can be understood on either of these levels, either as a concatenation of charges (charged particles, or waves, or the effects of strings in a multidimensional universe, depending on one's approach to quantum physics), or as a singular charge. However, the paradox of the charged object, or subject, is that each singularity is, in fact, relational: that is, it is dependent upon the tension between the positively and negatively charged poles, in traditional electromagnetic terms. A sign(al), then, is that which moves us on, gives us a jolt, changes our behaviour, whether this be a sign or collection of signs (a word, a map or an item of news) or a signal or set of signals (an electric shock, a scent, or some set of circumstances that produce a subconscious sense of threat). In other words, in the concept of the sign(al), no discrimination is made between the conscious and the unconscious or subconscious.

As the Structuralists and others have made clear, objects only exist in relation to their opposites. Light only means anything in relation to darkness, body in relation to mind. By the same token, the charged, relational object is only an object by means of its encounter with a subject, itself relational. Therefore, how I respond to a sign(al) depends on my history and the context I am in, each of which is dependent on my relations with others, human and non-human.

In simple terms: first, we learn through experiences. Secondly, what we experience is real, not merely an abstract gloss on a concrete reality; our experiences are our involvements in events. Thirdly, every experience – every event – is unique as the set of relations that determines it is unique; we only exist, and everything only makes sense, in relation to many kinds of Otherness, and we are only ourselves insofar as we are related to other people and other non-human entities.

In general, this is a Deweyan position, though arrived at rather differently. As explained in Chapter 1.6, John Dewey is widely regarded as the 'father' of modern theories of experiential learning. Whitehead, like Dewey, has experience as firmly grounded in the present. Derrida, however, has experience and meaning as deferred (Derrida, 1982), so the present has no essential being. At first sight, these positions seem incommensurable. However, if we put aside the issue of essential presence (which can be construed as little more than an argument about Plato, although there is insufficient space to discuss this here), their accounts of experience bear a remarkable similarity as yet unexplored in the literature. In their implications for education there may, however, be significant differences, that will be discussed below.

On this set of process-orientated accounts, how do human beings (at least) learn, develop and generally 'go on' with life? All three accounts seem to agree that experiences are incremental. Each experience impacts on future experiences, *via* memory and conditioning. Whitehead refers to this as pre-hension: apprehension depends on prehension. Derrida refers to traces (Derrida, 1976). Dewey argues that perceptions determine stimulus as well as response (e.g. 1896, 1912) and that learning is therefore 'conative' as opposed to 'cognitive' or 'behaviourist'. On all these accounts, a person is implicated in his or her experiences and so learns to anticipate them, and such anticipation affects but never totally determines forthcoming experiences. As experiences mount, we re-classify. Life is thus a process of emergent patterning. This patterning is heavily influenced by culture (as meaning-making is always relational) and yet is in part unique to the individual. My context is always, to some degree, unique, yet, as a being of relations, I am positioned within my culture. Thus there is no patterning without meaning and no meaning that is utterly predictable. Much of this is Deweyan. However, as I shall argue in Chapter 2.2, outcomes actually lack the predictability on which Dewey's educational philosophy partly depended.

To understand this with respect to a concrete example, consider response to a flag consisting of black and white halves. (This is intended purely as an example, with apologies to any who recognize this as flag as their own.) The black half is a concatenation of charges, generally understood as wavelengths, that produce the effect of black; similarly the white. Although I have a set of generalized responses to black and white, my response to them as they constitute this flag is determined by a host of cultural influences, and by my (perhaps shifting) position *vis-à-vis* these. Conversely, my other responses to black and white may well be affected by my feelings relating to the flag. Furthermore, my response to the black-and-white flag cannot be simply computed by adding together my responses to a black piece of cloth and a white piece of cloth; sign(al)s are not singular and plural in that mathematical sense.

Everyone nowadays is aware of the contentiousness of the concepts, 'flag', 'black' and 'white'. Whatever my response to this flag is, it is likely to be similar to that of others in my cultural group, but this flag will have its own particular connotations for me as well.

On the above account, the attempt to isolate the sign(al) precisely fails. The sign(al) is both the series of charges that produces the colour effect and the flag in its cultural and historical context, as it affects the subject. However, whether it be small, large, singular or multiple, it remains the unit of meaning. However, it is a unit of analysis only insofar as we are prepared to abandon the concept of 'unit', for meaning cannot be broken down into units, or measured with respect to size or location in any way whatsoever. The basic 'unit' is perhaps best conceived as one of difference – that which produces a charge – as Derrida and Deleuze and Guattari (1994), among others, have posited. The construal of a unit of meaning as a unit of difference puts this semiotic, pragmatic account of meaning-making and purposeful activity at odds with the dominant pragmatist educational perspective, that of John Dewey, in one important respect, which will be explored more fully in the next chapter.

In conclusion, a view of all living as *semiosis* ('sign-use') is inevitably biosemiotic or pansemiotic. That is, it regards everything a living thing does (if not non-living things too) as response to a sign, or sign(al). This is, of course, only a valid perspective if it can be argued first that there is no absolute qualitative distinction between a 'sign' and a 'signal' as I have argued and, indeed, this is a tenet of the Poststructuralism of Derrida, Lyotard and others. One might argue that it is also implicit in the later analytic philosophy of Ludwig Wittgenstein – Wittgenstein, 1967 – in which he describes all human activity in terms of 'forms of life' or 'language games' without drawing a firm distinction between the two. This view, therefore, is not simply located in one particular corner of Continental philosophy or 'Parisian Theory'.

To sum up: in everyday speech, we tend to think of a sign as a human construct and a signal as an unconscious prompt; we respond to signs consciously and signals automatically. This kind of thinking, which draws such a clear and firm line between the thinking mind and the unthinking body is, I argue, a legacy of Cartesian substance dualism: that is, René Descartes' conviction that mind and body are quite different kinds of substance. It is in this tradition that we tend to see the universe – even animals – as merely mechanical, and regard human beings as the only rational creatures, with a duty therefore to control, exploit and manage natural resources. Of course, elements of this thinking predate Descartes (elements are in Plato and Aristotle), but the strongly held view of the universe, and of non-human nature, as purely brutish, mechanical and unintelligent is very much a product of Enlightenment, and underpins Newtonian physics as well as various forms of modern Humanism. Aristotle, for example, believed the differences between people and animals were of degree rather than kind, yet in the Cartesian tradition, animals are regarded as no more than machines.

A fully semiotic position thus refuses to draw a clear distinction between sign-using human culture and signal-responding animal and non-animal nature. As far as theories of language, from which Postructuralism developed, are concerned, this is a quite consistent stance. For decades, Structuralists and then Poststructuralists have challenged the view that a 'text' or work of art is simply the product of an author's creative mind, with various theories stressing the role of political ideology and individual readers' responses in constructing the text as a unit of meaning. (See, for example, Roland Barthes' 1968 essay, *The Death of the Author* [Barthes, 1977].) On the fully semiotic account, therefore, *semiosis* refers to both signs and signals, since there is no clear point at which one ends and the other begins.

It is not new to challenge Cartesian dualism; indeed, there will be few philosophers alive who would subscribe to it. However, I argue that the implications of its refusal have simply not been fully realized, at least in education and our conceptions of childhood. Perhaps the most important philosopher of education since Plato and Aristotle, John Dewey, certainly challenged it. In *Experience and Nature* (1925), Dewey employs the term 'body–mind' to describe the human organism. However, as I shall argue more fully in Chapter 2.2, Dewey did not simultaneously problematize the sign–signal distinction though it would seem, in retrospect, to have been a logical move to make. Consequently, Dewey did not question habits of schooling and education in quite the same way as a fully semiotic perspective may do.

If we can regard all living as a response to signs/signals, with no clear distinction between them, then certain implications flow.

First, we must accept that the world is, to us, as we know it. Responding is meaning-making. Living is no longer a case of responding to signals and then interpreting this basic living through cultural artefacts such as rituals, language and art. Rather, the processes of responding and making meaning are inseparable. It is simply meaningless to conceive of a world existing beyond meaning, as every living thing (perhaps everything) is engaged, in varying degrees of complexity, in the activities whereby meaning is made and we, as human beings, make human meaning. Whatever the stuff of the universe is that enables us to carry on making sense of it, we can only know it through our existing cultural practices – though these cultural practices themselves evolve, or change, over time.

Secondly, we are all, child and adult alike, semiotic engagers or meaning makers. This does not mean that we all make the same meanings!

Thirdly, while we all engage in forms of meaning-making that we recognize as rational, there is no absolute rationality, whether God-given or not, that somehow resides in the human organism, as potential or actuality. As a corollary of this, we need to think carefully about what we mean by 'learning', and this forms the matter of the following chapter. Before that, some of the more general implications of a fully semiotic perspective are introduced.

2.2.2 Foundational for What?

A view of living as semiotic engagement carries certain implications for our understanding of the human condition generally. These will be considered briefly in the remainder of this chapter, prior to a more extended discussion of the implications for childhood and education in the remainder of Part 2. Some material in this section is quoted from my article, *From Semiosis to Social Policy: The Less Trodden Path*, originally published in *Signs Systems Studies* (Stables, 2006c)

Is this 'foundational statement for a post-foundational age' any more than a truism? To examine its implications for our understanding of what it means to be human more broadly, it may be helpful to return to a context in which people are more used and content to take a semiotic perspective: that of response to literature, film and works of art.

Reading a book involves responding, half-consciously, to a complex, evolving series of signs, in terms both of their incontrovertible denotations (what everyone agrees they mean) and their endlessly varied connotations (what different people 'read into them' based on their own experiences and expectations). Texts operate on a spectrum characterized by Barthes as from 'readerly' to 'writerly' according to how open they are to multiple interpretation. However, when the response to text is taken to include subsequent action, it becomes clear that no text, however simple and apparently ambiguous, is closed to interpretation; ultimately, it is impossible to prescribe how people will respond to any text. (Consider the variety of responses to a speed restriction sign on a road, for example.)

Insofar as living is both textual and intertextual, therefore – as a fully semiotic perspective takes it to be – human responses, on all fronts, are always somewhat unpredictable. Signs are received in context, and context always varies. A word only makes sense within the context of a sentence, for example, and a sentence within a paragraph; thus response to signs and combinations of signs always varies. Interpretation is inevitable, therefore, even without any conception of the autonomous human 'mind'. This is the first major implication of a fully semiotic view of living for understanding the human condition generally: people are always somewhat unpredictable. This has implications for social policy, including educational policy, which will be considered in the following chapters.

The second, related implication is that all systems are open systems, just as all texts are intertextual. That is to say, just as the meaning of a particular text is determined partly by other texts and our experience of them, any human institution, understood fully semiotically, is a network of meanings, an 'imagined community' in 'discursive space' (Stables 2003a, b), a complex and evolving text, if you like, constantly countersigned (Derrida, 1992) and modified by the behaviour of those relating to it. Thus there are no firm boundaries to any institution or other form of social system; even outsiders are effectively insiders since, by merely knowing about any institution (in any way at all) they affect it through their actions, words and attitudes. Thus what everybody thinks and does changes the world, although each person's actions do not do so to an equal degree.

If there are no firm boundaries to anything, there are no firm boundaries to humanity: a fully semiotic perspective blurs the human/non-human divide (and may also blur the life/non-life divide, and thus the tensions between biosemiotic and pansemiotic perspectives, though that is not our direct concern here). In relation to this, it can no longer remain tenable to define the human condition by a series of exclusive attributions, including those of 'language' and 'feelings'. This is not tantamount to claiming that sheep speak English (as Sebeok, 1995, has pointed out, there is no evidence of anything beyond the human using syntactic structures, as we understand them), but amounts simply to a claim that the general kinds of behaviour, including mental operations relating to spatial awareness, recognition, tool use and memory, that Classical Humanists and many of a religious persuasion have been used to seeing as unique to the human species, and fully developed only in adult humans, can also be found in other life forms. What it means to be human is thus problematized by a fully semiotic conception of living. This has implications for the ways in which we, as human beings, should relate to the natural world; it has implications for the ways in which we regard categories within humanity (such as social class, personality and gender); and it also has implications for they way in which we view adult–child relations, which will be explored in the next chapter.

Overall, therefore, looking at living as semiotic engagement changes the way we look at human life generally. While Aristotelian in certain respects, it is anti-Aristotelian in others. Like Aristotle, it undermines the Enlightenment view of human beings as the only natural creatures that cannot be understood as machines. Unlike Aristotle, it does not regard the child as only potentially human, as all people are equally semiotically engaged, if we collapse a firm sign–signal distinction. While there is always a sense in which the child is less than the adult, or represents adult potential, the power of this explanation is significantly diluted from this fully semiotic perspective.

The Meaning-Making, Semiotic Child

2.2.1 'A Mind of His Own':
The Wilful, Intentional Child

The previous chapter summarized the case for seeing living itself as 'semiotic engagement', and indicated where a fuller exposition of this argument can be found. It is inferred from this that human life may properly be seen as contiguous with non-human life rather than as quite separate from it. Furthermore, both within and beyond the category of the human, it is valid to think of both social categories (such as class, gender, and youth and age) and institutions and organizations (such as education and schools) as open rather than closed: that is, as not purely self-contained and clearly marked off from neighbouring categories. For example, it is difficult to see where the adult ends and the child begins. Related to this is the realization that a person is never fully predictable. On this basis, the present chapter will consider what it means to be a child 'in her own right'.

Paradoxically, on one level a child cannot be a child 'in her own right', since, by virtue of being a child, the child is not an adult, or full member, of any society, and cannot therefore enjoy full adult rights – just as he or she cannot be expected to accept full adult responsibilities. From the ancient Greeks to the present day, children have been denied full membership of society; indeed, there would be no meaningful concept of childhood if this were not so. Whether children have enjoyed no legal rights or limited rights, they cannot enjoy full adult rights. Rather, they are adults in the making, who must be trained, or educated, so as to be fit to be granted such rights. There remains, however, a considerable difference between the situation in which they are granted no rights at all, and that in which – as in the UK now – they are granted a degree of legal protection. To both Plato and Aristotle, for example, infanticide was not only an excusable but a recommended strategy under certain circumstances, particularly (but not exclusively) where children were clearly disabled. While later historians of childhood have found his argument exaggerated, there is no doubt that

Lloyd deMause (1974) reveals a significant amount of evidence of infanticide over a long period. On a less dramatic level, it must often have been the case in the past – and must sometimes be so now – that many children were regarded as unwanted and serious burdens to their parents and were afforded little if any respect as persons.

At the same time, legal status does not fully determine social and cultural status, nor does it explain everything about the regard in which a person is held. Someone with no protection under the law could still be held in high regard, if the law is either ineffective, insufficiently extensive, or even unwanted, as in some hypothetical anarchist or even extreme libertarian state. If we regard both children and adults primarily as persons rather than as categories of person, the situation is somewhat less clearly marked. In terms of the rights enjoyed by adults in modern liberal-democratic states, neither adults nor children would be fully autonomous under Plato's or Aristotle's prescriptions, yet each of them urged educators to work with, rather than against, children's natural propensities to play and restlessness. Insofar as modern liberal democrats take issue with Plato and Aristotle, the issue relates to the rights of all persons, not merely children.

Nevertheless, the Classical view remains as one in which individuals are evaluated in terms of their capacity for reason and their usefulness to the state, and neither of these conditions is strongly problematized. Self-expression, being a person 'in your own right', or standing against society as a matter of conscience or conviction, as opposed to merely fulfilling a role within it, largely post-date not only Plato and Aristotle as widely accepted virtues, but also the Medieval tradition that drew so heavily on them. The Postmodern world is, as was explained in Chapter 1.8, increasingly 'individualized': in existential terms, we are increasingly 'compelled to be free', responsible for a bewildering range of lifestyle choices – or so, at least, it seems. Being, or feeling, in charge of one's own life-trajectory is now seen as desirable, hence the ubiquity of advice on lifestyle management and the employment of life-coaches and other personal advisors. We live in a world in which a good child is one who can be entrusted to 'make something of themselves in the world' – a world that is largely indifferent unless they do – and a good education will breed a strong sense of personal self-directedness through increasingly developing the capacity for reasoned choice. Again, this is not an entirely anti-Aristotelian perspective, for Aristotle also preached the virtues of deliberation, but it is nevertheless anti-Aristotelian to a significant degree.

Against this background, it is not surprising that society's view of the self-willed child has not been consistent over time. At its most extreme, the view has been that the child's will is the result of demonic possession and must be firmly extinguished before it can cause significant harm. On one reading of Aristotle, this is actually quite a logical response. Aristotle's view of the child is as not yet reasonable, so any 'reasoning' the child does cannot come from the child. It is as though a child putting forward an opinion 'does not know what possessed him', and a society that believes strongly in the divine and the demonic often has little difficulty in believing in divine or demonic possession. After all, the idea of the 'Muse' of the Classical Greeks comes from a belief in spirits that invaded human psyches, inspiring them to do certain things for good or ill (literally, from the Latin *in-spirare*, 'breathing into'). Historians of childhood since 1500 have certainly identified cases of cruelty to children simply on the grounds that they must have their wills broken, but commentators such as Linda Pollock (1983) consider that this was always an extreme response and should not be taken ever to have been a universal norm.

Perhaps it is more accurate to state that Western society has long been ambivalent about children's self-expression and conscious desires, in part on the very understandable grounds that experienced adults feel the need to protect inexperienced children from harm, and in part on the equally understandable grounds that adults simply cannot afford either the time or the currency to give children everything they want. Neither of these considerations tells the whole story, however. The question of whether it is 'natural' or 'good' for children to be outspoken has always seemed problematic. Steven Mintz (2004) provides considerable evidence of the tensions evident here in the United States, where, as early as the nineteenth century, children often seemed assertive and outgoing compared to those in Britain, and where there were particular conflicts over whether girls should be encouraged to develop as 'tomboys' or 'young ladies'. Mintz suggests that often they were allowed to begin as the former, but end up as the latter. Pollock (1983) cites several examples of diary evidence that shows how avowedly Puritanical parents were torn between austere and indulgent treatment of their children, with the sentimental forces often as likely to win out as the severe: Pollock cites the case of one such father who disapproved of artists but nevertheless built a workshop for his daughter to develop her artistic talent! (Presumably God would determine how far this talent would actually be developed.)

As has been noted in previous chapters, historical evidence suggests a tendency towards greater enjoyment of children's more fanciful behaviour in the eighteenth century. Liberal Enlightenment values were generally more accepting of personal ambition and self-expression than had formerly been the case. This is starkly exemplified by comparing modern attitudes to ambition with the treatment of the theme in Shakespeare's *Macbeth*, where the tragedy emanates from the point at which the protagonist, urged on by his wife, begins to take matters into his own hands and actively aspire to the throne rather than waiting to see whether it was, as the Witches foretold, his destiny to become king. Nowadays, we generally encourage children to learn to 'take matters into their own hands' to pursue their ambitions, and often envy those who are most single-minded, even ruthless, in their pursuit as young adults. Ambition was a Pre-Modern vice and an Early Modern problem (as in *Macbeth*) but has become a Late Modern virtue.

The nature of the will has long been of interest to philosophers though, as with other abstractions, there is always a danger of stipulative definitions both prompting and issuing from explorations that seek a final clarity that cannot be attained. As with a term such as 'consciousness', it is never possible exactly to clarify what is at stake in the discussion. This explains why twentieth-century analytic philosophers tended to turn away from such questions: the terms of debate are just too vague. One of the symptoms of this vagueness is the difficulty one finds in picking apart overlapping terms. In this case, it is hard to differentiate between 'will', 'free will' and 'intention', for example. However, there is a good deal of philosophical discussion about the will and related terms, and a considerable body of work in psychology as well. From this work, it is possible to discover three orientations with respect to the present discussion.

The first is that the individual is somehow a victim of the will, which effectively invades and misleads the individual, as in the Classical and Puritan views of the child. Here the source of the will is outside the person.

The second is that the will resides in the person and gives the individual agency a sort of 'driving force'. This is a view more clearly associable with Liberal and Romantic views of the child. On this account, the will is a positive force that effectively comes from within the child, though it can still be construed as a universal feature that is lodged within the child, but for its own good.

The third view is the Late Modern or Postmodern view that the child is essentially a social construction who is 'agented' or 'individuated' by means of his own desires in relation to his social environment and position; here, the will has no independent existence, either within or beyond the person, despite the fact that the individual endlessly expresses preferences. All this is relevant to the present discussion because our ideas about where the will comes from, and whether it is good or bad, are important to our understandings of what children are and of how we should deal with them.

Significant philosophers, supplemented more recently by psychological theorists, have taken various stances, variously emphasizing one or another of the three orientations above. To Plato and Aristotle, the will existed separately from reason, but should become its servant. Thomas Aquinas in the thirteenth century and Descartes in the seventeenth adopted this broadly Aristotelian line. By contrast, philosophers in the Enlightenment empirical tradition, from Hume in the eighteenth century to Wittgenstein in the twentieth, often fail to find means to unite the wilful and the logical. For certain philosophers connected broadly with Romanticism, notably Schopenhauer, the will is the cause of everything, a view that encouraged mystical and occult practitioners such as Aleister Crowley who asserted, adapting a saying from Rabelais: 'Do what thou wilt will be the whole of the law' (retrieved from *The Book of the Law* 1:40: www.sacred-texts.com/oto/engccxx.htm 19 October 2007). Schopenhauer is also a likely influence on Friedrich Nietzsche, whose belief in the 'will to power' and the necessity of avoiding subservience to all existing doctrines makes him a seminal influence on the later Existentialists and Postmodernists.

At the turn of the twentieth century a more recognizably Late Modern view of the child began to emerge in which the person's actions and intentions cannot be divorced from environmental and cultural influences. The idea of 'intention' had been introduced into philosophy by Franz Brentano (1874) and was of interest to the developing field of psychology. One figure who straddled these fields and who was to become arguably the most influential philosopher of education of the modern era was John Dewey (1859–1952), whose early conceptions of the socially constructed individual child will be discussed in the section to follow.

2.2.2 The Socially Constructed Child

To Dewey, the will is not innate but develops with experience. 'Human nature' does not precede education; rather, learning and growth are processes of nature.

Nowadays, there is nothing surprising about saying that people exist and evolve in relation to their environments. In the late nineteenth century, however, this was still a radical view; after all, Darwinism had not been around for long. People were used to seeing themselves as above the material world rather than immanent within it, and certainly not as shaped by it. Their bodies might be material, but their souls were not. As is often the case with innovators, Dewey's naturalism, that seems unremarkable to us, was brave and controversial in its time.

Having acknowledged this, Dewey was a person of his time. Darwinism had altered the intellectual landscape. The discipline of psychology was beginning to make serious headway in its own right. Also, the social situation in the United States called forth new forms of thinking. Just as (as Pollock, 1983, suggests) Americans were consciously aiming to do things differently from the British – including, perhaps, bringing up children – there were also more impersonal social forces that demanded new solutions. First, Americans were supposed to be free and equal, yet there was a huge gap between the rich and the poor. The response to this was to inaugurate research programmes at the University of Chicago to investigate and come up with appropriate policy responses. Dewey was part of this experiment, from which–in part–can be traced the development of the twentieth-century tradition of social science. Secondly, American cities were multicultural well before those of Europe. America was the home of the immigrant. The American context was recognizably twentieth century in this respect well before, for example, the British.

In an early paper entitled *The Reflex Arc Concept in Psychology*, Dewey responds to the theories of stimulus and response that were held to explain mental development, stating:

> The older dualism between sensation and idea is repeated in the current dualism of peripheral and central structures and functions; the older dualism of body and soul finds a distinct echo in the current dualism of stimulus and response. (Dewey, 1896: 2)

The 'dualism between sensation and idea' is that found in Locke (see Chapter 1.6). In his comments on 'peripheral' and 'central structures and functions', Dewey is trying to get us away from thinking in terms of a 'mind in here' and a 'body out there' that responds to the brain's instructions. Rather, we operate as whole human organisms:

> . . . what is wanted is that sensory stimulus, central connections and motor responses shall be viewed, not as separate and complete entities in themselves, but as divisions of labor, function factors, within the concrete whole, now designated as the reflex arc. (1896: 2)

The idea of the reflex arc is that the environment does not offer a 'stimulus' to a blank slate of a mind, to which the mind (as a separate immaterial entity) responds. Rather, human response develops as the human develops so that each stimulus is interpreted as a stimulus in the light of previous responses; the development of the individual mind and its environment cannot be separated. Dewey's perspective here (and elsewhere) places emphasis on conation (broadly, the willingness and ability to act) rather than cognition or affect. As he points out a little further on in the paper (1896: 4), a sound, for example, is not merely a stimulus but rather 'an act . . . of hearing'.

A considerable strength of Dewey's account, implied rather than made explicit, is that it helps to explain the gradual growth of human consciousness from infancy. Each human act, which is an act of meaning, makes sense only in terms of expectations:

> From this point of view the discovery of the stimulus is the "response" to possible movement as "stimulus". We must have an anticipatory sensation, an image of the movements that may occur, together with their respective values, before attention will go to the seeing . . . (Dewey, 1896: 7)

For a significant time, Dewey was a Professor of both Philosophy and Education. (At this time British universities did not have Departments or Professors of Education.) During the first half of his career, up to and including the publication of *Democracy and Education* in 1916, he wrote a series of immensely influential works on education and ran a Laboratory School which, though not entirely successful in itself, marked the beginning of the Progressive Education movement. In his later career, Dewey was disillusioned by the progress of this movement, and his copious philosophical output paid much less attention to issues of youth and schooling.

The first, and perhaps most forthright, Deweyan work on schooling is *My Pedagogic Creed*, published in 1897. The following extract adorned the homepage of the website of the John Dewey Society in 2007:

> I believe that education is the fundamental method of social progress and reform. All reforms which rest simply upon the law, or the threatening of certain penalties, or upon changes in mechanical or outward arrangements, are transitory and futile. . . . But through education society can formulate its own purposes, can organize its own means and resources, and thus shape itself with definiteness and economy in the direction in which it wishes to move. . . . Education thus conceived marks the most perfect and intimate union of science and art conceivable in human experience. (Dewey, 1897: v)

In *My Pedagogic Creed* (1897), *The Child and the Curriculum* (1902), *The School and Society* (1915) and *Democracy and Education* (1916), Dewey laid the foundations of both the modern belief in mass education for liberal-democratic societies and the child-centred curriculum. His vision, in the Liberal tradition, was powerful and optimistic. It went beyond Classical Liberalism in seeing the individual not as simply autonomous but as an individual agent who is always part of something bigger; there is something in Dewey's vision to appeal to both Liberals and Communitarians in our own time. Nevertheless, in his more extreme statements, such as that quoted above, it can be argued that he went too far, or was insufficiently critical. 'Through education', Dewey claims, 'society can formulate its own purposes [and] organize its own means and resources *and can thus shape itself with definiteness and economy*' (my italics).

If meaning is deferred and outcomes are unpredictable, as on the fully semiotic account offered in Chapter 2.1, this simply does not follow. Even if social agreement on the premises were possible, they would not be sufficient to ensure the conclusion. Nor does Dewey's conclusion necessarily follow from the premises as grounded in his philosophical and psychological work, where he compellingly explains both that individual perspectives are grounded in necessarily social experience and that prior experience helps to shape current and future experience. This cannot be tantamount to claiming that third parties, however well intentioned or learned, can either guarantee social agreement over purposes, means and resources or predict the outcomes of interventions in the experiences of others, for they do not share their various prior experiences. This critique of Dewey will be developed in the following chapter.

As has already been noted, views about the source of the child's will are influential in determining how the child should be treated. To Dewey, the child's will develops through social interaction, that is, in an environmental context, though Dewey does not consider the role of the non-human environment here. To that extent, Dewey can be seen as an early Social Constructionist. Social Constructionism (or, for our purposes, 'Social Constructivism', since the terms are used synonymously in many debates, though not in all) is arguably the dominant educational philosophy at the time of writing, at least in the European and English-speaking worlds. While Schopenhauer and Nietzsche saw the will as individual and the means to individual empowerment, to Social Constructionists, the individual cannot be divorced from society. If, under Liberalism, the individual is held to precede society, under Social Constructionism, society is held to precede the individual.

An even greater influence on Social Constructionist thought than Dewey is Lev Vygotsky, a Russian psychologist whose work was undertaken in the 1920s and 1930s but not published in English until the 1960s. In recent years, Vygotsky has arguably replaced Jean Piaget as the greatest educational theorist of the past hundred years. The Swiss Piaget, working in the Liberal West, understood cognitive growth as both biologically determined and individually realized (e.g. Piaget 1954); the Russian Vygotsky, working in the Communist Soviet Union, understood it as socially determined. Interestingly, neither questioned the feasibility of understanding mental development in strictly hierarchical terms, as rising in stages towards full adult reasonableness; in this, they were both Aristotelians.

Vygotsky is best known for two ideas: that of 'inner' *vs.* 'outer' speech, and that of the 'Zone of Proximal Development' (ZPD). In *Thought and Language* (1962 – in English), he took a different line from Piaget in interpreting infants' babbling, or 'egocentric' speech as an important element in the learning process, and not merely as commentary on experience. Vygotsky argued (*a*) that language is important to thought, and (*b*) language and understanding develop through a dialectical interaction of speech with others and half-formed speech inside the head; infants utter this speech aloud whereas older children and adults cease to do this – until old age or the onset of mental illness, perhaps.

Vygotsky's ZPD (1978) has perhaps been even more influential on educational theory. Whereas Piaget simply thought that the developing mind would process information differently as it matured, Vygotsky believed that appropriate social interaction was necessary to this process. While Piaget felt a child would attain a higher level of cognitive processing provided that environmental stimulation had been merely adequate and biological growth was normal, Vygotsky put far more emphasis on the quality of tutor–child interaction. Vygotsky believed that the cognitive gap between child and parent, or student and teacher, was a zone of 'proximal development' or potential growth, and that the quality of interaction across this gap would determine whether the child could reach the next level of mental operations. (Note that the concept of a level of mental operations is not problematized by either of them.)

There are now many educationalists and social psychologists who regard themselves as 'post-Vygotskians'. However, in terms of direct application to pedagogy and curriculum, perhaps Vygotsky's greatest influence is in the application of his ZPD concept as 'scaffolding' learning, by David Wood, Jerome Bruner and others (Wood et al., 1976). The scaffolding image is fairly self-explanatory: teachers and parents construct stepped processes by which children can come to understand things they could not otherwise understand. When the building is complete, the scaffolding can eventually be removed, thus enabling the child to undertake the cognitive operations on her own.

Vygotsky's remains a limited form of Social Constructionism, however, because it does not question a single, universal, gender and ethnic-neutral and hierarchical concept of reason. That is to say, despite the Vygotskian emphasis on dialogue, Vygotskian reason remains essentially monological rather than dialogical (e.g. Wegerif, 1998). Some more recent conceptions of social learning do not rest on this assumption. According to Berger and Luckmann (1966), for example, all social interaction empowers, as people learn that authority structures are not fixed (as others have different views of them) and thus realize they can potentially change them. To Rom Harré and others, the aim of learning is not the attainment of a Platonic or Aristotelian state of pure reason, but rather the enrichment of personal and social identity. Harré's work in this area will be discussed more fully in Chapter 3.3. (See also Stables et al., 1999, and Stables, 2003a,c, 2005a.) More recently, some commentators have questioned even this, arguing that education offers endless possibilities as much to disrupt as to reinforce identities (Chapter 3.3). On this account, which I shall develop later, education exists more to disrupt fixed notions of the individual, society and identity than to enact them. This deconstructive tendency is evident in the argument about learning that forms the matter of the next chapter.

Learning and Schooling: Dewey and Beyond

2.3.1 What is Learning?
A Fully Semiotic Perspective

This chapter critiques Deweyan and subsequent Social Constructionist assumptions about learning and schooling from the fully semiotic perspective offered in Chapter 2.1. However, it argues that the semiotic perspective is broadly compatible with some recent approaches in social and critical psychology.

One of the most contentious inferences that can be drawn from a fully semiotic perspective is this: there really is not as much to 'learning' as most people think. It is often assumed that there is something very special about 'learning behaviour' and that teachers and concerned parents are skilled at promoting such behaviour. School inspectors and others who sit in on classrooms feel qualified to judge whether 'good learning' is taking place. However, if all living is responding to signs and signals through the employment of signs and signals, what differentiates 'learning' from any other form of living?

Consider the following.

If all living is semiotic engagement, then learning is semiotic engagement. However, as not all living is characterised as learning (though the saying "we live and learn" comes close to doing this on occasions), then learning must be either a distinct form of semiotic engagement or a term applied to general semiotic engagement in certain contexts.

The following empirical claims can be made with some confidence, grounded in ordinary language:

1. living (semiotic engagement) in formal educational contexts (e.g. "doing things in school") is often referred to as learning, and

processes leading to the award of qualifications are often referred
to as learning processes (e.g. the Maths GCSE course);
2. experience recalled subjectively as pivotal in the development
of the autobiography is often recalled as learning experience (e.g.
"I learnt a lot from *X*");

These both posit learning as living in certain recognised contexts, with
perhaps the further demand, in at least the second case, that something
(some thread in the life story) must recognisably have changed or
grown since the behaviour occurred, yet none of these definitions gives
learning any privileged position as a form of living in any other respect.
If learning is to be identified as the factor that causes changes in "scripts"
or "schemas" –our patterns of making sense of the world–it is very difficult to locate. It is clearly not "in" an event that occurred, so must relate
to the learner's responses to it. It seems plausible that, thus understood,
it is a term applied retrospectively to changes, whether trivial or profound, in the life story, and that it may be most unstable, in the sense
that a particular event might be recalled as "learning" in one context but
not another. If this is so, there can be no direct evidence of observable
"learning behaviour" or "learning processes", regardless of the widespread use of the term in relation to, for example, the inspection
of schools and evaluation of teaching. It is simply impossible to gauge
how much will have been learnt from a teaching event. (Stables,
2006b: 6–7)

On this account, learning is not something we do at any particular
time. Rather, it is something we find we have done. Furthermore, whether
we regard an experience as a learning experience, in retrospect, seems
to depend on the cultural context. In one context, we will say we learnt
from something we did in school, or from something we regard as positive; in another, that we learnt from something we did by accident, or
from something negative. The meaning of learning seems to be both
'deferred' and relative. In itself, 'learning' may be rather emptier of content than many have tended to assume. Obviously, this has significant
implications for how we understand teaching, schooling and education
more broadly. All these issues will be tackled more fully in subsequent
chapters. The following section offers a more detailed account of how
a fully semiotic perspective partly concurs with, and partly goes beyond a
Deweyan one.

2.3.2 Alongside and Beyond Dewey

The fully semiotic perspective outlined in Chapter 2.1 has the following implications for teaching and learning. (See also Stables, 2008b.):

1. All human experience involves responding to signs and signals ('sign[al]s') through the use of signs and signals. Alternatively, we might say that all human experience involves the modification of patterning, whether or not it is subsequently credited as learning. Here, 'patterning' can refer to both cognitive models (such as recognizing a particular shape as a triangle, or a particular act as an act of kindness) and to cultural practices (such as a tendency to approach or see a particular situation as requiring a mathematical solution, or as inviting a kindly gesture). Cognitive and behaviourist learning theories therefore offer inadequate accounts. Cognitive approaches underplay the importance of prior experience (whether described as habit, conditioning, prehension [Whitehead], memory, or 'traces' [Derrida]) in determining how we understand new stimuli, while behaviourist approaches underplay the importance of context and the uniqueness of the individual position, and thus the unpredictability of outcomes. 'Whatever our children learn cannot be exactly what we know. Whatever our students learn cannot be exactly what we teach' (Stables, 2003a: 130).
2. All experience, including that which will be regarded as learning experience, involves tension and disruption of the known. The sign(al) operates as a prompt, a charge. Thus, just as learning can be either good or bad, so is teaching equally interpretable as either positive identity development or more-or-less controlled identity disruption. Students must therefore expect to be challenged, upset or offended from time to time, and no educational practice or initiative will be uniformly universally received; it is not a case simply of building social progress towards prespecified ends through shared activity. For example, a particular teacher setting a class of children a particular task may have her words ignored by some, regarded as a welcome challenge by others, regarded as a threat by others, and regarded as 'boring' by yet others. However classroom teaching is developed, it seems inconceivable that this variation of responses can be eliminated.
3. Everything to do with teaching and learning is cultural practice. However, diversity of habituation ensures that experience is always varied, though the words used to describe it (for example) may not reveal the extent of the variation. To take the example from (2), a teacher might

set a particular homework to a class, who then all complete ostensibly the same task. This by no means indicates that all the students have had the same experience. People are thus more different than they seem to be; teaching, research and policy all need to recognize this variation. Furthermore, identity politics and multicultural education should no longer proceed on the assumption – conscious or implicit – that individuals are treatable as products of their cultural, social and ethnic groups; as everyone is different, assumptions about 'greater' or 'lesser' difference according to group membership can have limited validity. This is a claim with radical educational consequences, particularly in countries that recognize affirmative action/ positive discrimination. For a fuller exposition of the justification and possible implications of this non-deterministic view, see Stables 2005b.

4. However, what we experience is experientially real, whatever the continuing doubts about its ontological status. We experience actual events. Events constitute the universe. Learning really is experiential, and experience always holds the potential for learning.

5. Formal education does not, therefore, enhance learning *per se*, but rather attempts to channel it in socially desirable directions. However, outcomes remain unpredictable: Learners never quite learn what teachers teach, nor do they share the same assumptions about what constitutes (valuable) learning. Therefore, the conscious aims of the channelling are of limited validity; in this sense, education cannot be 'provided', and insofar as educational 'opportunities' can be provided, whether they will be received as opportunities, and how, cannot be adequately pre-specified. Finally:

6. The unit of meaning is neither free-standing, of standard size, spatio-temporally locatable nor divisible. Meaning-events (experiences) cannot therefore be atomized: broken down and reconstructed. Effective teaching, for example, cannot be identified in one context and transferred to another. 'Evidence-based good practice', a mantra of British schooling in recent years, is therefore largely illusory: part of a broader strategy to standardize the unstandardizable and to pre-specify inevitably unpredictable outcomes. On the semiotic account, good teachers create rich experiences for students that come to be seen as having fulfilled social/ cultural functions, as experienced by the individual student and by significant others: the more the emphasis on standardized, formal education, the more restricted the conception of the functions. Although created in liberal societies for quite opposite reasons, formal education in such societies can therefore serve to inhibit rather than enhance experience. A good education, whether formal or informal, will leave the learners assured that they have undergone a series of significant personal

events that have promoted their (and, by implication, others') human flourishing.

Dewey was one of many important influences on the above work, though the semiotic approach draws on a variety of traditions (Stables, 2005a). However, there are grounds for questioning whether the semiotic approach, notwithstanding its eclecticism, takes the debate beyond Dewey in any significant respect. One possible response to this is that the semiotic approach provides an elaborated, or alternative conceptual framework into which (most of) Dewey's work fits very well, thus offering some new perspectives on Dewey, and suggesting possible future implications, as yet unrecognized. The alternative – to be expanded below – simply attempts to locate those aspects of Dewey's thought that are clearly resonant with, and those that clearly depart from that proposed in Stables 2005a and elsewhere, offering tentative explanations for the key disjunctures.

The present argument does not attempt to draw on Dewey's full, and extremely wide, output, but rather focuses on a selection of texts representing expressions of his direct thinking about education and related aspects of his philosophy. The earliest (*The Reflex Arc Concept in Psychology*: henceforth RAC) dates from 1896; the latest (the Introduction to *The Use of Resources in Education*: henceforth URE), from 1952, when Dewey was in his nineties. The principal focus, however, will be on *Democracy and Education*, first published in 1916 and Dewey's most extended and philosophically developed work with an explicitly educational focus.

Points (1)–(6) above will now be considered individually with respect to the above.

(1)

A central element in Dewey is that of the conative, as opposed to cognitive or behavioural, nature of learning. In *RAC*, he points to the tendency of the still-young discipline of psychology to adopt discredited dualisms relating to mind and body. Rather:

> ... what is wanted is that sensory stimulus, central connections and motor responses shall be viewed, not as separate and complete entities in themselves, but as divisions of labor, function factors, within the concrete whole, now designated as the reflex arc. (Dewey, 1896: 2)

Dewey's perspective here (and elsewhere) places emphasis on conation (broadly, the willingness and ability to act) rather than cognition or affect.

As he points out a little further on in *RAC* (1896: 4), a sound, for example, is not merely a stimulus but rather 'an act . . . of hearing'. Each human act, which is an act of meaning, makes sense only in terms of expectations:

> From this point of view the discovery of the stimulus is the "response" to possible movement as "stimulus". We must have an anticipatory sensation, an image of the movements that may occur, together with their respective values, before attention will go to the seeing . . . (Dewey, 1896: 7)

To this extent, at least, Dewey concedes that there may be little, if anything, distinctive about 'learning' experiences *per se*, though he rarely makes this point explicitly in the texts under consideration. An exception occurs in *The School and Society* (Dewey, 1915– hereafter *SS*):

> Learning? – certainly, but living primarily, and learning through and in relation to this living. (Dewey 1915: 36)

Frequently, Dewey refers to life/living in a way that incorporates educational practice, and seems to leave little or no space for a distinct conception of learning. At the beginning of *Democracy and Education*, for example (Dewey, 1916 – hereafter *DE*), he states, '. . . all communication, and hence all social life, is educative' (1916: 5).

However, insofar as living is learning (and *vice versa*), it is always dependent on prior experience. Dewey is frequently critical of any educational scheme that regards the mind as independently able to make sense of a world it has not experienced. In *DE*, he stresses that

> . . . the supposed original faculties of observation, recollection, willing, thinking etc. are purely mythological. There are no such ready-made powers waiting to be exercised and thereby trained. (Dewey, 1916: 62)

And in *URE*, at the very end of his career, berates the progressive education movement (largely owing its existence to him) for confusing ideas with 'inherent essences' (in Dworkin, 1959: 133).

On the uniqueness of individual response, however, Dewey is, particularly in his specifically educational writings, much more ambiguous. Throughout – but arguably most forcefully in his earlier writings – he combines a strong commitment to individual sense-making with an at least equally strong commitment to the school as cultural transmitter. 'Through education', Dewey claims in *My Pedagogic Creed* (hereafter *PC*), and as was noted in Chapter 2.2, 'society can formulate its own purposes [and] organize its own means and resources *and can thus shape itself with definiteness and economy*' (my italics) (Dewey, 1897: V). On examination, however, there is little evidence in any of Dewey's work of a definite set of desired or feasible outcomes. Rather, there are periodic reminders that people will make sense of things in their own ways. Indeed, in *Progressive Education and the Science of Education* (1928: *PSE*), he promotes the experimental, 'laboratory' school on the grounds that 'compared with traditional schools, [there is] a common emphasis upon respect for individuality and for increased freedom' (in Dworkin, 1959: 115). In fact, in the spirit of some of his later work rather than *PC*, he seems to have moved towards a more pluralistic, perhaps less naïve, conception of schooling, claiming in *PSE* that, 'As the working operations of schools differ, so must the intellectual theories derived from those operations' (Dworkin, 1959: 116-17).

As, for example, the extended discussion of 'vocationalism' in the latter stages of *DE* suggests, perhaps the real, and only identifiable clear aim of schooling is a commitment to lifelong learning – and Dewey can certainly be credited for raising awareness of this. ('The criterion of the value of the school curriculum is the extent to which it creates a desire for continued growth and supplies means for making the desire effective in fact' [Dewey, 1916: 53].). However, he does make extremely strong claims for schools in *PC* and *SS* that barely take account of differential outcomes and pupil responses. At the opening of *SS* he asserts, 'What the best and wisest parent wants for his own child, that must the community want for all its children' (Dewey, 1915: 7). But surely Dewey's belief in the social construction of mind does not extend to any sort of guarantee that everybody (even the 'best' people!) will share the same values, or that schools can somehow ensure they are passed on. There is more than a little paternalism in the normative tones of 'best', 'wisest', 'must', and 'all'. The implication here is that the likes of Dewey know what is best for children as much as the most traditional didact.

There is some evidence of Dewey softening his line on this in later writings, though by then, it might be argued, the die had been cast in terms of schooling practices: The experimental school had had its day and the progressive schooling movement was well underway. In *DE*, Dewey notes, 'The things with which a man *varies* are his genuine environment' (Dewey, 1916: 11), but there is no recanting of the lofty claims made in *PC* and *SS*. Perhaps the distinction between 'man' and 'child' is carefully drawn here, or perhaps Dewey was simply not inclined to dwell on the contradiction between such acknowledgments of inevitable diversity and the earlier blinding faith in schools. The nearest he comes to an acknowledgement of values dissonance in *DE* is in his insistence of the importance of that which schools do *not* pass on in his portrayal of them as selective environments (1916: 20).

(2)

Dewey sees education as always building on previous experience without ever, it seems, challenging it in uncomfortable ways, despite the emphasis on education as communication (particularly *DE*) and on individual liberty. The assumption is of education as an unqualified, and unproblematic, good. Students must undertake socially desirable tasks to which they will bring their prior expectations and because everyone (of good taste, anyway) wants the same thing, and intelligence is collective, neither prior experience nor subsequent evaluation will differ from the norm to the extent that ill-feeling will ensue. Rather, he tells in *CC* of 'the race-experience which is embodied in that thing we call the curriculum' (Dworkin, 1959: 53), implying that the diverse backgrounds of many of the citizens of his time had already been assimilated into a harmonious and homogeneous Americanism. If such a collective culture existed at the time, it is evidently long gone. Although Dewey defines experience in terms of 'trying' and 'undergoing' (1916: 139), he does not discuss the experience of schooling in terms even of challenge and difficulty, let alone potential incomprehension, unwillingness or disaffection. Rather, his naturalism leads him to stress – particularly in the earlier, more specifically educational texts – that all roads can lead to Damascus. When he writes in *SS* that 'The children begin by imagining present conditions taken away until they are in contact with nature at first hand' (Dworkin, 1959: 61), he is quite at odds with a semiotic perspective, for language and cultural meaning do not seem to constitute the bottom line for Dewey in any sense.

It is pertinent to note at this point that Dewey's relative interest in education seems to decline. In the extensive *Experience and Nature* (1925: *EN*), for example, neither 'education' nor 'school' deserves even an index entry, and there is no major work on education after *DE* (1916) until the very late and much less regarded *Education Today* (1940). The rugged naturalism is undiminished in *EN*, however: Dewey dismisses those who see 'qualities as always and only states of consciousness' (1925: 74) as naïve dualistic cognitivists. Rather:

> It is a reasonable belief that there would be no such thing as "consciousness" if events did not have a phase of brute and unconditioned "isness," of being just what they irreducibly are. (Dewey, 1925: 74)

(3)

Dewey, as has already been shown, not only believed that people are products of social groups (and that this is compatible with individual liberty) but that American society was, or easily could be (for he does not address the problems) a culturally coherent social group despite its diverse origins. His naturalism leads him to suggest that people are less different than they seem to be rather than the reverse. While many may have taken Dewey's prescriptions for active learning as pedagogically desirable for multicultural populations, Dewey does nothing to problematize them himself in this regard; indeed, he seems uninterested in cultural difference in his key writings on education, despite an evident interest in international affairs (e.g. Dewey, 1929).

Interestingly, given the recent emphases on evidence-informed policy and practice on both sides of the Atlantic, Dewey promoted the use of multiple case studies to determine good practice in teaching and learning, writing of the need for 'A series of constantly multiplying careful reports on conditions which experience has shown in actual cases to be favorable and unfavorable to learning' (*PSE*: in Dworkin, 1959: 125). In this, he promoted a belief in isolating and potentially transferring 'best practice' that characterizes the contemporary policy scene but which is regarded with deep suspicion from a fully semiotic perspective (e.g. Stables, 2005a).

It is clear that Dewey did not see reality as significantly constructed by language, or semiotic interchange more broadly. His view, expressed in *DE*, of 'life as a self-renewing process through action upon the environment' (1916: 2), and education as enacted through communication, should not be confused with later perspectives on language *as* action (such as Austin, 1962; Wittgenstein, 1967; Habermas, 1984/1987). There is no primacy of language in Dewey. For Dewey, things are invested with meaning (become signs as opposed to merely signals) because of collective human activity; they do not determine that activity. Consider the following from *EN* (italics in original):

Animals respond to certain stimuli . . . Let us call this class the signaling reflexes . . . Sub-human animals thus behave in ways which have no *direct* consequences of utility to the behaving animal . . . Signaling acts evidently form the basic *material* of language . . . [but] . . . The hen's activity is egocentric; that of the human being is participative. The latter puts himself at the standpoint of a situation in which two parties share . . . The characteristic thing about *B's* understanding of *A's* movement and sounds is that he responds to the thing from the standpoint of *A* . . . To understand is to participate together, it is to make a cross-reference which, when acted upon, brings about a partaking in a common, inclusive undertaking . . . The heart of language is not "expression" of something antecedent, much less expression of antecedent thought. It is communication; the establishment of co-operation in activity in which there are partners . . . Primarily meaning is intent. (Dewey, 1925: 147–9)

Dewey's view of 'symbols' as 'condensed substitutes of actual things and events' (1925: 71) does not have communicative activity grounded in sign systems, as would , for example, poststructuralist perspectives (given considerable latitude in the use of 'systems'). Perhaps as a legacy of the body–mind dualism he sought to escape, Dewey's system relies on an absolute qualitative difference between humans and other species that allows the former to engage in meaningful action which, while a response to some underlying reality, exploits language and other communicative tools without being dependent upon them. In this, he appears to replace the Classical Liberal belief in autonomous rational agency with one of collective rational agency. Whence this agency originates, other than as some mysterious force of nature, remains unclear. To Dewey, action invests meaning in language. His is not the direction that the mass of twentieth-century philosophy and cultural theory would be able to follow.

(4)

Nevertheless, the still widely held claims that learning is experiential and that 'we experience actual events' are entirely Deweyan and, indeed, have been formulated more clearly and effectively by Dewey than by anyone else. On this account, subjective experience is not merely a commentary on an objective world but contains within it both the means and the content of learning. Experience matters; indeed, it is all that really matters. What Dewey underplays, by contrast to many later perspectives, is the role of language and other semiotic systems in creating and defining that experience.

(5)

However, this falls far short of an argument for any form of formal education, particularly as Dewey stresses in *DE* that 'No thought, no idea, can possibly be conveyed as an idea from one person to another' (1916: 159). Neither is it an argument against formal education.

Dewey's strong advocacy of schools as the breeding grounds, or sites of renewal, of democratic societies is achieved by means of a combination of perspectives that, in most other systems, are at odds. In short, he manages to combine a Lockean belief in school as a place in which children can be taught to think for themselves with a happy acceptance of school as an institution for channelling activity to produce social coherence and positive compliance. Later, Marxist and post-marxian theorists would understand this dynamic in terms of Ideological State Apparatus (Althusser, 1971) or even symbolic violence (Bourdieu,1991): hegemony 'bought into' by a willing public. There is no sense of immanent critique in Dewey, however, who argues that purposeful human activity is individually liberating and socially cohesive at the same time, requiring no sense of liberation *from* social norms and practices. Dewey sees individual liberty as entirely compatible with community action in his best-known writings on education.

(6)

The implications for educational policy and practice from a fully semiotic perspective therefore seem quite at odds with those from Dewey in certain key respects, though each perspective can be construed as liberal-pragmatic and post-Cartesian, and each emphasizes the primacy of human experience (rather than, say, structural measures or mere credentials). While the semiotic perspective sees schooling as deeply problematic (and educational largely insofar as it is problematic), Dewey assumes that both social aims and their implementation *via* schooling are largely unproblematic, given good pedagogy – itself relatively unproblematic. Dewey's is a one-size-fits-all prescription for thriving democracy in which the school as social institution is a site for cultural revivification. No wonder it has an enduring appeal for social democrats and educational optimists.

In conclusion, there are many defining parallels between Dewey's philosophy of education and the fully semiotic approach I have attempted to develop elsewhere. Chief among these are the belief that mind, meaning and behaviour are inextricably linked, and the commitment to active involvement in education, such that it produces significant events for students.

The major point of departure concerns the recognition and valorization of difference. Although Dewey depicts humans as inescapably relational, and communicative, the emphasis in the best-known works on education is always on shared purpose and outcome; little or no account is taken here of differences in individual contexts of reception and response. Savery (1951), for example, depicts Dewey as an 'emergent naturalis[t]' (1951: 498), for whom natural events are cohesive and progressive and for whom (as for Hegel, an early influence on Dewey), human dialogue has a synthetic and purely positive role. While, at the very end of his career, Dewey denied his position was 'holistic' (Dewey, 1951: 570), it nevertheless depends on a faith in the reality of historically verifiable events. By contrast, a fully semiotic perspective, while not necessarily fully relativistic, denies that what lies beyond the perceptual (broadly understood) is verifiable.

To Dewey, the value of educational activity is immediate and shared; on the semiotic account, it is deferred and shared in part. To Dewey, the school is a force for unquestionable good, provided that the pedagogy is right; on the semiotic account, schools, like activities, have no intrinsic value, but have potential as sites of valuable activity and will be variously received. To Dewey, problems are to be solved; on the semiotic account, problems are to be explored and reworked. To Dewey, everyone well educated will take the same values from school; on the semiotic account, everyone will take something different from school (or from whatever alternative experiences to schooling they may have).

To Dewey, therefore, there is not a great gulf between Political and Comprehensive Liberalism: school, for example, can respect individual liberty simultaneously with insisting on shared activity and compliance, since society (educated society, at least) will share commitment to a set of values to be transmitted. On the semiotic account, Political Liberalism renders Comprehensive Liberalism untenable, in John Rawls' terms (Rawls, 1993), as religious and other cultural differences belie the possibility of all adult members of the broader community agreeing on what values and practices to pass on. This implies that the educational value of schooling comes not from integration and the standardization of best practice, but rather from the exploration and juxtaposition of many kinds of difference, without expectation of complete resolution. This further implies preference for a system of schooling characterized by competing models and a degree of internal inconsistency.

In summary, while the fully semiotic approach to education shares most aspects of Dewey's philosophical scheme, the degree to which it differs is sufficient to suggest a widely differing, much more pluralistic approach to education as public policy.

2.3.3 Alongside and Beyond Social Construction

A fully semiotic perspective shares with Social Constructionism the belief that the individual develops in relation to his or her environment. However, it does not assume that the individual is simply determined by her environment, nor that the 'environment' is entirely 'social'. The fully semiotic position is, in this sense, 'Post-humanist': that is, it does not regard the human world as existing entirely separately from the non-human.

While Classical Liberalism can be criticized for regarding the individual as an autonomous rational agent, offering an account in which the individual is effectively prior to society (though Locke's writings on education, for example, do not work on this assumption in relation to the child), the Social Constructionist view can be criticized for effectively arguing that society precedes the individual. In a sense, of course, both views are true as well as false: an effective society is impossible without thinking individuals, while society, by existing before we were born, does precede us as individuals. However, each has an extreme tendency that can surface in, for example, discussions about social policy. A fully semiotic view does not allow for this polarity. On the semiotic account, we respond to the world as we read a book. Extending the analogy, we use a public language in a private way, using a common stock of words and phrases to develop an endlessly original stream of utterances. Over time, the 'common stock of words and phrases' itself changes. On this account, we are never entirely private and individual nor entirely public and communal, and it makes no sense to draw a firm distinction between the private and the public or the individual and the social. Indeed, it might be argued that the assumption of too firm a distinction tends to lead to a situation in which 'private sector' enterprises operate with an inadequate sense of moral duty towards other citizens, while 'public sector' institutions operate with insufficient attention to what people actually want – to 'market forces'. (This argument is developed somewhat in Stables, 2005a, Chapters 13–17.) Just as nobody's utterances can be fully predicted by their circumstances (though a degree of prediction is possible), so can no individual be seen merely as a product of their society, even though each of us acts in a partly predictable and conditioned way. Note that if an outcome is partly predictable and partly unpredictable, then it is unpredictable!

With respect to the six points discussed in the previous section, the following points of similarity and difference emerge between a fully semiotic and a social constructionist account.

1

Learning and development are indeed conative rather than merely cognitive or behavioural. Human acts are cultural and intentional. A recent cultural and discursive turn in social psychology recognizes this. Jerome Bruner, for example (1983), shows how even the actions of newborns are goal-directed. While the desire for milk and comfort is likely to be common to all cultures, human actions become increasingly differentiated from place to place and time to time as they become more sophisticated. Response is indeed dependent on prior experience, but is also dependent on context, and each person's context of reception is always different; again, these differences increase as we get older. So not only are there no grounds for separating learning behaviour from other behaviours; there are also no grounds for believing any two people will react the same to an environmental stimulus – even if it were possible to identify a single stimulus in most contexts.

When we encounter others, we are always in a 'zone of proximal development', in that we are engaging with other worldviews. Sometimes these views have higher social status than our own: such is the experience, more often than not, of the student talking to the professor, the child to the adult, or the worried man to the lawyer. All the time we are potentially learning through dialogue. There are inevitable asymmetries in dialogues. Thus while we are always within this 'zone' in our dealings with others (we even learn from our children and our students!), it is no simple matter to ascertain what we are 'proximal' to and 'developing' towards. As with Dewey, therefore, we can share a faith in schools as potentially rich and stimulating environments without any faith in them as precise tools of social engineering.

2

Indeed, school can no more single-handedly create an individual than society as a whole can. As any parent knows, every child develops a personality that, while clearly influenced by its background, is almost guaranteed to surprise – and brothers and sisters within the same household often turn out very different from one another. Clearly each child has drawn on the cultural resources available – there are no others on which to draw – but each in a different way. One way of explaining this in psychological terms is with reference to the discursive psychology of Rom Harré. (See also Stables et al., 1999; Stables, 2003a,c) Harré explains how we position ourselves, and are positioned, as individuals by evaluating the options available to us in any given situation, bearing in mind what course of action seems congruous with our existing views of ourselves, and will preserve a necessary balance between our social and personal identities (Harré, 1979, 1983; with Langenhove, 1999). Put simply, we think 'What should I do now?', bearing in mind what it is characteristic of me to do, what will enable me to retain acceptance by others, and what will continue to mark me out as an individual. In other words, each of us feels a psychological imperative both to fit in up to a point and to be different up to a point: in Harré's parlance, we must develop and keep in balance both our personal and our social identities. Thus society – and its institutions, including schools – gives us the resources on which to draw but does not, in any obvious way, determine how we each draw on them.

3

If we are not careful, Social Construction can offer us a very thin view of a person: simply as a member of a group. Thus 'identity politics' can all-too-easily lapse into an 'us-against-them' fight for resources and recognition. Concepts such as multiculturalism and pluralism are of minimal use if they rest on the assumption that persons can be reduced to ethnic allegiances and treated accordingly, and the world bears witness to the extent to which this currently occurs. For example, Abdullah (2007) shows how pluralist policy in Malaysia rests on such assumptions, with the result that each group merely 'tolerates' others while one (Malays) continues to enjoy a privileged position. Abdullah suggests that instead of defining people as Malay, Chinese, Indian, Islamic or whatever, mutual respect should be developed through dialogue, on the grounds that ethnic identity (for example) forms an element of a person but does not define the whole person. Thus people's differences can be respected as constitutive of persons, who deserve respect in their own right, rather than the other way round. On this basis, we can respect others as persons and be genuinely interested in their views, sexual orientations and allegiances even where they differ from our own – because we are genuinely interested in them as persons in their own right.

4/5

Experience is everything – but not just social experience, if by 'social' we mean that which is widely recognized as shared. Experiences always occur in context; by the same token, an experience cannot be fully prescribed, and a fully social experience (i.e. one shared by everybody) is impossible; note how children in large comprehensive schools divide into small social units with competing interests and aspirations, for example. This has implications for a view of education as offering 'opportunities'. Inevitably, adults must make decisions about the situations children will be put into. However, as intentional, and increasingly differentiated, beings, children will not all respond to the same situation in the same way. One person's 'opportunity' is another person's 'so what?' and a third person's 'threat'. Educational policy built on a fully semiotic view, acknowledging the full agency of the child, must take account of this; the issue is returned to in Part 3.

6

As with Dewey, social constructionism runs the danger of overlooking the irreducibility of difference. Human experience, simultaneously private and public (though not all equally intended for public broadcast!), individual and social, is inevitably new and evolving. Borrowing a term from Hannah Arendt, life is characterized by 'natality' (Arendt, 1958). Perhaps most strikingly when it comes to children, we are engaged in constantly bringing new life into an old world, and the world itself changes as a result (see also Biesta, 2006). This responsibility – to introduce the old to the new, so that it is renewed – is the responsibility of the educator, and it is to specifically educational issues that we turn in Part 3.

Part 3
Education Reconsidered

3.1

The Roots of Compulsory Schooling

3.1.1 Compulsory Schooling as Right and Requirement

It is one of the ironies of the powerless state of childhood that the United Nations deem it a basic human right that you must go to school. Article 26 of the *Universal Declaration of Human Rights* states: 'Elementary education shall be compulsory'. At the World Education Forum in 2000, delegates of 164 countries adopted the *Dakar Framework for Action*, incorporating the aim of 'free and compulsory education of good quality for all by 2015'.

Making schooling compulsory frees children from the whims and abuses of desperate or otherwise unreliable parents. It also ensures that the young of any nation state have some grounding in literacy, numeracy and whatever other skills or knowledge the state considers important. Furthermore, it frees them from having to work for a living. This does not remove the irony, however: only when you are a child is it virtually universally accepted that you are empowered by having no say in what you do each working day; in the adult world, such a condition is regarded as a necessary evil. Of course, this is to ignore the varied ways in which 'schooling' can be interpreted, many of which might be child-friendly and enjoyable. Indeed, certain forms of home-schooling can be tolerated. It is, however, interesting that people in general in the richer countries are so used to school being part of the social fabric that this basic assumption – that children must be removed from the home to the normative environment of the school – is accepted not as a preferred option in certain situations, but as a basic human right.

Such uncritical acceptances can be dangerous, potentially masking either inefficiencies, cruelty or unwarranted interference in the system. It is therefore important that compulsion in education remains a live issue, even where younger children are concerned. Whether it really is a live issue is itself a matter of debate. In 1990, Kevin Williams wrote:

The practice of compulsory schooling is animated and sustained by an almost universal prevailing public consensus that the practice is in the child's interest . . . the law making education compulsory could be said to be one of the achievements of civilisation. (Williams, 1990: 289)

In 1999, Christopher Winch and John Gingell attempted to reignite interest in the debate:

> . . . if we compel people to do something, then we need to provide good reason for that compulsion. The fact that in this case those compelled are children alters the matter somewhat – because we expect children to be subject to some compulsion – but that does not affect the basic thrust of the question that concerns compulsory schooling . . . hopefully this important issue will now generate continued philosophical interest. (Winch and Gingell, 1999: 39-40)

There is no strong evidence at the time of writing of this renewed interest. In any case, what is a child? As we have seen, the concept is by no means a closed one, nor is it clear where childhood ends and adulthood begins. Should sixteen- or eighteen-year-olds be in compulsory education? Are they children?

This valorization of compulsion is, in fact, a particularly modern conception. The history of compulsory education goes back a long way but until the nineteenth century, it was not associated with Liberal or democratic values. Far from it.

As discussed in Part 1, the documentary evidence supporting compulsory schooling goes back to Plato's *Republic*. It is important to bear in mind that this is a Utopia, and not an existing state of affairs. It merely suited Plato's philosophical scheme to prefer a system in which the most promising young people could be removed from their possibly inadequate and sentimental parents to prepare them for social leadership. Arguments for compulsory education have always rested, to a considerable degree, on the perceived inadequacies of parents – often for good reason, one might feel. The Athenians refer to other city-states, specifically Sparta, as employing rigorous means of military training. Aristotle, as was discussed in Part 1, pulled back slightly from Plato's preference for removing infants, arguing that the most effective and individuated early care is offered through the household (Chapter 1.3). As argued in Part 1, the philosophical basis for this imposed education is not one that most Late Modern or Postmodern citizens would wish to endorse.

Actual instances of compulsory schooling going back more than two hundred years are relatively rare. The Aztecs required all male children to attend school up to sixteen (Mann, 2005). In Scotland, the Education Act of 1496 required the children of noblemen and freeholders to go to school. However, modern compulsory education was effectively born in the German-speaking countries in the eighteenth century.

As with Plato, the rationale for introducing compulsory education in Prussia leaves a good deal to be desired. The effects, however, were extremely far-reaching. In the 2000s, England and Wales have a National Curriculum with emphases on literacy, numeracy and preparation for citizenship, compulsory attendance for students, standardized testing and a national system of teacher education; Prussia had most of these by the end of the eighteenth century. In 1763, schooling was made compulsory for children between five and thirteen, and in 1794, all schools and universities were made institutions of the State. In 1810, State certification of teachers was introduced. The model quickly spread to Austria and throughout Europe, and was largely adopted in the late 1800s in the United States. It is a system recognizable in modern Liberal states, yet its inspiration was far from Liberal.

The seeds of the modern school system were set in Lutheran Germany as early as the 1500s. An early elaboration of the potential role of public schools was written by Martin Luther in his 1524 letter to the German authorities. In 1524 Luther wrote:

> I maintain that the civil authorities are under obligation to compel the people to send their children to school. . . . If the government can compel such citizens as are fit for military service to bear the spear and rifle, to mount ramparts, and perform other material duties in time of war, how much more has it a right to compel the people to send their children to school, because in this case we are warring with the devil, whose object it is secretly to exhaust our cities and principalities of their strong men. (Richman, S., 1994 Chapter 3 page 1, retrieved from www.sntp.net/education/school_state-3.htm 26 October 2007)

Within thirty-five years, compulsory attendance had been inaugurated in Wurttemberg. According to Richman:

> Luther himself drew up a plan for Saxony. The purpose of all those school systems was to impose Lutheranism. Similarly, in the mid-16th century, John Calvin set up mandatory schools in Geneva, which were used to stamp out dissent. Under Calvin's influence, Holland followed suit in the beginning of the 17th century. It is important to understand that the purpose of the schools was to *indoctrinate the citizens in the official religious outlook* [italics in original], for, as Luther put it, "no secular prince can permit his subjects to be divided by the preaching of opposite

doctrines. . . . Heretics are not to be disputed with, but to be condemned unheard." Unsurprisingly, it was in Calvinist New England that compulsory schooling first arrived in America. (ibid.)

Compulsory schooling was not introduced to provide equal opportunities for children, or to develop their potential to the full. It was not provided because either parents or children wanted it. It was not intended to produce inquiring, successful individual citizens. It was introduced partly to instil universal literacy, as Postman (1994) suggested (Chapter 1.8). However, the literacy required was obedience to a certain form of Biblical teaching; what was required was a compliant and dutiful population who would positively endorse – as opposed to merely tolerate – the form of Lutheranism that the monarchy approved (bearing in mind its scepticism about the power of the established church). Goldberg (1996: 88) quotes the German philosopher, Johann Gottlieb Fichte (1762–1814), who stated that schools 'must fashion the person, and fashion him in such as way that he simply cannot will otherwise than what you wish him to will'.

It is not necessary to rely on the historical accounts of committed Libertarians such as Richman and Goldberg (both associated with the Cato Institute, a Libertarian 'think-tank' in the USA). Andy Green, for example (1990, 1997) discusses schooling as a major form of nation-building (ironically, less in Britain than elsewhere). The development and reinforcement of national identity remains an explicit aim of educators around the world, and an implied aim of many more; it is clear what call there would be for a 'national curriculum' otherwise.

Of course, the initial reasons for instituting something are not sufficient to render it invalid in its present form. Think, for example, of the relatively tolerant and compassionate modern cities founded on profits from slaves, tobacco, opium or other forms of ruthless exploitation. Modern state schools are not a bad thing merely because Prussian leaders were totalitarian. However, given the historical sources of modern compulsory schooling, it is surprising that it is not more openly and fully questioned at the level of compulsion rather than merely effectiveness.

Notwithstanding the general willingness to accept compulsory schooling, there have been articulate voices raised against it.

3.1.2 Critics of Compulsory Schooling

Perhaps the best known of these voices are those of Ivan Illich and John Caldwell Holt, though Paul Goodman's *Growing Up Absurd* (1960) and

Compulsory Miseducation (1964) can be regarded as the literary instigators of the modern de-schooling movement. Illich's *Deschooling Society* critiques schools for weakening the will and dampening the desire to learn, replacing it with a conditioned desire to be instructed. Illich sees a credential-driven, goal-oriented education as displacing and subverting creative human growth, effectively damaging the human spirit by quantifying the unquantifiable. Illich saw schools as providing a series of disappointing substitutes for real motivation and learning: identifying grades and qualifications with achievement, the quest for learning with the expectation of instruction, attendance with achievement, and shallow procedures with substantial, principled work (Illich, 1970).

This final point is picked up in one of the most influential accounts of schooling from a later and more hopeful perspective: that of Derek Edwards and Neil Mercer in *Common Knowledge: The Development of Understanding in the Classroom* (1987), in which the authors warn against the danger of schools substituting mere 'procedural' knowledge (i.e. knowing how to get on well in school!) with 'principled' knowledge within the various disciplines (history, science etc.). Indeed, many of Illich's criticisms have been heard from educators themselves in recent years as England, in particular, has moved strongly to a school system characterized by benchmarks, targets and other accountability measures. As Jean-Francois Lyotard would have it (Chapter 1. 8), the system has become increasingly bound by ideas of 'performativity' in the postmodern confusion over abiding and overarching values. Illich's argument precedes Lyotard's and is not reliant on any sense of 'incredulity towards metanarratives' (Lyotard, 1984: xiv), arguing rather that modern society has merely 'got it wrong' when it comes to schools, but in this way, too, Illich's view has called forth many subsequent echoes. Finally, Illich argued for learning networks that would allow people to share and develop mutual interests, an aspiration that has been advanced by the internet, though it has not replaced the school.

Holt's argument (1974) is about civil liberties. He believes that it is a fundamental human right that, as far as possible, we are free to choose what we attend to, and that this right is simply violated by compulsory schooling. To Holt, freedom of thought is more precious still than freedom of speech, and yet children are routinely denied it.

Other arguments are more specific. Some commentators believe that the state has interfered unnecessarily in that most parents would want their children educated regardless of compulsory schooling (e.g. West, 1974); others that compulsory schooling is rendered less effective by the presence of either ineducable or merely disruptive children. Rothbard (1978), for example, argues that human variety determines that not all will respond equally to standardized education which, in its turn, merely serves to repress individuality and diversity. Rothbard questions the government's right to attempt to impose its view of what a citizen should be like. He even sees publicly funded education as exacerbating social class divides by, effectively, reinforcing 'ghetto' mentalities and taxing the poor to subsidize the children of the rich. He believes in education as a right, but states that this is not the same as the right for authorities to impose any form of educational provision.

John Taylor Gatto (2003) and Robert Epstein (2007) focus on the gap between aspirations for compulsory schooling and its achievements. Gatto sees present schooling as a sort of *reductio ad absurdum* standardized to the point of a lowest common denominator that is so low that it is dehumanizing. He wants a radically decentralized, voucher-based system that disrupts the hegemonies of central control, subject specialism, standardized testing, abstract theorizing (as opposed to real-world problem solving) and an insistence on the same provision for all. Epstein argues that schools smother initiative, offering nothing to either under-, or potential over-achievers. He believes that the insistence on having young people in school rather than work is an anachronism from the Industrial Revolution, and, furthermore, that the introduction of Western educational practices precedes increasing social problems with youth in developing countries insistent on following the Western model.

These recent critiques are broadly – in many cases, explicitly – Libertarian, so why has compulsory schooling become so generally an accepted part of espousedly Liberal societies, even when criticisms abound about its effectiveness?

3.1.3 Compulsory Schooling and the Liberal-Democratic Tradition

Arguments for compulsory schooling in England and Wales came to prominence in the mid-nineteenth century. As explained in Chapter 1.6, eighteenth-century Classical Liberalism was not generally sympathetic to State control of education. None of the best-known versions of the Social Contract argue for this. Even Hobbes, arguably more an authoritarian Conservative than a Liberal, who believed in absolute power for the sovereign, stopped short of this, though less than Locke, and, in particular, Rousseau. Hobbes saw education as a necessary means of socialization, inducting naturally self-interested people into the values of citizenship for their own safety and security. As in all things, the sovereign would have the right to intervene in this process. On the other hand, to Hobbes, as to his more obviously Liberal successors, society of itself has no power or agency: It is held together by individuals who transcend their own self-interest to cede to authority for their enlightened self-interest. Indeed, to the Millennial observer, Hobbes' attitude to education seems deeply ambivalent; as James Marshall has noted, it is not dissimilar to Michel Foucault's late-twentieth-century notion of 'governmentality', whereby people are inducted into accepting the existing power structure such that they accept it voluntarily. This, in turn, reminds us of Fichte's advice to the Prussian leadership (above) (Marshall, 2000; Foucault, 1979). Marshall states:

> There is something of a paradox then as what is said about the duty of the citizen, namely obligation, seems to be inconsistent with the duty of the Sovereign, namely education; if the Sovereign desires peace then one cannot educate, whereas if one desires education then one cannot ensure peace.

> Hobbes states explicitly that the Sovereign does have duties of an educational nature in these areas. Thus whilst the Sovereign is responsible primarily for the safety of people, 'safety' is not to be interpreted as 'bare preservation' but rather as 'general providence', ". . . contained in public instruction both of doctrine and example". As it was contrary to the Sovereign's duty to relinquish any aspect of his power and authority, so also was it against his duty, "to let the people be ignorant, or misinformed of the grounds, and reasons of those his essential rights; because thereby men are easy to be seduced, and drawn to resist him . . . "

> . . . Hobbes suggested that a special day should be set aside for this education. Laws and duties are to be told and read – hardly education. Yet on the other hand they are to be expounded and the people must come to know and understand "the grounds and reasons of these his essential rights". That sounds more like education.

> (Marshall, 2000, retrieved from <www.vusst.hr/ENCYCLOPAEDIA/ hobbes.htm> 29 October 2007)

By contrast, Locke (1692) is deeply sceptical of the effects of schooling rather than private tutoring. To Locke and other Liberals, human nature is perfectible. However, it can only attain fully rational autonomy if influenced in the right way in childhood. This explains not only Locke's distrust of servants (with whom children necessarily interacted a great deal), but also his almost impossibly high expectations of tutors (Chapter 1.6). Of the company children are likely to keep at schools, Locke is deeply suspicious, though he acknowledges that the 'tutor *vs.* school' dilemma is not an easy one to resolve:

> I confess both sides have their inconveniences. Being abroad, 'tis true, will make him [*sic*] bolder, and better able to bustle and shift among boys of his own age; and the emulation of school-fellows often puts life and industry into young lads. But . . . as for that boldness and spirit which lads get amongst their play-fellows at school, it has ordinarily such a mixture of rudeness and ill-turn'd confidence, that those misbecoming and disingenuous ways of shifting in the world must be unlearnt, and all the tincture wash'd out again, to make way for better principles, and such manners as to make a truly worthy man. He that considers how diametrically opposite the skill of living well, and managing, as a man should do, his affairs in the world, is to that mal-pertness, tricking or violence learnt amongst schoolboys, will think the faults of a private education infinitely to be preferr'd to such improvements. . . . Virtue is harder to be got than a knowledge of the world; and if lost in a young man, is seldom recover'd. (Locke, 1692: S69, retrieved from www.fordham.edu/halsall/mod/ 1692locke-education.html 27 September 2007)

Given that the Romantic followers of Rousseau were even more opposed than Locke to early socialization into the accepted ways of the State, it is ironic that it was one of the greatest educational thinkers of the Romantic and Liberal-humanist traditions – Matthew Arnold, 1822–1888 – who would perhaps do more than anyone else to argue for compulsory State education in England.

In both England and Wales and the USA, compulsory education was adopted in admiration of the Prussian model. In America, this followed the visits of Horace Mann and others in the late 1800s; in Britain, Arnold's influence was felt earlier. In 2000, Brendan A. Rapple described Arnold's fulsome recommendations of Prussia's successes to his political masters:

> Thus when more public institutions of various kinds have been established, when, for example, there has been increased State involvement in secondary and higher education in England, there will necessarily result more intelligence, more culture, more Geist in society. Then the "children of light", the "lovers of culture" will exist in greater abundance; then in their capacity as "aliens", as the saving "remnant", they will somehow express the 'best self' of the collective character of the State.

Because of the ambiguity in Arnold's treatment of the State, it is not surprising that quite different interpretations of his views have been proffered ranging from the opinion that he was a staunch defender of the liberal and democratic viewpoint to the conviction that he was an authoritarian and espouser of totalitarian regimes. (Rapple, 2000: 4, retrieved from http://findarticles.com/p/articles/mi_m2242/is_1634_280/ai_85370548/pg_4 29 October 2007)

In fact, as would John Dewey some years later, Arnold had developed a conception of the (ideal) State as the embodiment of what is best in each individual. This view of the State provides the basis for the Social Liberalism that is now Liberalism's dominant strand. *Contra* the Libertarians, such as those quoted in the previous section, Social Liberals believe that individuals working together can be stronger than if autonomous, and ceding to collective rules and norms can be much more positive than Hobbes envisaged. This shift of perspective was strongly motivated by a desire to do something about the conditions of the poor. (See also Chapter 1.6.) Arnold, therefore, believed that the State could, potentially, improve things for people, but only if rightly motivated. In his seminal work *Culture and Anarchy* (1882), Arnold strongly contrasts a state of 'anarchy' with one of 'culture', on the grounds that a free-for-all (preferred by Libertarian individualists and callous Utilitarians) does no good for society as a whole. Arnold witnessed the decline of religion and felt that the arts, particularly poetry, could take its place. (He was Professor of Poetry at Oxford.) Thus, what was needed was a society in which the children of the poor would be inducted into the 'sweetness and light' of high culture, thus developing them as fully human beings. In Arnold, perhaps more strongly than in any other influential writer about education, we see overt prescriptiveness on the grounds that it is 'for their own good' – as opposed to 'for the good of the State'. For example, he urged the British government to eliminate the Welsh language on the grounds that its use would disadvantage Welsh people. Thus he leaves a legacy that combines Romantic aspiration, public accountability, curricular anti-vocationalism (i.e. a 'liberal education' in the common usage of the phrase) and central control: a particularly English mix, some might say nowadays.

Although Arnold seems an anachronism in many ways, much of his thinking about education remains influential today. Indeed, unless checked, the contemporary tendency seems to be towards ever more compulsory education. This condition will be examined in the following chapter.

The Extension of the In-Between Years

3.2.1 The Dominant Discourse

As was made clear in the previous chapter, current arguments for compulsory education in countries such as the UK tend to be grounded in a rights-based form of Liberal thinking that embraces a more thoroughgoing social egalitarianism than was the case under Classical Liberalism. To Locke and his followers, individual strength of character was of more importance than perceived equality of opportunity, while in the current dominant educational discourse, the emphasis tends to be the reverse. Thus the policy debate in England and Wales (between which there are minor differences) is predominantly concerned with issues such as the proportion of eleven-year-olds reaching average or 'expected' standards in literacy and numeracy, and the disparities in educational achievement between the rich and the poor. Compulsory schooling is thus seen as a benign means of social reform, an approach that might be contrasted with one of Conservative Nationalism, in which schools exist to serve the existing social order, or one of Revolutionary Socialism, in which they exist to overturn it. This position begs several questions, which are addressed in the remainder of this chapter, concerning conceptions of equality of opportunity, the validity of standardized measures of achievement, the importance of social and economic inequalities, and the capacity for formal education to address them. If (*a*) the issues reflect agreed social aims, and (*b*) compulsory education is an unquestionable social good, then increasing compulsory education should gradually serve to tackle the issues. If it does not, then the grounds for the increase can be questioned. Both premises (*a*) and (*b*) are, indeed, open to question.

3.2.2 Equality of Opportunity as a Basis
for Educational Policy

'Equality of opportunity' is a compound term. It is also a policy slogan, and one which enjoys wide, if often tacit, support. Policy slogans must be catchy and memorable; they do not need to be unambiguous. Indeed, Norman Fairclough (1995: 113) has pointed out that 'ambivalence potential' is important in slogans and other policy formulations designed to maximize public response.

One might go further and argue that slogans such as 'equality of opportunity' are not only ambivalent but openly paradoxical or oxymoronic. (Other candidates for this include 'parity of esteem' and 'sustainable development'.) That is to say, policies in democracies have to appeal to the maximal number of potential voters, and so aim to attract support from those with differing, even opposing, political orientations. On this account (first developed in Stables, 1996), the collocation of 'opportunity' with 'equality', though now widely accepted and unquestioned, rests on the juxtaposition of two opposing concepts. 'Opportunity', in ordinary language, relates to subjective judgment and experience; individuals have opportunities. 'Equality', on the other hand, refers to objective, transpersonal measurement of people's treatment of others, whether linked to an ethical virtue such as respect or a material condition such as income. Whether something is an opportunity or a threat depends on personal response; others might try to convince you that a particular career move, for example, presents you with a good opportunity, but the judgement is finally yours. With equality, the situation is reversed. While an individual may insist she is being treated 'equally', or complain of the reverse, 'equality' remains an interpersonal rather than an intrapersonal construct. (Applying the same logic to 'parity of esteem', one might argue that 'parity' refers to measurable equality between people, whereas 'esteem' is a relative value measure, reliant on one value being 'higher' than another. Regarding 'sustainable development', what is 'sustained' remains unchanged, whereas what is 'developed' cannot remain unchanged.) In such cases, the political rhetoricians who coin slogans are attempting to draw in as wide a range of sympathies as possible.

In effect, such compound policy slogans mask conflict by attaining to cohesion. Imagine a future government were committed to 'freedom and fairness'. That sounds very attractive – who could object? – yet freedom entails the permission to act unfairly. The political reality is that aspirations for freedom must be balanced against those for fairness, for they often act against each other. As a politician, however, you can only tackle the real issues once you have been elected. Only a policy with a wide initial appeal will put you in that position.

On this account, it is hardly surprising that commitments such as 'equality of opportunity' run into problems at the policy formulation and implementation stages, for a slogan does not amount even to a policy, let alone to a means of enacting it.

A particular problem in this case concerns whether opportunities can be provided. Certainly, goods and services can be made available to people, even made compulsory for them, but this does not determine either that the recipients of the goods and services will respond positively to them or that they will act sensibly on receipt of them. This problem becomes more acute when people have not chosen to receive the goods and services in question, and thus have not formulated either a reason for receiving them or a plan of what to do with them. This is likely to be the case for many children in school – though not all of them, and not all of the time. Many school students receiving instruction in curriculum subjects have not elected to take that instruction to achieve something they have decided for themselves. Many younger children may work hard in school because they require the praise and protection of adults. Many older students will acknowledge that there is a point in having good grades in public examinations, and will make an increased effort accordingly. What, however, is there to motivate many 11 to 14-year-olds for whom (in the English context), dependent infancy is a thing of the past and the search for chosen credentials lies beyond their current horizons? They are in a sort of no-man's-land. They might find, of course, that they enjoy studying things regardless, but this will only occur if the teaching is responsive to their existing interests, aspirations and attainments, and this is difficult to achieve in a context of standardized content and instruction.

'Equality of opportunity' is, then, a very broad term, and its meaning-in-use can vary enormously in significance. At the simplest, purely formal, legal level it merely 'requires that positions and posts that confer superior advantages should be open to all applicants' (Arnesen, 2002: 1), and even then, it only applies within a specific area of government, such as a particular nation state. Purely formal equality of opportunity, therefore, has no impact on educational provision, except in peripheral areas such as the employment of teachers. It does not imply a commitment to ensuring that all people (or as many as possible) are in the position to apply for the advertised post in the first place.

A more substantive commitment to equality of opportunity does, however, entail such a commitment. This raises highly problematic issues for formal education. It is at the level of implementation of the slogan that the debate begins in earnest. At one extreme, Libertarians such as Robert Nozick (1974) and Richard Epstein (1995) regard equality of opportunity as the condition under which people are as free as possible to pursue their private interests, regardless of inequalities of outcomes: 'The libertarian view is that people's opportunities are equal in the relevant sense when each person equally faces other possible interaction partners in a regime in which everyone's Lockean rights are respected.' (Arnesen, 2002: 23. 'Lockean rights' here refer principally to private property in the broadest sense.)

By contrast, John Rawls' 'equality of fair opportunity' (2001) assumes that children of equal natural talent should be equally equipped to aspire to, and apply for the vacant post referred to above; privileges of background, including social class and gender, should not be allowed to increase one's chances. In effect, Rawls is asking systems such as education to create a classless society, which in turn demands a quite invasive social policy that wrests control from (for example) parents and turns it over to (for example) schools. Even then, the policy rests on an assumption of native talent, which not all will share, and there is no effective commitment to equalities of outcome. Furthermore, it is unclear how differences in effort should be handled; some children may deserve more success than others, but, again, this additional effort might be explained by external factors. Thoroughgoing outcome egalitarians, therefore, will seek a system that ensures that no one is disadvantaged in the end – but this requires extreme intervention and the denial of any private sphere in which advantage can be conferred.

In conclusion, the greater the commitment to a substantive notion of equality of outcome, the more centralized educational provision must be, and the less individual freedom can be tolerated. Even among those with a very strong commitment, policy prescriptions will vary. For example, a believer in 'affirmative action' may recommend increased educational funding, and even a modified curriculum, for the least privileged, to counteract broader social inequalities, while others may insist on equal treatment of all at the school level as in all other contexts. Yet others might argue that society as a whole needs élite schools just as sport needs élite teams (Roemer, 2002). There are several authors who have committed to a 'Level Playing Field' conception, whereby equality of opportunity is inextricably linked to distributive justice (e.g. Dworkin, 2000; Roemer, 1995, 1998) and requires large-scale redistribution of wealth from the rich to the poor, but even this commitment does not offer any firm prescription for the conduct of compulsory schooling.

As Arnesen (2002: 28) puts it: 'Debates about the seemingly banal norm of equality of opportunity reveal profound disagreements as to the nature of fair terms of cooperation in the modern world.' David Corson has written of the 'secondary elaborations of belief' that render political policies so hard to enact consistently in education (Corson, 1988: 253). All the stake-holders in our schools may share a commitment to equality of opportunity, but such a commitment does not take us very far in agreeing how exactly education should be conducted. The same holds true for alternative policy formulations, even though not all are compound: the terms 'inclusion' or 'diversity' for example, can be interpreted in quite conflicting ways (noting that 'diversity' is often paired with 'equality', thus creating yet another potentially paradoxical, or oxymoronic, policy commitment). A key issue is that of whose conceptions predominate, and this cannot be separated from the issue of what schools are supposed to achieve. This, in turn, raises broader questions about the nature of schools and other ostensibly public and private institutions.

3.2.3 Whose Expected Standards?

Representatives of government, academics and employers often inform us that standards in schools are too low, but how are these standards set in the first place? These are, of course, judgements: expert (but not all-knowing) opinions informed by relevant (but selective) experience. In many coun-tries these judgements are backed up by quantitative data from standardized tests of various sorts. Some may argue that the judgements are 'based on' such data, though this may often be disingenuous, since no testing régime can enjoy absolute validity or reliability. Data inform, but do not determine, judgements.

In England and Wales, for example, a matter of significant political concern is the proportion of students judged as failing to attain 'average' competence in literacy and numeracy, where 'average' means National Cur-riculum Level 4 at age 11 and GCSE Grade C at age 16. The first obvious objection to this is that the notion of 'average' carries with it expectations that some must be below average: not everyone can be average or above. Also, note that thirty years ago, the equivalent of GCSE Grade C was only attained by about a fifth of the population and there was no mass standard-ized testing of eleven-year-olds. One is therefore justified in wondering where the notion of average competence comes from in this case. It is cer-tainly not valid to assert that it is in any way obvious whether people can, say, read and write to an 'average' or 'satisfactory' level. The demands to be met for so-called functional literacy – the level of literacy required to cope with everyday tasks (e.g. Stables, 2003a) – are very different in England now from a century ago. Then an average farm worker, for example, hardly needed to read and write at all; now he or she has to deal with complex instructions on bags of fertilizer, feed and other chemicals, apart from the out-of-work demands posed by self-assessment tax return forms, vehicle maintenance and insurance, and a host of other regulations.

Purportedly-objective assertions about educational standards are always actually contextual and contingent. It is always pertinent to ask who is making the judgements, and on what basis, and to retain a sense of perspective in relation to them. While this implies that, on the one hand, there are grounds for mistrust of such judgements, on the other it is inevitable that concerns about a human cultural activity such as schooling should vary from place to place and time to time. Thus, Matthew Arnold's support of the Prussian system was based on his perception of its successes *vis-à-vis* the English, and should not be taken as explicit or tacit support for the questionable motives behind its inception. Arnold's case was made in good faith as, I dare say, most of the public statements about educational standards are in our own time.

Nevertheless, reflection on the standards issue prompts two related questions: who is actually in charge of what happens in schools, and who should be? The problem of expected standards cannot be divorced from the expectation itself: whose expectation it is, and what purpose it serves.

On a modified Aristotelian conception of childhood, children themselves can have no say in this: they are being prepared for adult society and so cannot partake in its judgements. If, as I have argued, there is a strong Aristotelian legacy in current attitudes to children, it is not surprising that the public discourse about education, while urging choice at one level, is nevertheless dominated by voices preoccupied with performance on a narrow range of standardized tests, implying that such results tell us pretty well all we need to know about compulsory education. This narrow, top-down approach to schooling has takes no account of 'secondary [let alone tertiary] elaborations of belief': the assumption is that certain students do worse than others, not because of cultural and personal factors that result in their 'seeing education differently' but because of bad teaching or institutional management. While, again, such judgements are made in good faith, they rest on a simplistic set of assumptions about schools as closed 'delivery' systems. From a fully semiotic perspective (for example), there are no closed systems.

I have argued that schools, and other social institutions, are constituted by the meanings they have for those engaged with them: in short, that they are 'imagined communities' in discursive, or semiotic, space. Material in the following five paragraphs is adapted from Stables, 2003b:.

The concept 'imagined community' is most strongly associated with Benedict Anderson's work on nationhood, and his analysis of international tensions in relation to this (Anderson, 1983).

> Just as the boundaries of nationhood are not always clear, nor are those of schools, nor of other cultural institutions. Where do we find a school? In and among its buildings, perhaps, yet these buildings cannot of themselves constitute the school. A school only exists in relation to its being imagined: if it is the sum total of anything, it is the sum total of perceptions and experiences of it. Such perceptions and experiences are certainly refined through the school's social networks, but these are themselves indefinite and elusive, linking those who work in the institution, those who have personal connections with it and those who know it only at second or third hand. One aspect of this is that its cultural practices pay limited heed to notions of internality and externality as these relate to its buildings, or even its teachers or students. For example, students do homework and fieldwork; games are played outside the school (sometimes at other schools), books are marked at home; friendships are forged and played out within and beyond its physical confines; cigarettes are smoked in dark corners; individual and collective life trajectories are inextricably bound up with it, as are aspects of adult domestic and economic life. Even the amount of time spent within the physical boundaries of the school varies greatly between, for example, the boarding school and the liberal Sixth Form College (to take examples from the British context). Perhaps most importantly, schools are conceived or construed *via* the perceptions of those who are not presently students or teachers within them, and are often not directly related as parents of students, past or present. The imagined school, in its complexity, is a part of the imagined community within the imagined nation, each of which will be variously imagined. (Thus conceived, it is easy to understand how sensitive to broader cultural and social currents issues of schooling are: for example, with respect to religion and ethnicity.)

It might be countered, however, that Anderson's argument does indeed relate to nations and not to smaller groupings. Perhaps understandably, since nations are his concern, he is somewhat ambivalent about the degree to which other, smaller communities are imagined. For example:
   "In fact, all communities larger than primordial villages of face-to-face contact (*and perhaps even these*) are imagined." (Anderson, 1983: 15. My italics)

There are certainly aspects of Anderson's formulation that do not apply neatly to schools, including his assertion that nationhood implies a sense of 'deep, horizontal comradeship' (1983: 16); it would be a rare school that could boast this, and many school leaders might not hold such aspirations. However, schools are similar to both nations and cities insofar as 'they are sociological entities of such firm and stable reality that their members can even be described as passing each other on the street, without ever becoming acquainted, and still be connected.' (1983: 31) (Friends of mine recall their daughter waiting for the bus to take her to her comprehensive school, happy with her friends and apparently oblivious of the behaviour of other groups of waiting students; I recall a former pupil returning to school for a day to observe classes, when considering teaching as a career, only to conclude, 'I had no idea this school was like this'.) Furthermore, all but the smallest primary schools are unlikely to bear much resemblance to the primordial village, the status of which, *vis-à-vis* imagined communities, Anderson seems unclear. Nobody knows everyone else in any but the smallest schools. Even if they do, they do not live permanently at the school; there are out-of-school lives that remain private and distinct. There was no such regular escape from the primordial village community, when even the hunting party must have acted with a strong sense of mutual purpose and transparency.

To the poststructuralist, all communities are imagined. In Derridean terms, the meaning of school is 'deferred' (Derrida, 1978): that is to say, not precisely spatially and temporally locatable. Just as the current experience of nation, according to Anderson, has its roots in previous contexts, so our images of schools are constructed retrospectively and from distance. Much, perhaps most, of the debate about schools, that shapes them in the public imagination, comes from those whose experience within their physical boundaries is spatially and temporally distant. By contrast, actors within schools often speak of them in the third person; school is "it" and not "we". Only certain speakers, at certain times, and in certain contexts, will refer to "my" or "our" school; at other times, and in other contexts, participants speak of themselves in relation to "this school".

School, therefore, is both there and not there; it stays with us throughout the lifespan yet we are detached from it during our schooling; it both is and is not its buildings; it belongs both to some (its professionals, its students) and to all. As such, it is not easily researchable, and is best understood in terms of stakeholders' perceptions of it. (Stables, 2003b: 895–7)

An implication of this view is that protestations from above can never fully determine what will happen within schools, however well intentioned, thought through or backed up by financial resource. This is not to assert that what social leaders want from schools will have no effect, but rather that it can have only limited effect. Schools cannot be the delivery systems that many desire. Ironically, perhaps this explains Arnold's admiration for the Prussians: maybe they had intended to produce a servile population but unpredictably produced one with greater initiative than the English. Such conjectures can never be proven, any more than the outcomes of schooling can be guaranteed.

If we were to regard children not as not-yet-ready for society, but as already part of it – or were to go further and question how far schoolchildren can validly be regarded as 'children' at all, these debates would take on a different character. As adults looking down on young people, we would no longer be asking 'What are they doing for us?' so much as 'What are we doing for them?'

3.2.4 Are Schoolchildren Children?

Who runs a school? If a school is an imagined community, effectively constructed by those who act and speak in relation to it – and given that quantitative measurements cannot be made of such things – then the most influential group in a school must surely be the students. The children (*sic*) define the culture of a school more than any other group. Looking beyond them, the next most influential group would seem, on this account, to be the parents. Then there are the teachers, the management and the governors. Of course, these last can wield considerable influence, such is the power structure of schools – but they cannot control them, and educationalists and policy-makers can control them even less. Indeed, one of the ironies of schools is, as Locke seemed aware, that placing young people together in large numbers increases their power to define the culture thus, in one sense, making them less rather than more malleable in terms of adult wishes.

In short, schools are not simply the creations of adults: no more of current governments than of John Dewey, Matthew Arnold or the King of Prussia. Of course, governments can influence them. One such possible influence is to attempt to equalize outcomes between them by controlling the mixture of students within them. However, policies such as 'bussing' cannot tell children how to think or react; they might, as all changes, have some effect, but what that effect will be cannot be pre-specified, and may not be altogether positive. The greatest irony of schooling is that it is arranged on behalf of children yet largely controlled by them; what is provided and what is taken are two different things. An Aristotelian perspective is incapable of acknowledging this for, from such a perspective, children are not yet able to manage, for they are effectively only potential persons. Indeed, we must acknowledge that children are not able to manage as adults do – one would not wish to see them driving cars or passing laws, for example – yet they do manage; indeed, they manage a great deal.

On this account, 'children' are simply not children. The assumption that *Child 2* (the person of limited years) is synonymous with *Child 3* (the novice) is only partly true. Children are less good than adults at things that adults excel at (indeed, they cannot be trusted with all such things), but they are extremely influential. They engage semiotically with their worlds as vigorously as adults – arguably often more so – and reshape their environments continuously and inexorably. They do not, as the extreme Romantics suggest, 'come from another planet' from adults, but they do, as the Romantics observed, operate creatively and responsively. They cannot, in general, be 'superior' to adults, as social status, and thus conceptions of superiority, rest more in the adult world than the child's, yet they can be equal to, or even superior to, adults in certain specific requests. This is not to say, of course, that students would run a school better than adults; merely to acknowledge that they do, in fact, play a much greater part in the running of such institutions than is acknowledged in the current political discourse.

Educational policy – perhaps all social policy relating to children – remains intensely paternalistic, however. Children (as simultaneously *Child 2* and *Child 3*) are seen as recipients of it merely, as though they are entirely dependent on adults. Not only does such an approach fail to acknowledge the social and cultural trends of the Millennium (as described in Part 2), under which the child–adult divide has been significantly problematized; it also fails to acknowledge its own internal inconsistency, for if children were entirely dependent, they could not go to school.

Even neonates are goal-directed according to, for example, Jerome Bruner (Bruner, 1983). However, infants are not sufficiently independent to attend school. To attend school, you have to be able to manage without your Mummy. Even young primary pupils have already attained a degree of independence. By the early teenage years, young people have not been physically dependent for years, and they are largely socially independent, yet they are not financially independent. Indeed, they may not be such for many years to come.

The effect of the educational thinking of the past two centuries has been effectively to stretch the age of financial dependency more and more, so that now fewer and fewer people enter their twenties in the position of earning their own income and therefore acting as fully productive members of adult society. At the same time, it should be noted, life expectancy has increased. An increasingly typical life trajectory nowadays comprises twenty or more years of being paid for by others, including a period of building up debts that will have to be repaid later (though the young person has no experience of earning to repay debt), a working life of about forty years, and then at least twenty further years paid for somehow.

In other words, increasingly rich capitalist societies have systematically reduced the proportion of the lifespan in which someone can function as a financially non-dependent citizen. We teach people to spend before we teach them to save. We tell them what to do for longer and longer before we leave them to work out what to do for themselves. The inevitable result of this may be that working life will have to be increasingly heavily taxed to pay for the long periods of dependency, and succeeding generations will not be able to accrue capital, in the form of property or investments, that recent generations have. Put starkly, the current emphasis on ever-increasing education could be squeezing the life out of society. Education is, it might be argued, valued when it offers people a return on their cultural capital; in other words, when having pursued it enables you to do better than you would otherwise have done – better than your parents did, for example. When it fails to offer such a return, it will lose its value.

3.2.5 The Case Against Ever-increased Compulsory Schooling

Note that this section is not entitled, 'The Case Against Compulsory Schooling'. Although such a case can well be made, it would be unfeasible as well as unwise simply to remove compulsory schooling in the short term. Schools exist as part of a complex social structure, and cannot suddenly be removed without undermining that structure. Nevertheless, short-term policy provides a steer with respect to long-term ambitions. The continuing extension of the in-between years, during which physically, and largely socially independent young people are kept from full civic responsibility by virtue of their economic dependence, may also be causing damage to the social structure. We have accentuated *Child 2* (the years before autonomy) and *Child 3* (the sense of unreadiness to take a full role in economic life), at the same time as reducing the time left to the adult to earn, produce and invest. We (i.e. in countries such as the UK) have put pressure on the supply side of education by artificially stimulating the demand side. Instead of providing educational services when people feel ready to invest in them, we insist on providing them before people enter the world of work, and often have to provide more and more to make up for the used inefficiently beforehand.

For example: contrast the time it takes to learn conversational skills in a foreign language as a motivated adult anticipating an important business trip with the time it takes in the compulsory school system. It is clear that schooling serves certain functions, but whether it serves them efficiently is another matter. Its rationale is part historical, part unquestioned and part political, and on all these grounds is open to question. Schools keep young people out of the employment market, but need young people be exploited now as they were in the early nineteenth century if they were in employment rather than school? School keeps children in a protected environment in which they can learn, but is school really protective, and do children learn most efficiently there? Finally, schooling exists to provide equal opportunities, compensating for inadequate parenting and unearned privilege, yet the massively increased spending on education in Britain in recent years has not witnessed a closing of the gap between the rich and the poor. Surely there should be a better response to this situation than to recommend ever more compulsory education, whether this entails considering education vouchers, decentralizing powers over provision and curriculum or opening up employment opportunities.

In conclusion, premises (*a*) and (*b*) stated at the beginning of this chapter are both inadequate. Compulsory schooling can never fully simply reflect societal aims, even when the formulation of such aims is seen as the prerogative solely of those in power; when it is acknowledged that children themselves largely shape their schools, the assumption is weakened further. Compulsory education achieves a great deal for a great many, but it is certainly not an 'unquestionable social good': There is no guarantee that going to school will prove a positive experience, in the short or longer term. Given the weakness of these premises, it cannot be assumed that ever more compulsory education is worthwhile.

Given a long-term intention to reduce compulsion in education, short-term policies might focus on increasing empowerment of students and the development of their choice and initiative. This, in turn, requires a reorientation in thinking about the aims of the curriculum and of teaching, away from the existing emphasis on standardized outcomes. This is the concern of the following chapter.

Teaching for Significant Events: Identity and Non-Identity

3.3.1 Planning for the Unpredictable

The question addressed in this chapter follows on from those posed in the last. If educational outcomes are unpredictable, but schooling remains inevitable, at least in the short term, how might the aims of formal teaching and learning be reformulated? This issue is tackled first in relation to outcomes, and second with respect to processes.

3.3.2 Desirable Outcomes

A centrally led education policy based on measurable benchmarks and output targets rests on certain assumptions. These include: (*a*) the assumption that the output measures are valid and reliable: that is, that they measure what they purport to measure (and that this is what is most important to measure) and that the standards are consistent across place and time; (*b*) that the outcomes are more or less equally valid for all who achieve them.

The following objections might be raised with respect to these.

Regarding (*a*):

For the purposes of this discussion, the output measures discussed will be test and examination results. In England and Wales, it is these which provide the bulk of the data for the evaluation of schools in those countries, including the construction of performance tables (often known as 'league tables'). Test and examination results (hereafter 'tests') can only act as proxies for full competence, for the following reasons:

a 1: A test can only focus on a section of a subject.
a 2: A test must relate to the school syllabus, which is itself a selection from a disciplinary tradition. (Deng, 2007, for example, shows how successful

science teachers are more reliant on a knowledge and understanding of school science than of science in the academy).

a 3: A test can only 'test' certain kinds of knowledge, skills and understanding.

a 4: A test tends to focus on well-established aspects of a subject rather than that which is new or controversial.

a 5: A test 'tests' certain attributes that are not subject-specific, including (for example) memory, writing skill and time management.

These selection issues render tests of no more than partial validity. The repeating of testing across large populations and across long periods of time raises other issues, specifically of reliability:

a 6: Students can be helped to prepare for tests to varying degrees, both in terms of long-term advantage (home, school and cultural background) and in terms of immediate help (from peers, teachers, parents and others). These factors are accentuated where examination is by coursework.

a 7: There is a tendency for 'credential inflation' over time. That is, 'pass rates' will tend to increase year on year. While this can be attributed in part to teacher professionalism and the system becoming better embedded, this is unlikely to account for all the variation. If it did, one would expect to find increases in pass rates in, say, mathematics and language arts mirrored in rises in scores on related tests of cognitive ability, such as spatial awareness and verbal reasoning; in other words, one would expect to find on other measures that students' understanding had increased commensurably. However, there is no suggestion that scores on verbal reasoning tests have risen in line with the proportion of English and Welsh students gaining GCSE Grade C in English (for instance). Also, those who provide the tests (in the UK, the examination boards) are responsible for the success of a product. If a syllabus or a test is successful, it will result in increased pass rates each year, as the system 'settles down' with students and teachers alike. This is not to assert that individuals involved in the system are not committed to the maintenance of standards, but the forces producing 'drift' are very strong. A falling pass rate on any syllabus would be a serious cause for concern, for providers at all levels: policy-makers, examination boards and teachers – and, indeed, this happens very rarely indeed.

With the best will in the world, therefore, no testing system can be totally valid and reliable, and will always, therefore, be an imperfect proxy for educational success, broadly understood. Furthermore, regarding (*b*):

b 1: There is no mechanism to ensure that every student puts the same value on a particular qualification as every other, and it would not necessarily be a good thing if they were to, as society demands variety and specialization and is not organized on the basis of homogeneity of interests, values and motivation any more than on total equivalence of skills; and

b 2: The same can be said of employers. There is no mechanism that can prevent employers from valuing students of certain personality types, or from certain schools and colleges, more than others – nor would it necessarily be desirable if it were so.

The idea that desirable outcomes in education are those that are equitable, measurable and transpersonal is therefore not fully sustainable. Of course, arguments can be mounted that the skills gaps are too wide between the most and less successful, or that poverty is exacerbated by lack of credentials, but neither of these propositions warrants universal standardization, or the judging of educational institutions merely on test results. Indeed, if such arguments are taken as hypotheses rather than self-evident truths, then the success or otherwise of interventionist policies can be more dispassionately assessed. The reduction of the formal education system to delivery of measurable policy objectives of this sort comes at a heavy price, however. It reduces the range of possibilities associated with the term 'education'.

It is instructive to consider how the terms 'education', 'teaching' and 'learning' are used in everyday speech. Such an 'ordinary language' analysis would have to consider usages such as the following: 'That was awful! That taught me a lesson.'; 'Getting married taught me a lot.'; 'Getting divorced taught me a lot.'; 'She was a brilliant teacher!'; 'He was an awful teacher in lots of ways, but I always remember his lessons.'

Two questions (at least) arise from such examples: 'Is learning/ education always good?' and 'When does learning happen?' Philosophy of education often fails to confront these questions fully. 'Education' is often accepted as a force for good, and as effectively provided by teachers in classrooms; indeed, this is the dominant sense in the policy discourse also. However, it is clear that in everyday discourse, 'education', while it clearly relates to values and preferences, is not universally cheerful, positive or encouraging, and that 'education' does not simply happen in sanctioned classrooms and lessons. Indeed, I have suggested elsewhere (Stables, 2005a, 2006a) that, in their most important senses, the meanings of 'education' and 'learning' are always 'deferred' (after Derrida):

> Thus if learning is to be identified as the factor that causes changes in "scripts" or "schemas" – our patterns of making sense of the world – it is very difficult to locate. Is "learning" "in" an event that occurred, or the learner's responses to it? It seems more plausible that it is a term applied retrospectively to changes in the life-story. If this is so, there can be no direct evidence of "learning behaviour" or "learning processes". (Stables, 2006a: 376)

At its most extreme, this can be taken to mean that learning, or education, is as likely to be as unpleasant as pleasant, and that formal education plays no enhanced role in it, other than by virtue of occupying a great deal of young people's time. Even without going this far, it is clear that formal education does not simply 'provide' learning, however convenient it may be for some policy-makers to hold to the reverse. Given that formal education does monopolize students' working lives, therefore, it seems sensible to shift the emphasis from outcomes to processes in evaluating it.

3.3.3 Desirable Processes

The most certain claim that can be made about teachers is not that they make people learn, but that they channel their activity. Teachers (attempt to) make students do certain things. This is the most basic fact of education, and the basis on which the present discussion will proceed. Teachers tell students what to do, though what they actually do is never quite what teachers envisage, since each person's experience is different. Let us begin by considering a little more extensively what is actually going on here.

Students are not passive recipients of knowledge. Indeed, knowledge only exists in the minds of people, or within persons (to avoid mind–body substance dualism). Thus knowledge and understanding are always filtered and renewed by personal processing, so that although several people may evidently know the same thing, what it means to them will always be varied and have a degree of uniqueness. Human beings are very complex, but the point can be illustrated by simple metaphors. If you throw a ball repeatedly against a wall, it will bounce back in ways that are partly predictable and partly unpredictable. The unpredictability is the result of differences across the surfaces of the ball and the wall, the trajectory of the throw, the wind and so on; in other words, there are specific contextual factors that are too subtle for an observer always to be aware of. Over time, in addition to this, both the ball and the wall surface are changed by these and other encounters: the ball more quickly than the wall!

Thankfully, living a human life is a rather richer experience, one hopes, than that of a ball bounced repeatedly off a wall, but the analogy makes a point: When we encounter something new the outcome is partly predictable but never fully so, we are changed a little by the encounter and, over time, the culture itself is changed through such encounters. Despite appearances, nothing remains the same; even human understandings of the Divine must change, albeit the Divine may not.

Similarly, every encounter between a student and a teacher alters each a little, but probably the former more than the latter, as the former is less experienced in such encounters and usually less experienced in life generally. This is not a hard-and-fast rule: school can seem dull and repetitive for students yet life-changing (in a good or bad way) for staff.

Teaching can thus be construed as more or less controlled identity disruption. That is, whenever a student encounters a new piece of information, or engages in a new activity, she encounters something that challenges some aspect of her existing experience of, and assumptions about the world. Education presents challenges to our existing worldviews, though schooling, very often, may present us with uninteresting mechanical tasks that challenge very little. Note that, from a pragmatic perspective, 'encountering a new piece of information' and 'engaging in a new activity' are both activities: the distinction between passivity and activity is fallacious in that students are always 'doing' something, even if 'only' listening or day-dreaming.

Much more importantly, note also that this is a view of teaching that is diametrically opposed to commonly held assumptions that teaching is about the reinforcement of identity: it is only about this given a prior acceptance that identity is not fixed. Thus an 'identity politics' view of teaching, based on the assumption that school should be about reinforcing our sense of cultural identity is positively anti-educational, unless cultural identity is accepted as fluid in the first place. This is not, of course, to endorse a view of teaching as simply destructive of identity: teachers who attempt to crush any sense of self-worth will, paradoxically, induce mechanisms of defence and withdrawal, as we see on the world political stage when less powerful groups simply fear annihilation by colonizers or their equivalents. Paradoxically, therefore, good teaching reinforces positive self-identity by challenging existing self-identity; it invites students to confront that which challenges their identity with a willingness to embrace the changes that will ensue. The simplest way of expressing this is that teaching always confronts students with that which is Other – or should do, if it is to have any effect. Education is (positive) disillusionment, making us see that what we held self-evident is not self-evident after all.

There are various accounts in recent philosophy and psychology of how and why this process occurs. Two will be considered here: Julia Kristeva's account of the development of subjectivity *via* 'abjection', and Rom Harré's conception of the identity project.

Noelle McAfee (2004) offers a concise introduction to key ideas in Kristeva's thought. Kristeva combines perspectives from Poststructuralism and psychoanalysis. She understands self-development in terms of subjectivity, the process whereby we use language and other symbolic systems to generate a sense of ourselves as distinct from others. However, the neat orderliness that we seek is constantly challenged by reminders of that which problematizes it. In *Powers of Horror* (1982), Kristeva is particularly interested in what she terms 'abjects'. Abjects exist on the borders of what we are and what we are not; they repel and fascinate us. Corpses are the strongest abjects; excrement and vomit also cause strong feelings of abjection. Many children, for example, will reject or eject food as part of a psychological struggle to fix and maintain a sense of what is and what is not 'them'; this may give them a sense of emotional control, however fragile. In the more rarefied context of schooling, not explicitly addressed by Kristeva, students are also likely to react in a range of ways, including rejection, to that which is offered to them as a challenge to their ordered senses of who they are. Any education that retreated from such challenge would be very weak. On this account, education inevitably offers the possibility of causing offence, and the educable person expects to be offended from time to time.

The implications of Harré's conception of the identity project have been discussed elsewhere (e.g. Ross et al., 1993; Stables et al., 1999) so will be summarized only briefly here.

Harré's concern is in how we develop both a social identity (fitting in with others) and a personal identity (being different from others) and keep these in appropriate balance. In *Personal Being* (1983), he offers an account of this process in terms of an ongoing cycle comprising four stages: appropriation, transformation, publication and conventionalization. When a student appropriates a new piece of information, he makes sense of it in relation to his experience; when he transforms it, he makes it do work for him in a particular context; when he 'publishes', he offers his transformations up for judgement (e.g. he gives his essay to his teacher); the results of the publication affect the culture itself to some degree, and particularly the student's conception of it, which then offers new opportunities for the cycle to be repeated.

As to how we negotiate our 'identity projects' *via* this 'social reality matrix' (Harré, 1983), Harré later developed the idea of 'positioning' (Harre and van Langenhove, 1999). When we are placed in a new situation we undergo a sort of tacit internal dialogue in which we ask ourselves how we would be likely to act in this situation, given our sense of self-identity, and what the various consequences will be of the possibilities for action in this case, bearing in mind the need to balance fitting in with others against being an individual.

Harré's model offers opportunities for teachers to gear their teaching towards the positive self-identity of their pupils, by turning lessons and activities into 'significant events' for them (Stables et al., 1999). At the same time, his idea of positioning reminds us, as does Kristeva, that there are deep-seated reasons why students will often not react as teachers would wish, or indeed, react positively at all to every 'opportunity' educators present them with.

3.3.4 Guidelines for the Good-Enough Teacher

If all this sounds a more downbeat account of teaching and learning than many, then so be it. Life is never simple and not always cheerful, nor can education be. Well done, however, teaching can still be immensely influential, but only when appropriate account is taken of the diverse human beings on, or with, whom it is practised.

The idea of the good-enough teacher is inspired by D. W. Winnicott's account of the 'good enough mother' (Winnicott, 1951). It is currently being developed in the work of Derek Pigrum (Pigrum, 2005). According to Winnicott, the infant has to learn, and be comfortable with the knowledge, that certain things are 'him' and certain things are 'not him'; like Kristeva later, the concern here is with the boundaries of the self. Normal identity development depends on the infant being able to trust that the mother will depart from and return to him. Abusive and unreliable parents thus render normal emotional and psychological growth impossible. On the other hand, there is no demand on the caregiver to be superhuman: as long as the mother (or her equivalent) shows an appropriate commitment to her child, the initial stages of development should proceed unproblematically. The good-enough mother ensures a secure personal space for exploration and growth for her child. Winnicott refers to this as 'potential space' in which 'transitional objects' such as teddy-bears help the child realize his subjectivity through his play with them.

Adapting Winnicott's conception for the schoolteaching context involves a degree of licence, given that schoolchildren are not neonates and classroom teaching is not 'natural' in the sense that motherhood is often construed as being. On the other hand, just as there is part of us that is always child – always experimenting and developing our ideas of self – so there is some value in seeing a classroom as a potential space in which explorations can be undertaken that further a child's sense of who he or she is. The 'good enough teacher', therefore, is charged with making the classroom such a protected space for exploration. This implies that the classroom must not be a threatening place, either because of the teacher who is overbearing or because the other students are antagonistic; so there are considerable management skills required by the 'good enough' teacher, even if this represents simply a 'lowest common denominator' view of what teaching can achieve. It is no mean achievement to have a classroom in which students are sufficiently comfortable that the curricular work they are doing is also identity work, yet a wealth of literature on 'deep learning' and related ideas shows that the best students are those who relate the subject matter to their own personal experience (developed from Marton and Saljö, 1976). This connection of 'deep learning' and identity development helps to explain how our judgements about learning and education tend to be deferred. It is not obvious at the time what the significance of a particular classroom event will be; it is rather retrospective judgment that enables us to evaluate our education. As these are relative value judgements, most will not be remembered as 'good' on this measure, but all should hope to be 'good enough'.

This being so, how might a teacher be remembered as 'good' rather than 'good enough'?

As noted above, the most basic fact about teaching is that teachers channel students' activity. Students are continuously involved in semiotic engagement: in responding to, and reacting to, the signs and signals in their environment. What they do is prompted by their contexts for action and teachers have significant control over those contexts, though less over how any individual student will respond to them. On this semiotic perspective, all students are always active. It is not a case of whether they are 'paying attention' so much as what they are paying attention to, and even simply paying attention actually involves doing something.

On this basis, I have argued elsewhere (Stables, 2005a) that good teaching should be 'activity-centred' and 'learner-aware'. The recent debate has often been cast as an opposition between 'content-centred' and 'child-centred' or 'learner-centred' approaches. From a fully semiotic perspective, however, each of these definitions entails a problem. Pragmatically, 'content' is meaningless in isolation from process. For example, the food chain or thermodynamics might form part of a science curriculum, but while understanding these concepts appears to be a matter of mastering content, on closer examination such knowledge is always knowledge of 'what happens if' and 'what happens when', for unless we understand these concepts in these ways, we do not understand them at all. Similarly, the teaching of such concepts involves sharing with students a series of actions – experiments, explanations, discussion and so on. What is at stake here is the disciplinary practice of science, not merely a series of 'facts' in isolation; indeed, facts cannot exist in isolation. As Ludwig Wittgenstein put it in the *Philosophical Investigations* (1967), understanding is effectively 'knowing how to go on' (e.g. 1967: n. 155).

  Similarly, the child, or student, is also in an ongoing process of development (as, one hopes, is the teacher). Teaching is not simply an appeal to 'what the child already is', but is rather an invitation to the child to become something more as a result of the insights she may gain from the activity. Insofar as child-centred teaching involves gearing activities to suit the way children already are, it is limited and limiting. As Vygotsky's 'zone of proximal development' suggests, teaching should always be orientated towards growth. In terms of 'pitching' the lesson, this implies that children should be repeatedly given tasks to do that they cannot yet do, and helped to do them, rather than being given tasks they can already easily undertake on the grounds that they will move on to more difficult work when they are 'ready'. (This last approach amounts to an unfortunate interpretation of Piaget's developmental theory. It is also grounded in the Aristotelian assumption that the child has preordained innate potential which teaching simply has to realize. A fully semiotic perspective denies such a fixed notion of potential.) Nevertheless, there is a danger in stating that teaching should not be child-centred in any sense. Subjecting a five-year-old to an undergraduate lecture on quantum mechanics would be foolish. An appropriate balance, therefore, is to approach teaching with a view to its being activity-centred and learner-aware, offering challenges to students that they are willing and able to confront without undue fear, and from which they have a reasonable expectation of success, bearing in mind that complete prediction of student outcomes is impossible.

  Good teaching, then, is a matter of appropriate task-setting in an appropriate working environment, where 'appropriateness' involves a sensitivity to the twin demands of disciplines (science, history, music and so on) and of students' personalities, prior knowledge and expectations. A classroom event occurs at the intersection of personal and interpersonal narratives. It is dialogical on a number of levels: dialogue between the subject and the teacher, the subject and the student, the teacher and the class as a whole, the teacher and individual students, students and other students, and students and texts, or even their own thoughts. This can be summarized in terms of three 'conditions' of classroom dialogue (Stables, 2003c.): teacher-student, between-student, and within-student. The richest classroom experiences are likely to be those that engage as many of these possibilities for dialogue as possible. The aim is that we should look back on as many such experiences as possible as having been of significance for us.

Part 4
The Child In Society

4.1

The Child and the Law

4.1.1 The Scope of the Law

This brief chapter offers a cursory overview of the differing ways in which childhood is defined by law across the world. It does not aim to be exhaustive, but rather to point to the degree of consistency and inconsistency both within and between states. It also offers a more speculative discussion on the role of legal definitions in cultural practices, where further variation may be found. This survey of the legal status of children will then form the basis for the final chapters, in which social policies relating to children will be discussed, with particular reference to education. The factual information in this chapter is drawn from a variety of sources, formal and informal, which are not individually cited; every effort has been made to ensure that these sources are current and accurate, by cross-checking where possible.

4.1.2 The Protected, Western Child: All or Nothing?

Superficially, there is not much variation in the legal age at which adulthood begins around the world: in most countries this is 18, and this appears as the norm in the U.N. Convention on the Rights of the Child. Twenty-one in Iran and 17 in Saudi Arabia represent upper and lower limits. In Britain and the USA, it is 18, but in some Canadian territories 19: hardly a dramatic contrast.

As to what 'adulthood beginning' means, there is greater variation in effect. In general, the greatest change on attaining the age of majority is that one can enter into legal contracts in one's own right. This relates not merely to business deals, but also to less obviously commercial transactions such as voting in elections, or accessing 'adult-only' films or literature. However, in certain countries, parents retain effective control over children, more or less protected by law, that renders such regulations of limited validity. Some interesting examples relate to marriage – arguably the most significant contractual arrangement most people will ever make.

Countries differ somewhat even in the legal framework around marriage. In Scotland, as in England and Wales, someone can marry with parental consent at 16 – when young people are not held responsible enough to vote – though until 1929 the age was 12 in Scotland: the old Roman law. In China, a male cannot marry until 22 (a female until 20) without parental consent. (In a number of countries, the ages are different for males and females.) On the other hand, children can marry with parental consent at puberty in Sudan and at any age at all in Brunei Darussalam. The implication in cases such as these last two is that marriage is not a contract entered into between bride and groom but between families on their behalf. Where such beliefs, which were common in the Western world in fairly recent times, still hold, some parents may feel that they are exercising their responsibilities best by arranging marriages for their children before they reach the age of majority.

Such cases reveal how conceptions of choice, freedom, duty and responsibility can vary dramatically between cultures. For example, while it is unthinkable that an infant could consent to marriage, Sudanese law insists that children who have just reached puberty, or the age of 10, must consent to their parents' choices for them. To many Western liberals, such a concept of 'consent' will seem alien. In Brazil, the normal minimum age for girls to marry (16) is waived if the girl is pregnant; given Brazil's huge cultural and geographical mix, it is possible to come up with a number of explanations of why this might be. In Iran the ages are 15 for boys and 13 for girls, with exceptions made for younger marriages if a court agrees – yet the age of majority is 21. On the other hand, young people in Sweden may not marry without special permission before 21. The point here is that a relative uniformity in legal provisions between nations may serve to conceal a huge range of cultural assumptions and practices. Even what 'marriage' means may be subject to considerable variation, as it has been through British history. It is not always assumed that it is a contract solely entered into by the husband and wife to be.

Another important area in which laws vary widely is that of employment and its converse, a protected right to education. In Brunei, where the age of majority is 18, a child is defined as under 14, and employment can begin at 16. In Sudan, employment only becomes legal at 18 and marriage without parental consent at 21. In Brunei there is no legal right to schooling; in Sudan there is eight years of schooling specified by law. In the UK, very limited employment is allowed from 13, though full employment is only allowed from 16, which is the school leaving age (likely to be raised to 18 by 2010). Again, there is a wide scale of apparent consensus on the issue, with many countries allowing full-time employment and the leaving of education from 16, with full adulthood deemed to begin at 18. Differences are often minor. For example, Belgium sets its school leaving age at 15, but insists that those between 16 and 18 engage in at least part-time education. Again, however, the differences in reality are likely to be greater than the figures suggest, particularly outside the most 'developed' nations.

Wider discrepancies occur with respect to children's protection from the criminal law. Although not held ready to vote or marry without permission, young people under the age of majority are generally held to be responsible for their crimes. In England and Wales, a child under 10 cannot be convicted of any crime. Between 10 and 14, the situation is fluid, depending on whether the court decides the child understood the consequences of his or her actions. Children (or 'young people' – use of these terms also varies from system to system) over 14 are assumed to understand the difference between right and wrong, though they will probably not receive fully adult sentences. Under this system, 10 is the official age of criminal responsibility, but this varies from country to country, even though the age of majority does not. Thus in Sweden, Finland, Denmark and Norway, the age of criminal responsibility is 15, whereas it is 18 in Belgium, 8 in Scotland, and lower than that in several countries, including a number of states of the US.

Two rather more trivial cases are those of the consumption of alcohol and the driving of cars. Teenagers in the US can drive from 14 upwards, depending on the state, but not drink in public until 21; 17 and 18 are common driving ages. Although many countries have 18 as the cut-off point for either the consumption or the purchase of alcohol, some have no limits and others ban alcohol entirely. In many countries, in Asia and (perhaps surprisingly) Australia, alcohol is only available to certain ethnic groups or in certain regions.

This brief, and by no means entirely representative, survey serves to reveal both a general pattern and a considerable degree of vagueness and potential confusion. All countries recognize an adult–child distinction in law. However, few are entirely consistent. It is evident from the range of practices that childhood is not an 'all-or-nothing' condition that suddenly stops at the agreed age of majority. (If it were, then the twenty-first birthday party would lose its meaning in Britain, for example.) The age at which one is deemed fit to vote and enter into a contract may or may not tally with the age at which you can drink, marry or be held responsible for a crime. To some extent differences between nations may reflect underlying differences in emphasis about the nature of childhood itself. For example, many Asian countries, where arranged marriage is practised, may put relatively more emphasis on *Child 1* (the child as always child of the parents) than *Child 2* (the child as person of limited age), while all acknowledge *Child 3* (the child as novice) to some extent.

It is tempting for Anglophile Westerners to condemn certain countries for being less 'advanced' in relation to, say, laws relating to marriage or sexuality more broadly. However, such perspectives are themselves reliant on certain, always questionable assumptions about childhood. Some might argue that the Liberal West, with its firm laws on freedom from the age of majority (though these are not consistent, as American regulations about alcohol illustrate), coupled with its strict regulations concerning compulsory education and employment rights and restrictions until then, almost does offer an 'all-or-nothing' view of childhood, for one moment (almost) you are child, and have everything done for you, while the next you are free and without much protection at all. By contrast, it might be asserted, there is a much more gradual and compassionate approach taken in, for example, Asian countries where respect for, and obedience to, elders may be more deeply engrained in the culture than a legal conception of either childhood or adulthood, for in such a situation, you may be protected less by the law as a child, but you are also less likely to be left to 'sink or swim' as a young adult. In such matters, there is no absolute right and wrong, however strongly one is moved by the excesses and weaknesses of any one approach. How we conceive of childhood is affected, but never entirely determined by law. 'Law' and its related concepts, including 'justice', 'protection' and 'fairness', are not entirely synonymous, and each is culturally variable.

The broader issue of how children may be treated justly forms the focus of the final chapter. Prior to that, Chapter 4.2 will consider the ramifications of a fully semiotic perspective on social policy generally before the focus returns once again to children and education.

Semiosis and Social Policy

4.2.1 Semiosis, Posthumanism, Liberalism, Pragmatism

A perspective on living and learning as semiotic engagement inevitably has implications for social policy. These are explored in general terms in this chapter, with their particular implications for children and education forming the substance of the next chapter. Whether those implications must necessarily be those developed in this chapter is an issue over which there has, as yet, been insufficient debate. There are many examples of academics employing the techniques of semiotics to understand aspects of social life, but few have attempted to develop a political and social philosophy with *semiosis* as its basis (Stables, 2006c). As the position is new, it has not, as yet, been much contested.

There are, however, certain *sine qua non* aspects of a fully semiotic perspective, as discussed more fully in Stables, 2005a and 2006c. The first of these is the 'biosemiotic' or 'pansemiotic' proposition that humans are not the only sign users. My argument here is that the sign–signal distinction cannot be a firm one. All living things, at least, respond to environmental prompts of varying complexity in both conditioned and context-specific ways. For example, we approach a new problem in ways determined by the past: by biology and habit. However, the problem is, by definition, new, so our previous experience does not determine fully how we should solve it. Even if the problem were not new 'of itself' (whatever that means), the context in which we find ourselves is always slightly different from any previous context we have been in; we are always a little older than 'last time', for example.

Thus, how an individual responds to a set of environmental sign(al)s is never entirely predictable, and is less predictable the more complex the living being – so people are certainly not entirely predictable. The political implications are as follows:

1. As human beings are not the only sign(al) users, the boundary between 'human' and 'non-human' (especially animal) is not absolute or even

clear in every respect: it is not simply a case of 'us' having minds, or consciousness, and 'them' having none. (This is not the same as claiming a person is the same as a dog!)

2. There is always an element of unpredictability and individuality in human behaviour, just as there are always shared, cultural and habitual patterns (which themselves change over time). Thus human beings are partly predictable, partly not. However, when the partly predictable is mixed with the partly unpredictable, then complete predictability is lost.

Both (1) and (2) have implications for social policy, which I develop as follows – in the absence, as yet, of competing accounts.

I take (1) as (*a*) a challenge to Humanism, and (*b*) an admission that all systems are 'open' rather than 'closed'. Just as, according to Saussure, Structuralism and Poststructuralism, the meaning of a word or sign is defined by its relations to others (all of which are shifting on the Poststructuralist account), so a person or an organization only has an identity in terms of its relations with others. From this starting point can be developed (*a*) a certain form of Posthumanist orientation towards policy and ethics: an orientation arguably much needed at a time of environmental crisis, and (*b*) a view of organizations and institutions as 'imagined communities', as discussed in Chapter 3.2.

I take (2) as an invitation to acknowledge that the power of centralized State planning is limited, and so to prefer broadly Liberal (and sometimes Libertarian rather than Social Liberal) approaches to policy over those committed to heavy social control and social engineering, including traditional Conservatism, Nationalism, Socialism and even certain manifestations of Social Democracy. This does not amount to a full political commitment to Classical Liberalism or Libertarianism, however. Classical Liberalism/ Libertarianism relies on a belief in the unique rationality of the autonomous human agent: a belief that runs counter to a semiotic perspective, according to which there is no 'mind' operating on a separate plane from the interconnected physical body.

Neither does the semiotic perspective imply a belief in the absolute freedom of the individual. It could be argued, indeed, that the individual is, in fact, determined. However, this remains simply unprovable in either direction. If we knew everything, we might be able to show that we are all determined, driven by Fate. However, as we cannot know everything, we cannot know fully how people may be determined, so determinism is an unsafe basis for policy. To all intents and purposes, it remains a matter of faith, or interpretation, whether events are unfolding to a preordained purpose or we are altering them by our own free will.

The issue here is one of what can 'work', and on this account policy is more likely to succeed when it valorizes the inevitable unpredictability of human aspirations, preferences and achievements than when it attempts to foreclose on them. Politically, though not necessarily metaphysically, this implies a Liberal-Pragmatic orientation. Even if one combines a fatalistic orientation with a fully semiotic approach, the way our fates are played out are so complex that no government could ever have sufficient command of all the facts to make predictions sound enough to ensure the success of heavily interventionist policies. Thus a law of diminishing returns inevitably operates, with ever-increasing investment in a public service, on the grounds that it will produce a desired result, showing increasingly slow progress towards that result. The alternative is to hold that policies in all areas should acknowledge individual preferences as market forces. This implies that specific policy decisions must be taken in full recognition of immediate contextual problems and so be relatively short-term, but in the context of a longer term commitment to that which cannot change: the fact that people will develop individual and partly unpredictable orientations to action. According to this argument, a society that wishes to harness its human potential to the full should value this above all other social aims, however desirable the latter seem to those in positions of political power.

In the remainder of this chapter, I shall elaborate the implications of (1) and (2) in general political terms, before exploring their implications for children and education more fully still in the next, and final, chapter.

4.2.2 Posthumanist Politics and Ethics

If *semiosis* is the fundamental truth of all existence, and human beings are dependent on other beings for their survival, then political policy must take account of the semiotic engagement of non-human life. It cannot be pursued from a narrowly Humanistic perspective. However, it has been pursued from such a perspective for some time.

Modernity, or the period of Western history since the Renaissance, has been predominantly, though by no means exclusively, Humanistic. That is to say, it has been driven by a firm belief in the particular and exalted potential of human beings, and the resulting power of human reason. At a level of extreme generality, this might be understood in terms of three different manifestations or stages: the religious Humanism of the Renaissance (the period that many commentators regard as most strongly Humanistic, as a reaction to the Medieval view of people as weak, fallen creatures), the secular Humanism of the scientific revolution, and the social Humanism of the nineteenth and twentieth centuries. These periods overlap and are rarely, if ever, mutually discrete. Throughout this time, the major opposing trend has not (in European culture, at least) been one of pantheism, or commitment to the sacredness of all life, but rather a materialistic, mechanizing tendency that has occasionally lapsed into seeing not only non-human nature, but people too, as predictable machines. However, through all the embracing of a mechanical model for the universe, science has been seen as serving the human interest and has been applied largely to further that interest.

The Renaissance Humanism evident in the portraiture and depictions of the Virgin and Child by the great Italian Masters is deeply religious. Such art aims to reveal the Divine within the human, to show how God-given grace, intelligence, feeling and beauty can reside within the human form. Furthermore, the human beings are unique in being able to alter their spiritual value through their own efforts. The sense of harmony and tranquillity that the viewer of DaVinci's *Mona Lisa* has results partly from the artist's use of light and proportion to 'draw us into' her enigmatic smile. She exudes warmth and self-containment, while the landscape which surrounds her is wild, cold and rocky. The Renaissance combined the 'rebirth' of Classical learning with Christianity to exalt the human characteristics of humility, piety, reason and grace.

The scientific revolution of the seventeenth century was also driven by a desire to understand and represent the workings of God's creation. Most so-called Enlightenment thinkers were genuinely religious; the widely held sense of opposition of science and religion is a product more of Darwin and the nineteenth and twentieth centuries than of Francis Bacon, Descartes, Newton or Locke. The Enlightenment, like the Renaissance before it, was driven not only by human curiosity but by a belief that such curiosity was God-given, that people had been given rational minds by God to understand His ways. As discussed in Chapter 3.2, this had the side-effect of reducing the status of the non-human world to that of machine: animals were seen as merely brutish and the physical universe as operating like a clock. This materialist, mechanistic worldview would fill the void left by religion in later times.

The Enlightenment project was not merely concerned with understanding the physical world, however, but also with the progress of society, though this aspect of Enlightenment was the slower to flourish. It was not until the excesses of the Industrial Revolution had been realized, in the nineteenth century, that philosophers and scientists developed a systematic social science with the intention of reducing poverty and suffering. It is such concerns that form the basis of our current dominant political movements: Social Conservatism, Social Liberalism, Social Democracy and Cultural Marxism.

All of these mainstream political movements are concerned, as are many of the 'Nationalisms' evident in the world today, with increasing, and often equalizing, the wealth of peoples. Sometimes this wealth is defined in largely pecuniary terms; sometimes broader definitions are what is at play. Either way, the underlying rationale is essentially Humanistic: it presupposes (*a*) that human life is 'sacred'; (*b*) that human beings have creative and intellectual capacities that place them above other life forms and must be nurtured; and (*c*) that human beings can self-regulate and realistically aspire to high levels of self-fulfilment. To put it crudely, most current political doctrines are 'all about people' and 'all for people'. As economic systems, both socialism and capitalism rest on Humanistic values: wealth is defined in human terms and exists for human advancement; the success of the system rests on how it generates and distributes such wealth. (See also Stables and Scott, 1999.)

On this essentially Humanistic account, 'Nature' is bifurcated. On the one hand, 'human nature' is something precious, to be nurtured and developed; on the other, (non-human) 'nature' is of value as resource – or rather resources – for humans. It was not considered by Renaissance, Enlightenment or nineteenth-century thinkers (with some early exceptions) that these resources might run out or be damaged by human activities, yet it is these latter concerns which characterize the early twenty-first century tradition. This condition is not only Postmodernist, in terms of questioning the meta-narrative of science (Chapter 1.8; Lyotard, 1984) but also Posthumanist in terms of making us question our relationships with non-human nature.

The admission of, for example, human implication in global warming begs two responses with respect to this: either we must extend and refine what we mean by nature-as-resource, or we must stop thinking of nature as merely providing resources and instead work towards a different kind of relationship with the non-human world. The latter course is that preferred by, among others, 'deep ecologists' (e.g. Naess, 2005) and some philosophers who believe that a fundamental re-thinking of the human condition is needed, such as the philosopher of education, Michael Bonnett (2003). The former course is preferred by those of more pragmatic disposition for whom it seems inevitable that we shall use the non-human as resource in various ways (including to make us feel better!), but who urge greater awareness of, and response to, the consequences of our present ways of going about this (e.g. Stables and Scott, 2001; Stables, 2008c). In the present context, it is more appropriate to draw attention to the similarities than the differences between these two approaches, for each is agreed that we can no longer afford simply to make use of natural resources as we find them, and as technology allows, even if so doing improves people's material conditions for the foreseeable future. There are hidden costs to such exploitation which must be faced.

It should be noted at this point that this is not the only formulation of Posthumanism currently in the academic arena. Indeed, the alternative orientation is, as yet, more widely disseminated and discussed. This is the view that Humanism – indeed, the human condition itself – has become problematized by technological advances, from spectacles and prosthetic limbs (is an artificial leg part of the person who wears it?) to computer interaction, virtual reality and artificial intelligence. (See, for example, Haraway, 1991; Hayles, 1999.) Interaction with technology, as well as interaction with non-human nature, problematizes Humanistic assumptions about what it means to be a human being. In the following paragraphs, this perspective will be termed 'Posthumanism 1', and that relating to ecology and nature as 'Posthumanism 2'. What implications do both of these 'Posthumanisms' have for ethics and policy from a fully semiotic perspective?

It would seem to be of little ethical or political significance whether one wears spectacles or a hearing aid. Nobody is suggesting that such things should have rights, for example, or that they may feel pain. However, the extension of technology into human action entails many such issues. What, for example, if either conventional or bio-technology were to offer certain people unfair advantage: by improving the acuteness of their senses, their mobility, their strength, or their capacity to think? This is an extension of the 'drugs problem' in sport, where there is an ongoing debate about the acceptable boundaries of 'human' performance. What if advances in bio-technology and cloning were to produce a creature that, while largely artificial, had a nervous system, so could 'feel'? Or a respiratory system? Why would classifying such a creature as 'human' or 'animal' be any less acceptable than classifying a severely ill person as human when she is only kept alive by artificial means? Are people with heart pacemakers not human?

Such considerations render problematic not merely the question of what is unique about the human, but also what is in the human interest. Machines have replaced human labourers for two hundred years. As artificial intelligence develops, the capacity for human action might become less and less. Humanism, in whatever form, may have little to offer to the debates that will increasingly arise in this area. Of course, if a machine were made identical to a human, it would be a human, and there would be no problem (otherwise it would not be identical). The problem is in defining humanity under the disruption of its boundaries. This explains why this form of Post-humanism is often termed 'Transhumanisn'. Bostrom (2005) locates the roots of this form of Posthumanism in Renaissance Humanism's belief in the capacity of human beings to better their own lives. The (largely American) Transhumanist movement is particularly concerned with the capacity of new technology to improve, as well as problematize, the human condition.

In Posthumanism 2, the emphasis is on humanity as a species among many rather than as an exalted species (Badmington, 2000). As animals – specifically mammals – the interesting question for the Posthumanist is where 'they' end and 'we' begin. Do, for example, other animals have con-sciousness or any human feelings? Do they feel pain? Do they have 'language' or do they merely 'communicate'? Is all their behaviour instinctive, and what does that mean? Do they use tools? Do animals ever 'think for themselves'?

The answers we offer to such questions determine our stance on recog-nizably ethical and political issues: issues, for example, of what, if any, rights animals should have, of whether it is acceptable to eat them, and of what should count as cruelty towards them. Unlike the issues faced by the Transhumanists, these are concerns with a much longer history. Philoso-phers including Aristotle and Kant (1724–1804) were interested in animals. Aristotle believed each animal – as each person - had its own purpose in life, some of which included being food for humans; Kant tended to see animals as passive recipients of human morality, so that cruelty to them reflects badly on the instigator because cruelty is always bad. It is not a general char-acteristic of Western thought, however, to share the 'Pre-Modern' tendency to respect the 'spirits' of non-human creatures. Animism and mechanism do not make easy bedfellows. Despite this, the environmental crisis has inevitably increased awareness of human beings' dependence on the non-human world as resource of one sort or another. Also, recent scientific thinking has been more open than previously to the possibility that certain animals do use tools and a form of language, do feel pain and can be under-stood as having consciousness.

One of the problems regarding estimations of animal intelligence is that we tend to judge it from the point of view of human utility. Stanley Coren (2007) has devised a rank order of dogs with respect to intelligence, but here 'intelligence' means obedience and responsiveness, measured by how many times an instruction has to be repeated, and how quickly it can be learnt. Many cat lovers would wish to hold to a different view of intelligence! By narrow human standards, of course, other species lack intelligence; they are not human. However, even by these standards, estimations have begun to change in recent years, as evinced, for example, by recent work with chimpanzees focusing on both tool use and capacity to learn sign language (Goodall, 1990; Fouts and Waters, 2001). Donald Griffin (2001) is one biologist who has argued that animals have conscious minds. To some extent, however, the position taken on this determines the conduct and subsequent findings of empirical research rather than *vice-versa*. Scientists can only look for evidence of animal intelligence if they hypothesize its existence. The important point for the present debate is that the question of what is distinct about the human mind remains open. We have not fully come to terms with the Darwinian insight that we are one species among many, and that even the most important differences between ourselves and other species may be of degree rather than kind.

Taken together, Posthumanist perspectives call for reappraisals of policy, of ethical frameworks and, by extension, of educational practices. The mere fact of acknowledging the validity of a Posthumanist position does not determine what these reappraisals must be, but below are offered one example of how thinking in each of these spheres might change.

The policy example concerns the use of 'greenfield' sites for housebuilding. In a small but densely populated country such as England, with a rapidly increasing population and a rich agricultural tradition, this has been an issue for some time. The narrowly Humanist perspective applied to this issue in recent years has been that the immediate human interest is not merely of paramount, but of sole importance. This interest manifests itself in two ways: a demand for houses (or 'homes' as we are comfortably told, though a house only becomes a home when we make it one), and a counterdemand to preserve the countryside as amenity. Policy has sought to balance and satisfy these two interests. A Posthumanist might argue that a third imperative exists: that of environmental improvement rather than degradation. Thus a house-building scheme, or any other plan for landscape change, might also have to respond to the following challenges: it must increase rather than decrease the biodiversity of the area in question and its surroundings; it must increase and not decrease water and air quality; its lighting schemes must not block out the night sky; it must be carbon-neutral or carbon-negative (i.e. absorbing more than it produces); it must ameliorate rather than accentuate problems of traffic and access to public services elsewhere. This is not a simple matter, of course. A colleague responded to this particular idea in the following terms:

> One issue that immediately pops into my mind is that of advantages achieved through agglomeration, and the broader question of scale.

A steelworks (if such things still exist) might fail on all these grounds but produce a net benefit in relation to all of them at a regional, national or international scale. There's also the question of timescale. At the extreme one might argue, for example, that without the industrial revolution in all its smokey, gin-soaked glory our contemporary green thought, tastes and preferences would never have developed because they are only possible once certain other kinds of human needs are satisfied, and we don't have any other historically-validated way of rendering them satisfiable. There's more than one way of theorizing this. Finally, there's the issue of opportunity cost (as ever). What if a development fails on all these grounds but contributes to a measurable reduction in infant malnutrition? This is hard to imagine in Wiltshire, but perfectly possible in Sudan or North Korea. Not sure how that plays with posthumanism! (personal communication)

Nevertheless, without the Posthumanist concern, as construed here, these considerations would not come into consideration within the policy debate at all.

Ethically, a Posthumanist orientation demands some consideration be taken of non-human interests. While this by no means requires the arguably unfeasible demands of, for example, Paola Cavalieri (2001) that we regard all species of equal value, it does, as with the house-building example, require that we balance our interests with a concern for the health of the broader biophysical community. Again, it is possible to be very glib in suggesting examples without allowing space for detailed consideration of them. Acknowledging this, consider the following passage from Stables (2005a: 19):

The question of how far such limited rights should extend can be approached by asking what a particular animal requires to live 'naturally': i.e. to respond to sign(al)s without undue coercion or frustration caused by their interactions with humans. Such rights would not extend beyond what seem to be the capacities of the animal in question, so would not extend to protection against the possibility of becoming another animal's prey, or receipt of human medical care, but may well allow such an animal extensive freedom to roam, and thus potentially avoid capture. At the same time, any such rights cannot be granted without consideration of the human context. For example, Inuit peoples rely on the killing of seals while the British feel the need to conserve them. Rabbits are more verminous in Australia than in England, so need to be controlled more ruthlessly from time to time. From the human perspective, nonhuman creatures can never exist purely in their own right. Farm animals could thus remain farm animals, and be killed and eaten, but should also enjoy quality of life, including the least possible stress prior to death. The emphasis would be on 'working with the grain', on trying to avoid the fitting of square pegs into round holes. At the same time, talk of animal rights is human talk, and, on this level at least, the human interest remains foremost in all such discussion.

A notion of limited rights can accommodate the view that humans control land use to a high degree, and are not duty-bound to provide livelihoods to other species to their own detriment. Ecologically this is potentially sound, for we need biodiversity to secure the best futures for ourselves.

The above example deserves no privileged place within the debate. As in the housebuilding case, it merely illustrates the kinds of concern that might be 'brought to the table' when environmental ethics are discussed from an avowedly Posthumanist orientation.

4.2.3 Liberal Pragmatism from *Semiosis*

A fully semiotic perspective acknowledges that individuals make meaning in individual contexts, and that this inevitably entails individual differences in meaning and interpretation. This is far from Classical Liberalism, however. In the Classical Liberal tradition, referred to by some philosophers as Lockeanism (see, for example, recent debates between Harold Noonan, 1998, and David Mackie, 1999), individual human identity depends on the presence of 'thinking substance' (Noonan, 1998: 302), such that humans are uniquely rational beings. By collapsing the sign–signal distinction, a fully semiotic perspective allows us to consider the non-human as well as the human as capable of 'meaning and interpretation', albeit an animal will never have the same experience as a human, and bearing in mind that other animals will not recognize these two human concepts. More precisely, a fully semiotic perspective allows us to attribute meaning and interpretation to animal behaviour in an attenuated sense, since the concepts do not rest on a requirement of 'thinking substance' even in the human case, and human–animal differences are of degree rather than kind. Noonan and Mackie would refer to this anti-Lockean position as 'animalist', in that it regards the human as a species of animal. On first inspection, it seems incongruous to ally such a position to the Liberal tradition.

There are two further considerations that should be taken into account, however. The first is that the fully semiotic position attempts to problematize mind–body substance dualism as far as possible, and finds the legacy of such dualism in many aspects of contemporary thought. For example, our working concept of 'animal' is rooted in the Cartesian and Newtonian dismissal of animals as no better, or more worthy of regard, than machines. On this assumption, to state that humans are 'like animals' in almost any way at all (except, perhaps, in relation to certain aspects of physical prowess) seems belittling to humans. However, this is a problem caused by Cartesianism and Newtonianism, not by animalism or a fully semiotic view. It is a long-standing problem that beset initial reactions to Darwin, and continues to beset them in some quarters. On a fully semiotic account, neither people nor animals are machines; more precisely, they are only like machines up to a point. Machines do not have nervous systems nor are they as yet anything like as complex as the simplest mammal, let alone a human.

The more complex an organism, the more unpredictable its behaviour, on the semiotic account: unpredictable to a human observer, at least. On this account, it is a tribute to the complexity of the human being that acknowledgement is made of this unpredictability. Applying this to politics and management, a leader who wishes to work with the grain of human nature will, therefore, value this unpredictability, regarding it positively as creativity, enterprise or initiative rather than negatively as ignorance or incalcitrance. The unique virtue of the Liberal tradition, among the major lines of Western political thought, is that it does value it: its belief in human freedom need not rest on any Lockean assumptions about thinking substances and autonomous rational minds. Rather, a pragmatic judgement is made that leaving people to express themselves as they best see fit will, on the whole, produce a stronger society than will forcing them into high levels of compliance and agreement.

One of the best-known philosophers of recent times to adopt such a Liberal-Pragmatic position is Richard Rorty (1931–2007). Rorty argues strongly for context-dependent, ideologically light policy making. He does not address the environmental crisis. However, it is possible to adapt his Liberal Pragmatism to the current context in that respect:

Despite his apparent anthropocentrism . . ., Rorty's pragmatism can be applied to the ecological and environmental education debates. What seems to be lacking in Rorty's work is much concern with non-human agency, consequence or need. We suggest, therefore, that the concern of Rorty and others to shatter the grander illusions of modernity should be extended to post-Enlightenment humanism, arguably the major philosophical movement underpinning modernity. A post-humanist, as well as a postmodernist, critique is called for; at the very least, a retrospective on the aims and means of modernity; at its most ambitious, a reworking of humanist assumptions with a view to greater valorisation of the non-human, though this will inevitably emanate from and respond to human concerns: for example, increasingly recognising non-human life as necessary and not just as desirable and self-renewing resource. (Stables and Scott, 2001: 277–8)

It is hard to see how such an engaged critique can be carried out in anything other than a Liberal context, broadly understood: that is, a context in which certain basic human freedoms are enshrined as rights. These basic political rights comprise those of conscience, speech and expression (including freedom of the press), assembly and association. Except where safety and security, of individuals or communities, are in real and apparent danger, these rights should remain sacrosanct, regardless of whether they are objectifiable, ultimately legitimizable, or even potentially offensive to others. As people will continue to interpret their own worlds in their own ways, politicians should have the strength to work with this as opposed to against it. After all, none of the alternatives can have absolute legitimation either. We either learn to live with others or we are at war with them.

The particular focus here, however, is on childhood rather than international relations. Children cannot enjoy full adult rights by virtue of being children. On the other hand, 'being a child' has traditionally meant 'being less than an adult' in the broadly Aristotelian tradition. A fully semiotic perspective sees children more as 'different from' than 'less than' adults, albeit they lack many adult competences. The next chapter, therefore, considers how a Posthumanist, Liberal-Pragmatic political philosophy, based on a fully semiotic view of living, might be operationalized with respect to children.

Doing Children Justice

4.3.1 Bringing it all Together:
The Child (and Adult) Then and Now

The purpose of this chapter is to bring together the conclusions drawn up to this point and to examine their implications. It has been suggested that there are three aspects of 'what it means to be a child'. *Child 1* is the off-spring of parents. We are all children in this sense, particularly while our parents remain alive. *Child 2* is the person of limited years: the infant and the youth. In Britain and many other countries, we are children in this sense from birth to 18, or perhaps 21 in certain attenuated circumstance. *Child 3* is the person as novice, as not yet ready to take a full part in society, or live a fulfilled adult life. In many places, senses *2* and *3* are strongly inter-fused, partly insofar as the legal definition of childhood is of persons not yet able to enter into contracts on their own terms. When we think of child-hood in the UK, however, we rarely think in terms of lifelong duty to parents or ancestors, though this is a much stronger element of many other cul-tures, and it is possible to have a concept of *Child 2* in which 'the child is father of the man' (See Chapter 1.7).

Previous chapters also identified cultural influences on conceptions of childhood through history. (Here, I am using 'conceptions' loosely, in that much of the historical data can only lead us to speculate about how people actually thought.) Our basic framework for thinking about childhood is Aristotelian, in that children are construed primarily as potential adults, with their own childlike characteristics, for whom the importance of nur-ture and education is to allow them to realize innate, but unfulfilled, potential. Within this broad tradition there are, however, significant varia-tions. In the extreme Protestant, or Puritan tradition, the child is spiritually impoverished, even corrupt, and upbringing consists of bringing her to the path of possible salvation. In the Liberal tradition, the child is not born so tarnished, and has the capacity for real autonomy given correct early train-ing; this is perhaps the most optimistic view of education. In the Romantic tradition, the child is pure and gifted but the adult world is sordid and mean, so the child must be kept from it for as long as possible and encouraged to use her innate creativity before worldly duties are imposed on her; this tradition bears heavily on the child-centred educational practices of the recent past. In the Postmodern, or Late Modern context, by contrast, confusions abound as longstanding assumptions about adulthood are removed; when adults no longer have a relatively settled place within a relatively settled society, the whole idea of 'bringing children up' becomes problematized, so in contemporary societies there is simultaneously evidence of a cult of youth, a sophistication of childhood, and increased anxiety concerning the safety and well-being of children.

It is possible to map the three conceptions of childhood against the five cultural and historical perspectives on childhood, noting where certain conceptions of childhood (and, indeed, the concept of adulthood) are most and least highly regarded. This presents, admittedly, a crude and generalized picture, but one that offers potential for thought about how we deal with children and how we might, or should deal with them.

In Table 4.3.1, '+' indicates a relatively strong valorization of the aspect of childhood, '–' that the aspect in question is not valorized. '?' indicates a lack of clarity.

Insofar as childhood is a preparation for adulthood, note that adulthood itself is most highly valued in the original Aristotelian and Liberal traditions: in the first, the adult as rational dutiful citizen, in the second as rational autonomous agent and citizen. Respect for the established order embodied in parents and ancestors has weakened during Modernity; even the Puritans believed that many adult souls would not be saved. The emphasis on providing protection for the person of limited years seems strongest under the Liberal and Romantic regimes, but the purposes of each are quite different. To the Liberal, good education leads to a full and satisfying adulthood, while to the Romantic the adult world is often demeaning and should be kept at bay. Since the advent of Romanticism, faith in childhood

Table 4.3.1 Conceptions of childhood (and adulthood) in cultural traditions

	Aristotle	**Puritan**	**Liberal**	**Romantic**	**Postmodern**
Child 1 (respect for forebears)	+	+	?	–	–
Child 2 (limited years, needing protection)	? (Plato x)	–	+	+	?
Child 3 (unready, unfulfilled)	+	+	+	–	?
[Adult]	[+]	[?]	[+]	[–]	[?]

as a preparation for adulthood seems to have been dented. The Postmodern, or Late Modern consciousness seems generally confused, with no overwhelming consensus of respect for either the adult condition or the various traditional senses of childhood. The greatest contrasts, overall, seem to be between the Puritan and Romantic tendencies, which differ on every count. Indeed, a legacy of this set of tensions seems apparent in the conflicting demands on contemporary children in schools made by governments supporting high-stakes testing and basic skills training (evidence of the Protestant work ethic, embodied in both Puritan and Liberal traditions), and by child-centred teachers with values heavily influenced by Romanticism, for whom such prescriptions amount to a denial of childhood.

There is an overall trend evident in Table 4.3.1: a shift of emphasis from social reproduction to social renewal; from the established order to the emerging order (though 'order' may not be the most helpful term here). If we take a more positive than negative view of the social and cultural changes of Modernity, it would seem that we have increasingly begun to value cultural reinvention more highly than cultural preservation and, whether we like it or not, the globalization and individuation of Late Modern, arguably 'Hyper', capitalism increasingly remove any possibility of an 'established order'. On this account, the dangerous people are the cultural preservers – but where does this leave institutions such as schools? As arms of the State, what educational institutions do is dependent on policy, and policy may change more slowly than the *Zeitgeist*. The next section considers appropriate responses to current conditions.

4.3.2 A New Child for a New Age: Policy and Practice

We no longer live in a Pre-Modern world of certainties, in which each individual knows his place and daily rhythms and duties are prescribed as much by the demands of the climate and season as about anything that might seem arbitrary in culture or custom. Arguably, we also no longer live in a Modern world, in which nation states can build and empower themselves on their own terms, trading with others but relatively cohesive within their own boundaries, and using education to build nationhood. Increasingly, we inhabit a globalized world in which fewer and fewer places are culturally homogeneous.

While there have always been differences between individuals and groups within a society, societies themselves are less and less homogeneous mixtures. For example, the feudal pattern of local control and patronage within a largely White, English-speaking Britain has left few traces even in the agricultural hinterlands, where even the smallest villages have become unpredictable mixes in terms of professions, places of employment, life-styles and so on, and such places are generally much less ethnically diverse than the larger cities. Even in such villages, people may scarcely know their neighbours, not as the result of misanthropy so much as out of an assumption that what other people do is their business and not ours. Meanwhile, some of these individuated inhabitants are members of extensive international networks in terms of both work and family. As Manuel Castells has argued, ours is a 'network society' rather than one governed by a sense of established place and tradition. (Castells, 1996).

Of course, there remain powerful groups who are committed to particular traditions, and children brought up in such groups may feel themselves either empowered or repressed by the experience. However, the key point here is that such groups are merely 'groups', affiliations within a various world. What were dominant cultures have become sub-cultures in the global context where, perhaps, the only dominant culture is that of corporate capitalism, and an aspect of such capitalism is the demand on individuals to keep making individual choices. Again, it is possible to see this as both negative and positive. To those who feel their cultures are being usurped by Western imperialism, it is the former; to commentators such as Francis Fukuyama, whose book *The End of History* (1992) looks forward to a time when the whole world is content to embrace Liberal values and wars between competing ideologies are no longer possible, it is the latter. Indeed, recent events such as the *Al-Qa'eda* attacks will be interpreted by some from each of these perspectives, but however extreme the example, the diagnosis regarding the underlying situation can be much the same: people with proud traditions and comprehensive value systems can no longer exist 'in their own countries' without interference from other systems. Under these conditions, how can educators – and specifically educators in broadly Liberal societies such as Britain, Europe and much of the rest of the English-speaking world – help work towards as peaceful and successful a future as possible?

There is no one obvious resolution to the tension between value-pluralism and social cohesion. Even among avowedly Liberal theorists, perspectives differ. For John Rawls, for example (e.g. 1993, 1999), it is necessary to distinguish between 'comprehensive' and 'political' values. On this account, we must respect other people's right to value systems that are fundamentally opposed to our own, but each group must allow unhindered space for others, and for individuals within them, to follow paths they may not be comfortable with. Thus, for example, acceptance of the freedom of assembly implies that no parent has any right of redress against any adult child who dishonours the family, since the political value holds sway in such circumstances over both personal belief and cultural practice, including that which is sanctioned or even demanded on religious grounds. Note how alien this would be to a society in which *Child 1* (the child as ever indebted to the parents) was valorized over the other senses of childhood. As might be expected, other Liberal theorists, such as Ronald Dworkin (2000, 2006) regard Rawls' approach as inadequate, insisting that elements of Liberalism itself must form part of the shared comprehensive value system of any tolerant and multicultural society.

One possible way of uniting these perspectives is through the argument offered by, for example, Graham Haydon (2006) that what must be fundamental to pluralistic societies is an overriding respect for persons. This entails seeing an allegiance (such as one's ethnicity or religion), an orientation (such as sexual preference, or personality type) or an attitude or belief as an aspect of a person rather than that person's totality. Thus one is never simply 'a European' or even 'an outgoing, heterosexual, Socialist Norwegian' since however many affiliations are listed, the person as a whole is always more than the sum of these. On this basis, it is possible to take a genuine interest in others, since there is always an individual story behind the affiliations that, taken alone, might define the person as a definite threat.

Notwithstanding possible Poststructuralist concerns that a person is never a 'whole' – noting that this does not prevent conceptualization of a person as more than 'a sum of her parts' – such an approach can be broadly supported by the fully semiotic perspective developed throughout this book. The fully semiotic perspective makes no assumptions about individuals as holistic persons, and would deny that personhood is ever fixed, but it does encourage us to see differences as unavoidable and people as not entirely either predictable or trainable. (See the implications of this for moral education, specifically, in Stables, 2005b.) Pragmatically, the fully semiotic approach urges that none of it is 'the same' whether we want people to be or not, so policies and practices designed to restore homogeneity can never have more than partial and temporary success.

While this may not lead us as far as a Romantic view of 'the child as father of the man', it does invite an acceptance that 'the child can never be the same as the parent'. The child is a person, not a product of one or more social forces. Of course, if one were given omniscience, one might see that the individual is determined and is not ultimately free: we do not know, as we are not granted such a 'view from nowhere' (Nagel, 1989). Even if this is accepted, however, it does not recommend determinism as a guide to policy. Although factors such as religion, ethnicity, social class and gender clearly affect who we are, we cannot simply add them together to define who we are, if only for the simple reason that we are not all-seeing and so cannot identify all the pertinent factors, let alone the relationships between them. It is not necessary, therefore, to have a firm commitment to the absolute freedom of the individual to conclude that policies based on the assumption of such a commitment might work better than those regarding people as predictable machines, if only because they acknowledge the unpredictable outcomes of social interventions.

The fully semiotic perspective insists that children are just as much 'semiotic engagers' as adults (Part 2). This has implications for the consideration of policy which will now be considered in relation to (1) legal rights and responsibilities, and (2) educational policy and practice, with reference to (*a*) provision, (*b*) organizational management, and (*c*) classroom teaching.

4.3.2.1 Rights and Responsibilities: Deference to the Other

The dominant conception of the child in the UK and similar contexts is of *Child 2* informed by *Child 3*. In other words, the child is first and foremost a person of under 18 years, on the assumption that such a person is not yet an autonomous responsible agent. Note that there are many other ways this could be approached. For example, voting rights (a mark of attaining majority) could conceivably be awarded on the attainment of a certain level of civic and political knowledge. Alternatively, everyone could be given a vote, on the grounds that it is impossible to differentiate between those who can use it wisely and those who cannot. These might be seen as different interpretations of a conception of the child as first and foremost *Child 3*, whereby age is not a determining factor. By contrast, a society dominated by a conception of *Child 1* would have the young follow the elders' instruction, so voting would be redundant in most situations.

The danger of a *Child 2* conception is that it can be all-or-nothing: the legal framework can encourage parents and others to give too little freedom to those under 18, and to leave those over 18 to 'sink or swim'. The only way to avoid this 'sink-or-swim' outcome is to ensure that education and other relevant services for young people help them to take on adult responsibilities gradually. In other words, education is about the management of risk. All conceptions of childhood agree that it is a period of preparation, and therefore of supervision by adults; indeed, there could be no concept of childhood at all without this.

This implies that the child is in some way 'less' than the adult, but the ways in which this lack is understood can vary significantly. A fully semiotic perspective, as opposed to an Aristotelian one, has the child as just as engaged with the world and goal-directed as the adult, though the goals are different. Bringing children up is not, therefore, a question of teaching them how to learn, but rather of directing actions and the contexts for action; it is a matter of getting children to try appropriate things out in appropriate contexts. What is 'appropriate' is a matter of debate, of course, and there is insufficient space here to discuss the details of curriculum. However, decisions about what is appropriate should take into account the inevitable differences in how children will approach and interpret any task and its outcome.

Therefore, while education is inevitably a form of socialization, it is better seen as socialization into an open system. From a slightly different perspective, it can be argued that the upbringing of children is not done to reproduce the world of the adult for the world they are growing into is theirs, not ours – and should be theirs. As we have seen, there has been an historical drift towards seeing childhood in terms of cultural renewal rather than reproduction. (The philosopher Hannah Arendt employs the concept of 'natality' to understand education as constantly bringing newness into the world, so that both the 'newness' and the existing 'world' play their part in educational practice, and good education is a sort of dialogue between student perception and received knowledge: Arendt, 1958, and see also Biesta, 2006.)

From this perspective, how might we best approach the issue of the rights and responsibilities due to children? In non-legal terms, 'rights' pertain broadly to protection and permission; 'responsibilities' to expectations and duties. The issue, therefore, concerns what children should be discouraged from doing and encouraged to do at certain ages, on the assumption (accepting the arguments above) that by age 17, the young person should be almost fully autonomous.

It is unfeasible to produce a watertight list of items under these headings. There might be a consensus that children should be prevented from the following, at least: self-harm, harm to others, harm from others, undue dependence, restricting ignorance, too much self-consciousness, negative attitudes, disrespect and wastefulness. On the other hand, they should be developing personal virtues, positive attitudes, responsibility and autonomy, respect for self and others and financial self-sufficiency. The list could never be fully agreed nor the full meanings of its parts – yet, however construed, it remains the case that, if we consider it necessary to define an adult, we should be able to consider what it takes to become one. At the same time, there is an ever-present danger that attempting to 'pin things down' in this way will prove reductive and counter-productive. Given the unpredictability of outcomes, the inevitable choices that are involved in catering for the child should perhaps be balanced with an ever-present awareness of the unfathomable Otherness both beyond and within the self.

Philosophers of education including Gert Biesta and Denise Egea-Kuehne (2001), and Pradeep Ajit Dhillon and Paul Standish (2000) have drawn on the Poststructuralist thinking of Jacques Derrida and Jean-Francois Lyotard, each influenced by the philosopher Emmanuel Levinas, in their construal of justice, and therefore just education, as deference towards Otherness. On the Levinasian account, when I am confronted with the face of the Other, do I accept it (as Other) or try to destroy it by assimilating it to myself? The 'good' person does the former. This means that we can never fully 'know' the Other (within ourselves as well as beyond) as complete knowledge is complete assimilation. Here we have the link between Poststructuralism and Haydon's respect for persons. Respect for persons does not imply complete knowledge of them (or of us) but an interest in them (and in ourselves) as always Other, always becoming.

There are two potentially normative conclusions from this analysis. First, adults inevitably make decisions regarding what children are and are not allowed to do (and how far children themselves can be held legally responsible), but secondly, adults should not attempt to appropriate children by turning them into reproductions of themselves. Whatever legal rights they may need, children should surely have both the right and the responsibility to develop themselves as never finished but nevertheless discrete persons. As far as the minutiae are concerned regarding what they may legally be allowed to do at certain stages, and how the law should respond to their misdemeanours, this author has neither the legal expertise nor the space available to comment, except to stress that a more thorough survey of legal provision than has been possible here might well be undertaken from an explicitly educational perspective. This would be undertaken on the premise that 17-year-olds should have rights and responsibilities commensurate with being almost but not quite adults, while infants will require more comprehensive protections without any assumptions of responsibility – and, most challengingly, there ought to be a coherent progression from the latter to the former.

Unfortunately, existing educational provision, to which we now turn, might be said to embrace an Aristotelian paternalism to a significant degree.

4.3.2.2 Education, From System to Organization

In this section, I consider education from a fully semiotic perspective, from the top down, addressing the following questions: what is (or might be) education? What is (or might be) a school? What is (or might be) good teaching? In each case, I shall contrast the broadly Aristotelian perspective that is still widely accepted with a fully semiotic one.

What education 'is' cannot be divorced from what education 'is for', and it has been discussed at great length by many philosophers, some genuinely seeking answers, others excuses for committed action. To some, as to many sociologists, the concept only makes sense within a social system premised on certain assumptions about justice and progress, such that 'education' can only be 'educational' if it is good. Widely contrasting recent examples include the analytical philosopher Richard Pring (e.g. 2004) and the radical action researcher Jack Whitehead (1993). However, if we examine the use of terms such as 'education' and 'learning' in everyday speech, or what philosophers refer to as 'ordinary language' we see uses covering a wide range of experiences, good and bad, however. Indeed, an ordinary language analysis might lead us to question whether either 'education' or 'learning' can be provided at all. What 'educational provision' really is, on this account, is the provision of schooling; whether or not people find it educational, and to what degree, is something beyond the power of providers to determine.

The central point here is a simple one, but is more often conveniently forgotten nowadays than readily acknowledged. Schools can only be understood rightly in terms of their roles within a complex social organization – they are not free-standing, either as businesses or communities – and, as such, they have a variety of functions, some pleasant and desirable and others unpleasant and to be avoided if possible. One of many implications of this is that to evaluate school effectiveness, as if (*a*) schools exist solely to educate, and furthermore education solely comprises credentialization, or measurable and predictable outcomes, and (*b*) all schools are contextually and culturally similar, is naïve in the extreme. A more philosophical way of putting this is that it is a necessary but not sufficient condition of a school that it be educational, and that it is a necessary but not sufficient condition of education that it should lead to qualifications. Furthermore, as each school deals with a separate community, or subset of society, it is a further necessary but not sufficient condition of a school that it must differ in some respects from other schools. Therefore, schools are partly educational and education is partly about getting qualifications – but there is more to education than that, and more than schools can deliver. Furthermore, schools cannot 'deliver' education in exactly the same ways as each other. Unfortunately, a common response to this imnplication involves making schools ever more accountable. It is often felt necessary to standardize them even more, for only then (it is assumed) can the criteria for judging and improving them be validated.

Schools can alternatively be understood as 'imagined communities', the meaningful existence of which cannot be derived from the way they are understood or characterized in official policy. As such, any organization – any school – only has the value that those within its 'discursive space' (Stables, 2003b) endow it with, acknowledging that actors' perceptions do not all carry equal weight in terms of cultural, social or any other form of capital. (Pierre Bourdieu, 1997, distinguishes these 'forms of capital'. At the risk of over-simplification: cultural capital includes what you know, social capital includes who you know, economic capital includes what you own – and so on. Being well off with respect to one form of capital tends to result in increases in other sorts.) Ultimately, what people think or feel about a school, or about education more generally, will constitute its reality. By extension, its 'effectiveness' or capacity to deliver 'added value' cannot be convincingly externally measured.

Furthermore, to make this point about schools at the purely organizational level is to make it only half-heartedly. Schools are, indeed, somewhat unpredictable and diverse organizations, and are in some senses open systems even if they claim not to be so, as was discussed in Chapter 3.2. By the same token, educational systems as a whole are unpredictable and unstable, as are individual learners, lessons and even facts and instances. That is to say, each person encounters each new situation as a new context, a new combination of circumstances. Thus what each person makes of each new situation involves both an element of predictable, conditioned response and an element of original, context-dependent, unpredictable meaning-making – irrespective of whether people are held to have any meaningful capacity to 'think for themselves' in the sense assumed within Classical Liberalism. When the predictable is combined with the unpredictable, the outcome is unpredictable. Education is therefore unpredictable, as are schools.

In terms of our everyday assumptions and understandings, schools might be held to have three major, and often overlapping social functions: protection, education and socialization.

First, schooling protects the young and vulnerable from exploitation and the exigencies of economic life, to some degree. Infants, of course, are clearly physically, as well as socially and economically dependent, and are generally cared for in the home. As was noted in Chapter 3.2, the very possibility of attending school requires some degree of autonomy, however, for to manage at school demands being to manage without the direct physical and emotional support of your parents. Most schoolchildren can hardly be described as physically dependent, insofar as they can move, eat, dress, shelter and so on without adult help. Rather, they exist in an intermediate age between physical dependency and adult independence, increasingly socially independent but persistently financially so. Indeed, societies such as the UK have continued to stretch this period of financial dependence, not merely by extending compulsory schooling but, most recently, by removing student grants for higher education. Most 18 to 21-year-olds are now dependent adults, able to vote, move without restriction, marry, drive and so on, yet dependent on parental income for fees, food, clothing and accommodation. Forty years ago, university students (then far fewer in number) were more financially independent, insofar as they received state income, while remaining legally children until 21.

Why has this intermediate period been so stretched? The positive justification is that it increases credentialization and boosts skill levels in the economy, deemed essential for the survival of the most developed countries in a globalized world (e.g. Brown, 1999). However, there may also be an economic flip-side, as discussed earlier (Chapter 3.2). In a period in which (for example) young people are increasingly to be responsible for their own pensions, the long intermediate age of effectively compulsory schooling and strongly encouraged higher education both delays the accrual of salaried income and defers the motivation to save. It is ironic, and possibly dangerous, for a capitalist society to discourage young people from saving and investment; doubly ironic to spend longer teaching them about things they are actively discouraged from doing.

This leads us to the second, and central (it is often supposed) educational function of schools. 'You go to school to learn' is a truism, but it is a very partial truth. Everyone learns by being alive, in all contexts, all the time. The person suffering sensory deprivation learns to hold her breath; the elderly learn patience, forbearance and acceptance; the street child may learn advanced computational skills. Nunes et al. (1993), for example, studied street children in Brazil, focusing on how school mathematics can complement the understandings they develop through plying their trade. We learn what we can do and what we cannot do. Schools manage children's time and activity, and thus channel their learning. While this may include practising study skills or critical thinking, or coming to understand how factors such as nutrition and exercise can affect brain function, all this can be explained in terms of schools channelling learning rather than enhancing the capacity to learn.

Is there, in fact, any such capacity? I doubt it. The fully semiotic position holds that 'learning' is essentially a matter of retrospective judgement on certain experiences, and not a qualitatively distinct existential or biophysical state. (See Stables 2005a, Section 2). In other words, we cannot live without learning; there is nothing distinctive about 'learning behaviour' as it is happening.

Indeed, sometimes 'learning' is remembered as simply leading to existential change that is not even for the better. The person who, engrossed in the theory of education, is hit by an unseen passing car, may learn to pay more attention – or may learn a fear of cars. Either way, the learning involves no conscious effort or even awareness, and is certainly not the result of a positive experience. It is ironic, therefore, that mainstream philosophy of education claims to ground in 'ordinary language' the working assumption that 'education' always relates to positive value and progress. In fact, in ordinary language, 'education' and 'learning' are often terms used in reference to difficult, painful, negative, or even intractable situations. Even the fact that repeated practice tends to bring about improved performance does not of itself warrant a distinction between learning and other forms of living. Indeed, from this perspective, learning is inevitable: repeated actions often become faster and more efficient. Educational programmes channel human activity, often resulting in feelings of having learnt, but it cannot be shown that they enhance it. By the same token, the 'learning theory' that can be called upon to give import and lend respectability to much educational theorizing and policy making seems rather an empty vessel.

The education and socialization functions of schooling overlap in effect. After all, no knowledge exists completely irrespective of a social context, and part of the popular justification for schooling is that you 'need' to learn what you learn in school. Given the efforts to construct and control the curriculum (which Lawton has described as 'a selection from the culture': 1973), and given that failure to attend school means missing out on what others are learning, this must in part be true: ignorance is, and begets, social isolation.

On the other hand, by protecting young people against the real consequences of their actions – which are themselves highly constrained – school can isolate students from society. By denying or restricting personal wishes, ambitions, aspirations, interests, beliefs and preferences in favour of standard exercises with little or no perceivable immediate personal or social consequence, school could be held to deny the most valuable opportunities for learning. A great deal of knowledge (if not all) is knowledge of 'what happens if' or 'what happens when': we understand everything through an understanding of its effects and context. (To quote Charles Sanders Peirce: 'Consider what effects, which conceivably might have practical bearings, we conceive the object of our conception to have. Then our conception of these effects is the whole of our conception of the object', in Urmson and Rée, 1989: 256.) School, arguably, restricts the development of such understanding with respect to what motivates young people (who, let us recall, are largely socially independent of teachers and parents).

There is arguably a broader sense in which school can be viewed as socializing. That is, it makes us 'get on' with a wide range of people we may not otherwise have encountered, let alone chosen to encounter. Again, this must be true to some extent. On the other hand, by being at school, one of the things one is socialized into is school itself. As Edwards and Mercer (1987) have put it, within the school context much principled knowledge is received as purely procedural knowledge. That is, we learn at school how to get by with the teacher. Furthermore, studies of interaction sets show that it is quite possible, if not inevitable, that children in school will operate within numerically limited groups, sometimes of like-minded children. For example, Paul Willis's famous study of working class boys (1977) shows how such boys negotiate(d) school as a coherent yet subversive cultural subgroup.

So what should the future be for compulsory schooling? At present, the official policy drift is towards ever more emphasis on schools: their funding, governance, management, intakes and admissions, curriculum, teaching standards, facilities and resources, student outcomes and levels of attendance. Performance is closely monitored, by a number of methods, both quantitative and qualitative. For the 5–16 age group (in UK – and similar elsewhere), 'schooling' is effectively synonymous with 'education', insofar as school is where education is assumed and deemed to happen, and school is effectively compulsory. Shortly before the time of writing, British Chancellor of the Exchequer, Gordon Brown, pledged Britain to help developing countries achieve universal schooling, thus cementing the commitment to schooling on the overseas development as well as the domestic agenda.

However, while increased, even compulsory schooling, may well be welcomed as an uncontroversial step forward for many countries at certain points in their histories, this surely depends on the *status quo*. It does not render such schooling an unqualified good for all societies in all situations. Every social innovation has its day. The situation in countries lacking basic material provisions, social infrastructure and widespread literacy and numeracy is very different from that in largely affluent, pluralistic states. In the latter, future thriving in the global marketplace depends on an initiative-taking, autonomous (while socially aware) citizenry with a commitment to lifelong learning. We might at least consider that this may not come about through sustaining the belief that you go to school to learn when you are young (protected by the state), then work at much the same job until your sixties (funding yourself, but paying taxes), then retire on state, and other accrued benefits to enjoy a prolonged period of old age. Schooling, as we understand it, is part of a package of such old certainties, and, thus construed, there may be little point in making them ever more 'effective'. The first step in deciding how to handle their legacy must surely involve a more dispassionate investigation into their actual 'effects'. Unfortunately, there will inevitably be many who, perhaps unthinkingly, line themselves up against radical reconfiguration. Their ranks might even include a good number of educational professionals, for, as with any social change, a move away from compulsory schooling might remove power, as well as occupational certainty, from many.

This is not to argue that educational expertise is of no value – far from it. Nevertheless, the more we learn about learning, the more we realize that compulsory, formal school may not always be the best place to do it. In the long term, therefore, perhaps we should not simply be envisaging societies in which all young people enjoy extensive schooling, at least beyond an elementary level, but rather one in which life-trajectories are varied and as self-directed as possible, while a variety of educational provision is available for people to access in ways appropriate to their particular circumstances. There would doubtless be successors to our schools, where young people could come together, both for mutually agreed useful reasons and also so that their parents could go about their (other) business unencumbered by them, but this would be a society in which being a parent, as with being a student, would carry great responsibility, for there would no longer be a universal standard expectation regarding either children's current experiences or their eventual qualifications.

Although the above argument may seem radical, there are, I believe, some signs of a policy drift in this direction. Perhaps current UK policy, for example, for all its rhetoric about school effectiveness, standards and so on, is veering in this direction to some extent, in any case, by loosening and broadening both the concept of school itself (abandoning the 'one-size-fits-all' approach for one that is 'post-comprehensive') and the post-14 curriculum, allowing for greater differentiation and individualization.

In the short term, however, we have compulsory schooling and many unacceptable consequences would arise from suddenly removing it. Policy, however, must have a 'steer'. If the elimination, or reduction, of compulsory schooling were the long-term aim, what short-term policies might seem appropriate? Perhaps:

1. We might expect to find increased encouragement for schools to differ from each other, and decreased incentive for them all to be the same. In England, there has been a significant move to specialist schools during the early 2000s. ('Specialist schools are an important part of the Government's plans to raise standards in secondary education. The target of 2000 specialist schools has already been met 18 months early in February 2005'. www.standards.dfes.gov.uk/specialistschools, accessed 24 April 2006.)

2. We might expect to find increased emphasis on both parent and student choice. Such has been the commitment of both government and opposition in England/Britain for some time, and it remains a highly publicized, if still somewhat controversial, potential vote-catcher. (Up to 600,000 extra school places would be created to give parents in England more choice under new Tory plans.' http://news.bbc.co.uk/1/hi/uk_politics, accessed 24 April 2006.)

3. We might expect decreased centralized control over the curriculum. Here, the current situation in the UK is mixed. The Strategies for Literacy, Numeracy and subsequently Key Stage 3 (ages 11–14) have increased prescription in England, while proposals for 14–19 follow other recent initiatives (such as the removal of modern languages from the core curriculum) in increasing variety and choice. (See www.standards.dfes.gov.uk/keystage3/ and www.qca.org.uk/14-19), accessed 24 April 2006.)

4. We might expect a shift in officially sanctioned research priorities from a concern with the effectiveness and improvement of schools (with respect to external and supposedly objective standards) to a concern with the actual effects of schooling on the range of current and subsequent human experience, to achieve a better understanding of the effects schools actually have, across a much broader canvas. This is not evident as such. However, the intense emphasis on 'school improvement' and then 'school effectiveness' research during the 1980s and 1990s seems to have dissipated somewhat, although it is difficult to find appropriate evidence to confirm or deny this.

In conclusion, although certain changes post-2000 have continued to standardize and restrict variety (relating to school attendance and governance, for example), there is some evidence to suggest that the overall policy drift has been towards a deconstruction of what had become the accepted notion of 'school' in the UK. If policy makers, here and elsewhere, have the courage to continue in this direction, they will, at some point, have to confront the issue of the imposed and standardized curriculum – the expectations for young people to follow the same curriculum and gain the same qualifications, as well as attend the same kind of institution – and schools themselves will become increasingly responsible for attracting and retaining students, while being decreasingly subject to external forms of assessment, evaluation and demands to 'improve'.

Who knows how much of this current policy-makers have in mind. Within a Liberal society, a degree of trading-off between individual freedom and contracted constraint remains inevitable, though the degree to which it should affect the education of the young is by no means so clear: schooling has not always been part of the social contract. To illustrate the range of possibilities, a future state committed to comprehensive Liberalism would insist on all children being brought up according to Liberal values, implying a degree of (benevolent) prescription in educational matters, while (merely) political Liberalism insists on only a minimal view of the state in granting rights of association, belief and speech to adults and a limited form of rights to children. In a genuinely multicultural, globalized world, the challenge to achieve the latter may itself be great, while to attempt the former may be a step too far. Either way, the first task may be to free our thinking from a still largely Aristotelian set of assumptions.

4.3.2.3 Getting the Best From Our Classrooms

Whatever the arguments, there is no danger whatever of schools disappearing in the short term, or attendance at them becoming voluntary. Whatever their 'effectiveness', academic standards, or even desirability, they are an integral part of the existing social structure throughout the world. Although it is ridiculous to suggest that schools exist merely for child-minding, it is nevertheless the case that their function simply in keeping children out of the way while adults continue economic life in their absence is absolutely indispensible.

Chapter 3.3 considered how best teachers might use their time in classrooms, from a fully semiotic perspective. The following remarks serve as a final conclusion to this extended consideration of what children are conceived to be, and of how we might deal with them, particularly during that extended time that they are required to spend in classrooms.

First, children are as alive as adults; they are not learning to be alive, but live fully, interpreting the signs and signals for their environments in their own ways, drawing on the resources of the culture and adapting them to their own ends. They do not need to be taught to learn, or to know what to do. Childhood is not a preparation for life itself. However, they do need to be introduced to various aspects of the culture, and to legitimate ways of critiquing them, and they do need to learn both ways of thinking and the consequences their actions will produce. Thus a good education will combine rich experience with induction into disciplinary processes, such as moral reasoning and scientific enquiry. As, for example, Michael Young has stressed (2008), most children do not have access to certain socially powerful traditions, such as that of empirical science, other than through schooling – a point that deserves serious attention in any 'deschooling' argument, though no versions of the latter would do away with educational provision for those who want it.

Secondly, given that terms such as 'education' and 'learning' do not have clear and unambiguous meanings, and that experiences of them both vary and are very hard to locate and evaluate precisely, to base the effectiveness of educational interventions on simple outcome measures, such as test results, is shallow and itself ineffective. Rather, teachers should aim to help their pupils to experience significant events, given that the personal significance of something can be apparent either 'at the time' or only in retrospect. Of course, no teacher can make every hour of school life 'special', but the more teaching poses challenges to students, within an appropriately protective environment, the more it will enable them to rethink themselves and their position in the world. However, for an educational event to be significant, the child must (*a*) be presented with something about the culture, (*b*) be able to 'map' that knowledge onto her own experience, (*c*) be able to do something with that knowledge that has real consequences for her, and (*d*) be able to see how those consequences inform her responses to subsequent challenges. In other words, being a student in a classroom should feel like being a real person (not a person waiting to be real) doing real things (not 'learning activities' simply to gain a qualification) with real effects on self-identity, in all its possible forms. If the current culture of schools and classrooms is too narrow to deliver this, we should rethink it.

As a final thought, to acknowledge that the child is as much an engaged person as the adult is also to acknowledge that the adult is as much a player and an explorer as the child. One of the greatest failings of a worldview that conceptualizes children as less than adults is that it debars adults from everything that might be good about children. In our dealings with other adults – as friends, lovers, colleagues, managers – we would do well to remember that they, too, are engaged in ongoing identity projects, dependent on play, challenge, appropriate levels of protection and the management of risk. If our children do not live in an Aristotelian society of fixed roles and expectations, then nor do we. The shame is that all of our lives are sometimes held back by a sense that the way Aristotle described it is the way it ought to be. There are, indeed, plenty of things that we can learn from history, but one of them should be that what happened in the past does not fully determine what will happen next. We do not so much bring children up as help them change the world.

Bibliography

Abdullah, M. S. N. (2007), *Reframing Pluralism for Moral and Citizenship Education in Malaysia* (University of London Institute of Education unpublished PhD thesis).

Adorno, T. (1970), *Aesthetic Theory* (Minneapolis: University of Minnesota Press).

Alanen L. and Mayall, B. (eds) (2001), *Conceptualising Child–Adult Relations* (London: RoutledgeFalmer).

Althusser, L. (1971), *Lenin and Philosophy and Other Essays* (London: NLB).

Anderson, B. (1983), *Imagined Communities: Reflections on the Origin and Spread of Nationalism* (London: Verso).

Anderson, M. (1980), *Approaches to the History of the Modern Family* (Basingstoke: Macmillan).

Arendt, H. (1958), *The Human Condition* (Cambridge: Cambridge University Press).

Ariès, P. (1962) *Centuries of Childhood* (New York: Vintage).

Arnesen, R. (2002), Equality of Opportunity, in *Stanford Encyclopedia of Philosophy*, online at http://plato.stanford.edu, accessed 15 March 2008

Arnold, M. (1882), *Culture and Anarchy* (New York: Macmillan).

Austin, J. L. (1962), *How to Do Things with Words* (Oxford: Oxford University Press).

Badmington, N. (ed.) (2000), *Posthumanism* (New York: Palgrave).

Barthes, R. (1977), *Image/Music/Text* (London: Fontana).

Baumann, Z. (2000), *Liquid Modernity* (Cambridge: Polity).

Beck, U. (1992), *Risk Society: Towards a New Modernity* (London: Sage).

Benjamin, W. (1968), 'The Storyteller' (trans, Zom, H.), in H. Arendt (ed.), *Illuminations* (Cambridge, MA.: Harvard).

Berger, P. L. and Luckmann, T. (1966), *The Social Construction of Reality: A Treaty in the Sociology of Knowledge* (New York: Irvington).

Biesta, G. (2006), *Beyond Learning: Democratic Education for a Human Future* (St. Paul, MN: Paradigm).

Biesta, G. and Egea-Kuehne, D. (2001), *Derrida and Education* (London: Routledge).

Bonnett, M. (2003), Special Issue: 'Retrieving nature: education for a post-humanist age', *Journal of Philosophy of Education*, 37(4).

Bostrom, N. (2005), 'A history of transhumanist thought', *Journal of Evolution and Technology*, 14(1), available on line at http://jetpress.org/volume14/bostrom.html

Bourdieu, P. (1991), *Language and Symbolic Power* (Cambridge, MA: Harvard).

Bourdieu, P. (1997), 'Forms of capital', in A. H. Halsey, H. Lauder, P. Brown and A. Stuart Wells (eds), *Education: Culture, Economy, Society* (Oxford: Oxford University Press), 46–58.

Brentano, F. (1874), *Psychology from an Empirical Standpoint* (London: Routledge and Kegan Paul).

Brown, P. (1999), 'Globalisation and the political economy of high skills', *Journal of Education and Work*, 12(3), 233-51.

Bruner, J. (1983), *Child's Talk: Learning to Use Language* (New York: W. W. Norton & Company).

Buckingham, D. (2000), *After the Death of Childhood: Growing Up in the Age of Electronic Media* (Cambridge: Polity).

CACE (Central Advisory Council for Education, England) (1967), *Children and Their Primary Schools* ('The Plowden Report') (London: HMSO).

Castells, M. (1996), *The Rise of the Network Society* (Oxford: Blackwell).

Cavalieri, P. (2001), *The Animal Question: Why Non-Human Animals Deserve Human Rights* (Oxford: Oxford University Press).

Charles, S. and Lipovetsky, G. (2005), *Hypermodern Times* (Cambridge: Polity).

Coren, S. (2007), www.stanleycoren.com

Corson, D. (1988), 'Making the language of education policies more user-friendly', *Journal of Education Policy*, 3(3), 249–60.

Culler, J. (1976), *Saussure* (London: Fontana).

Cunningham, H. (1995), *Children and Childhood in Western Society Since 1500* (New York: Longman).

Cunningham, H. (2006), *The Invention of Childhood* (London: BBC).

Deleuze, G. and Guattari. F. (1994), *What is Philosophy?* (New York: Columbia University Press).

DeMause, L. (ed.) (1974), *The History of Childhood* (New York: Psychohistory Press).

Deng, Z. (2007), 'Knowing the subject matter of a secondary school science subject, *Journal of Curriculum Studies*, 39(5), 503–36.

Derrida, J. (1976), *Of Grammatology* (Baltimore: Johns Hopkins University Press).

Derrida, J. (1978), *Writing and Difference* (London: Routledge).

Derrida, J. (1982), *Margins of Philosophy* (Brighton: Harvester).

Derrida, J. (1992), *Acts of Literature* (New York: Routledge).

Descartes, R. (ed. Cottingham, J.) (1996), *Meditations* (Cambridge: Cambridge University Press).

Dewey, J. (1896), 'The reflex arc concept in psychology', *Psychological Review*, 3, 357–70.

Dewey, J. (1897), *My Pedagogic Creed* First published in *The School Journal*, LIV(3), 77–80.

Dewey, J. (1902), *The Child and the Curriculum*

Dewey, J. (1912), 'Perception and organic action', *The Journal of Philosophy, Psychology and Scientific Methods*, 9(24), 645–69.

Dewey, J. (1915/1944), *The School and Society* (Chicago: University of Chicago Press).

Dewey, J. (1916), *Democracy and Education* (Toronto: Macmillan).

Dewey, J. (1925), *Experience and Nature* (La Salle, IL: Open Court).

Dewey, J. (1928), 'Progressive education and the science of education', *Progressive Education*, 5, 197–204.

Dewey, J. (1929), *Impressions of Soviet Russia and the Revolutionary World, Mexico-China-Turkey* (New York: New Republic).

Dewey, J. (1940), *Education Today* (New York: Putnam).

Dewey, J. (1951), (ed. P. A. Schilp) *The Philosophy of John Dewey* (New York: Tudor).

Dewey, J. (1952), Introduction, in Clapp, E. R. *The Use of Resources in Education* (New York: Harper).

Dhillon, P. A. and Standish, P. (2000), (eds) *Lyotard: Just Education* (London: Routledge)

Dworkin, M. (1959), *Dewey on Education: Selections* (New York: Teachers College Press).

Dworkin, R. (2000), *Sovereign Virtue: The Theory and Practice of Equality* (Cambridge, MA: Harvard).

Dworkin, R. (2006), *Justice in Robes* (Cambridge, MA: Harvard).

Edwards, D. and Mercer, N. (1987), *Common Knowledge: The Development of Understanding in the Classroom* (London: Methuen).

Elias, N. (1978), *The History of Manners. The Civilising Process, Vol. 1* (New York: Pantheon).

Emmeche, C. (1999), 'The biosemiotics of emergent properties in a pluralist ontology', in E. Taborsky (ed.), *Semiosis, Evolution, Energy: Towards a Reconceptualisation of the Sign* (Aachen: Shaker Verlag), 89–108.

Epstein, R. (1995), *Simple Rules for a Complex World* (Cambridge, MA: Harvard).

Epstein, R. (2007), Let's abolish high school. Education Week. Retrieved April 18, 2007, from www.edweek.org/ew/articles/2007/04/04/31epstein.h26.html

Fairclough, N. (1995), *Critical Discourse Analysis* (London: Longman).

Foucault, M. (1979), *Discipline and Punish: The Birth of the Prison* (New York: Vintage).

Fouts, R. S. and Waters, G. (2001), 'Chimpanzee sign language and Darwinian continuity: Evidence for a neurology continuity of language', *Neurological Research*, 23, 787–94.

Fukuyama, F. (1992), *The End of History and the Last Man* (New York: Penguin).

Gatto, J. T. (2003), *The Underground History of American Education* (New York: The Oxford Village Press).

Gee, J. P. (2003), *What Video Games Have to Teach Us About Learning and Literacy* (New York: Palgrave).

Giddens, A. (1991), *Modernity and Self-Identity in the Late Modern Age* (Palo Alto, CA: Stanford University Press).

Giddens, A. (1998), *The Third Way: The Renewal of Social Democracy* (Cambridge: Polity).

Goldberg, B. (1996), *Why Schools Fail* (Washington, DC: Cato Institute).

Goodall, J. (1990), *Through a Window* (Boston: Houghton Mifflin).

Goodman, P. (1960), *Growing Up Absurd: Problems of Youth in the Organized System* (New York: Random House).

Goodman, P. (1964), *Compulsory Miseducation* (New York: Horizon).

Green, A. (1990), *Education and State Formation* (Basingstoke: Macmillan).

Green, A. (1997), *Education, Globalisation and the Nation State* (Basingstoke: Macmillan).

Griffin, D. R. (2001), *Animal Minds: Beyond Cognition to Consciousness* (Chicago: University of Chicago Press).

Guyer, P. (ed) (1992), *The Cambridge Companion to Kant* (Cambridge: Cambridge University Press).

Habermas, J. (1984/ 1987), *Theory of Communicative Action, Vols. 1, 2* (Cambridge: Polity).

Haraway, D. (1991), *Simians, Cyborgs, and Women: The Reinvention of Nature* (New York, Routledge).

Harré, R. (1979), *Social Being: A Theory for Social Psychology* (Oxford: Blackwell).

Harré, R. (1983), *Personal Being: A Theory for Individual Psychology* (Oxford: Blackwell).

Harré, R. and van Langenhove, L. (1999), *Positioning Theory: Moral Contexts of International Action* (Oxford: Blackwell).

Hawking, S. (2001), *The Universe in a Nutshell* (New York: Bantam).

Haydon, G. (2006), *Education, Philosophy and the Ethical Environment* (London: RoutledgeFalmer).

Hayek, F. von (1960), *The Constitution of Liberty* (Chicago: University of Chicago Press).

Hayles, K. (1999), *How We Became Posthuman* (Chicago: University of Chicago Press).

Holt, J. (1974), *Escape from Childhood* (New York: Dutton).

Hourd, M. (1949), *The Education of the Poetic Spirit* (Oxford: Heinemann).

Hoyles, M. (Ed.), (1979), *Changing Childhood* (London: Writers & Readers Publishing Cooperative).

Hutchinson, T. (1973), *The Poetical Works of Wordsworth* (Oxford: Oxford University Press).

Illich, U. (1970), *Deschooling Society* (New York: Harper and Row).

James, A. and Prout, A. (1997), *Constructing and Reconstructing Childhood* (London: Routledge).

Kress, G. (2003), *Literacy in the New Media Age* (London: Routledge).

Kristeva, J. (1982), *Powers of Horror: An Essay on Abjection* (New York: Columbia University Press).

Lanham, R. A. (1993), *The Electronic Word: Democracy, Technology and the Arts* (Chicago: University of Chicago Press).

Lawton, D. (1973), *Social Change, Educational Theory and Curriculum Planning* (Buckingham: Open University Press).

Leavis, F. R. (1930), *Mass Civilisation and Minority Culture* (Cambridge: Minority Press).

Locke, J. (first published 1692), *Some Thoughts Concerning Education* (Modern History Sourcebook). Retrieved June 20, 2008, from www.fordham.edu/halsall/mod/1692locke-education.html

Lyotard, J-F. (1984), *The Postmodern Condition: A Report on Knowledge* (Manchester: Manchester University Press).

Lyotard, J-F. (1988), *The Differend: Phrases in Dispute* (Minneapolis: University of Minnesota Press).

Mackie, D. (1999), 'Animalism vs. Lockeanism: no contest', *The Philosophical Quarterly* 49, 369–76.

MacPherson, C. P. (ed.) (1980), *Hobbes: Leviathan* (London: Penguin).

Mann, C. C. (2005), *New Revelations of the Americas Before Columbus* (New York: Alfred A. Knopf).

Maran, T. (2006), 'Where do your borders lie? Reflections on the semiotical ethics of nature' in C. Gersdorf and S. Mayer (eds), *Beyond Wild Nature: Transatlantic*

Perspectives on Ecocriticism. (in the series 'Nature, Culture and Literature'), (Amsterdam: Rodopi).

Marshall, J. (2000), 'Thomas Hobbes; education and governmentality', *Encyclopedia of Philosophy of Education,* available online at www.vusst.hr/ENCYCLOPAEDIA/hobbes.htm

Marton, F. and Saljö, R. (1976), 'On qualitative differences in learning I – outcome and process', *British Journal of Educational Psychology,* 46, 4–11.

Matthews, G. B. (1994), *The Philosophy of Childhood* (Cambridge, MA: Harvard University Press).

McAfee, N. (2004), *Julia Kristeva* (London: Routledge).

Mintz, S. (2004), *Huck's Raft: A History of American Childhood* (Cambridge, MA: Harvard).

Naess, A. (2005), Special Edition, *The Trumpeter Journal of Ecosophy,* 21(2).

Nagel, T. (1989), *The View from Nowhere* (Oxford: Oxford University Press).

Noonan, H. W. (1998), 'Animalism *versus* Lockeanism: a current controversy', *The Phlosophical Quarterly,* 48(192), 302–18.

Nozick, R. (1974), *Anarchy, State and Utopia* (Oxford: Blackwell).

Nunes, T., Schliemann, A., and Carraher, D. (1993), *Street Mathematics and School Mathematic* (New York: Cambridge University Press).

Opie, P. and Opie, I. (2001), *The Lore and Language of Schoolchildren* (New York: New York Review of Books). Piaget, J. (1954), *Intelligence and Affectivity: Their Relationship During Child Development* (Palo Alto, CA: Annual Review).

Pigrum, D. (2005), *Das Gegenwerk and the notion of the "good enough teacher."* Paper presented at the Philosophy of Education Society of Great Britain, Oxford University, New College.

Plato (trans. H. D. P. Lee) (1987), *The Republic* (Harmondsworth: Penguin).

Pollock, L. (1983), *Forgotten Children: Parent-Child Relations From 1500 to 1900* (Cambridge: Cambridge University Press).

Poster, M. (ed.) (1988), *Jean Baudrillard: Selected Writings* (Palo Alto, CA.: Stanford University Press).

Postman, N. (1993), *Technopoly: The Surrender of Culture to Technology* (New York: Vintage).

Postman, N. (1994), *The Disappearance of Childhood* (New York: Vintage).

Pring, R. (2004), *Philosophy of Educational Research* (London: Continuum).

Rawls, J. (1971), *A Theory of Justice* (Cambridge, MA: Belknap Press).

Rawls, J. (1993), *Political Liberalism* (New York: Columbia University Press).

Rawls, J. (1999), *The Law of Peoples* (Cambridge, MA: Harvard).

Rawls, J. (2001), *Justice as Fairness: A Restatement* (Cambridge: Cambridge University Press).

Richman, S. (1994), *Separating School and State* (Fairfax, VA: Future of Freedom Foundation).

Roemer, J. (1995), 'Equality and responsibility', *Boston Review,* April/May, 3–7.

Roemer, J. (1998), *Equality of Opportunity* (Cambridge: Cambridge University Press).

Roemer, J. (2002), 'Equality of opportunity: a progress report', *Social Choice and Welfare,* 19(2), 455–71.

Ross, M., Radnor, H., Mitchell, S. and Brierton, C. (1993), *Assessing Achievement in the Arts* (Buckingham: Open University Press).

Rothbard, M. N. (1978), *For a New Liberty: The Libertarian Manifesto* (San Francisco: Fox and Wilkes).

Rousseau, J-J. (1991), *Émile, or on Education* (London: Penguin).

Russell, B. (1945/1972), *History of Western Philosophy* (New York: Simon and Shuster).

Sanders, B. (1994), *A is for Ox* (New York: Vintage).

Savery, W. (1951), 'The significance of Dewey's philosophy', in P. A. Schilpp (ed.), *The Philosophy of John Dewey* (La Salle, IL.: Open Court), 479–514.

Schama, S. (1997), *The Embarrassment of Riches* (New York: Vintage).

Sebeok, T. A. (1995), 'Semiotics and the Biological Sciences: Initial Conditions', *Discussion Papers* 17 (Budapest: Collegioum Budapest, Institute for Advanced Study).

Shahar, S. (1990), *Childhood in the Middle Ages* (London: Routledge).

Shields, P. R. (1998), 'Some reflections on respecting childhood', *The Journal of Value Inquiry*, 32, 369–80.

Shorter, E. (1976), *Making of the Modern Family* (London: Collins).

Stables, A. (1996), 'Paradox in educational policy slogans: evaluating equal opportunities in subject choice', *British Journal of Educational Studies*, 44(2), 159–67.

Stables, A. (2003a), *Education for Diversity: Making Differences* (Aldershot/New York: Ashgate).

Stables, A. (2003b), 'School as imagined community in discursive space: a perspective on the school effectiveness debate', *British Educational Research Journal*, 29(6), 895–902.

Stables, A. (2003c), 'Learning, identity and classroom dialogue', *Journal of Educational Enquiry*, 4(1) (www.unisa.edu.au/JEE/) 1–18.

Stables, A. (2005a), *Living and Learning as Semiotic Engagement: A New Theory of Education* (Lewiston, NY: Mellen).

Stables, A. (2005b), 'Multiculturalism and moral education: individual positioning, dialogue and cultural practice', *Journal of Moral Education*, 34(2), 185–97.

Stables, A. (2006a), 'Living and learning as semiotic engagement', *Journal of Curriculum Studies*, 38(4), 373–87.

Stables, A. (2006b), 'Semiosis and the myth of learning', in *Proceedings of International Network of Philosophers of Education 10th Biennial Conference: Philosophical Perspectives on Educational Practice in the 21st Century*. (Malta: Allied Newspapers). Also electronically published at http://www.educ.um.edu.mt/INPE/proceedings.html *CHECK REF IN CH 2.3a*

Stables, A. (2006c), 'From semiosis to social policy: the less trodden path', *Signs Systems Studies*, 34(1), 121–34.

Stables, A. (2008a), 'The unnatural nature of nature and nurture', *Studies in Philosophy and Education*, www.springlink.com/content/102999

Stables, A. (2008b), 'Semiosis, Dewey and difference: implications for pragmatic philosophy of education', *Contemporary Pragmatism*, 5(1), 147–62.

Stables, A. (2008c), 'The song of the Earth: a pragmatic rejoinder', *Educational Philosophy and Theory*, www3.interscience.wiley.com/cgi-bin/fulltext/120120239.

Stables, A. and Gough, S. (2006), 'Towards a semiotic theory of choice and of learning', *Educational Theory*, 56(3), 271–85.

Stables, A. and Scott, W. (1999), 'Environmental education and the discourses of humanist modernity: redefining critical environmental literacy', *Educational Philosophy and Theory*, 31(2), 145–55.

Stables, A. and Scott, W. (2001), 'Post-humanist liberal pragmatism? Environmental education out of modernity', *Journal of Philosophy of Education*, 35(2), 269–80.

Stables, A., Jones, S. and Morgan, C. (1999), 'Educating for significant events: the application of Harré's social reality matrix across the lower secondary school curriculum', *Journal of Curriculum Studies*, 31(4), 449–61.

Steinberg, S. R. and Kincheloe, J. L. (1997), *Changing Multiculturalism* (Buckingham: Open University Press).

Stone, L. (1977), *The Family, Sex and Marriage in England, 1500-1800* (New York: Harper and Row).

Tooley, J. and Darby, D. (1998), *Educational Research: A Critique* (London: Office for Standards in Education).

Urmson, J. O. and Reé, J. (eds) (1989), *The Concise Encyclopaedia of Western Philosophy and Philosophers* (London: Routledge).

Vygotsky, L. (1962), *Thought and Language* (Cambridge, MA: MIT Press).

Vygotsky, L. (1978), *Mind in Society: The Development of Higher Psychological Processes* (Cambridge, MA: Harvard University Press).

Wegerif, R. (1998), 'Two images of reason in educational theory', *School Field*, 9, 77–105.

West, E. G. (1974), 'The economics of compulsion', in *The Twelve-Year Sentence*. Retrieved April 11, 2007, from http://www.ncl.ac.uk/egwest/pdfs/economics%20of%20compulsion.pdf

Wheelwright, P. (1960), *Heraclitus* (Princeton, NJ.: Princeton University Press).

Whitehead, A. N. (1978), *Process and Reality* (New York: Free Press).

Whitehead, J. (1993), *The Growth of Educatonal Knowledge: Creating Your Own Living Educational Theories* (Bournemouth: Hyde).

Williams, K. (1990), 'In defence of compulsory education', *Journal of Philosophy of Education*, 24(2), 285–95.

Willis, P. (1977), *Learning to Labour: How Working Class Kids Get Working Class Jobs* (Farnborough: Saxon House).

Winch, C. and Gingell, J. (1999), *Key Concepts in the Philosophy of Education* (London: Routledge).

Winnicott, D. W. (1951), 'Transitional objects and transitional phenomena', in D. W. Winnicott (1975) *Through Paediatrics to Psycho-Analysis* (London: Hogarth), 229–42.

Wittgenstein, L. (1967), *Philosophical Investigations* (Oxford: Blackwell).

Wittgenstein, L. (1974), *Tractatus Logico-Philosophicus* trans. D. F. Pears and B. F. McGuinness (London: Routledge and Kegan Paul).

Wood, D., Bruner, J. and Ross, G. (1976), 'The role of tutoring in problem solving', *Journal of Child Psychology and Psychiatry*, 17, 89–100.

Young, M. F. D. (2008), *Bringing Knowledge Back In – From Social Constructivism to Social Realism in the Sociology of Education* (London: Routledge).

Index